THE EMERGENCE OF

CHRISTIAN CULTURE

IN THE WEST

HARPER TORCHBOOKS

THE EMERGENCE OF CHRISTIAN CULTURE IN THE WEST

The Classical Heritage of the Middle Ages

HENRY OSBORN TAYLOR

Foreword and Bibliography by
KENNETH M. SETTON

HARPER TORCHBOOKS

HARPER & BROTHERS PUBLISHERS
New York

CONTENTS

FOREWORD
TO THE TORCHBOOK EDITION

By Kenneth M. Setton

Henry C. Lea Professor of History
University of Pennsylvania

If like an eighteenth-century novelist I may address you directly, gentle reader, it will be to commend your choice of this book. It cannot be read in a bookstore, however, leaning against a counter, standing first on one foot and then the other. It cannot be read in a subway or on a streetcar, but might be managed on a transcontinental train. The product of a leisurely scholarship, this book deserves a thoughtful, unhurried reading. The Roman poet Horace accuses his pedecessor, the dramatist Plautus, of bounding across the stage "with unfastened sock," anxious to stuff into his pocket the money he got for writing, indifferent whether his play fell thereafter or stood on a firm footing (*Epistles*, II, 1, 174–76). Henry Osborn Taylor did not write, and he cannot be read, this way. He was a literary craftsman. The times change, of course, and new historical evidence requires new syntheses. Grace of style is not enough in any age to give a book permanence. A book, however, which combines the gift of clear prose with a truly cultivated thoughtfulness can have a timelessness all its own, and needs no apology for its reprinting. Such a book is *The Classical Heritage of the Middle Ages*, reprinted in this edition under the equally appropriate and more expressive title, *The Emergence of Christian Culture in the West*.

There was a time, not so long ago, when men took in their stride quotations from Latin and Greek. They translated them as they read, or perhaps they had long before committed many of them to memory, and had only to glance at them and make silent comment on their aptness to the context in which they were employed. This delightful experience is inaccessible to most of us today. Our Latin and Greek wavers fitfully in mottoes and tags and the names of college fraternities. A generation which has lost its Latin and Greek is not a lost generation, to be sure, but it is one which moves chiefly on the surface of much of its literary and historical reading. It has lost the sense of continuity with the past for which it often reveals a groping need. Instead of whole patterns and distinct outlines it is confined to glimpsing shadows and bits of mosaic which never quite form intelligible pictures. It is a generation to which every old idea is new and must be newly considered.

In *The Classical Heritage* Taylor recalls to us, vividly and urbanely, a sense of continuity which is rich and satisfying, a comfortable confirmation of the truism that new traditions generally have roots in old traditions. He supplies abundant illustration of the fact that no language is dead which contains great ideas.

Henry Osborn Taylor worked very slowly and with great seriousness of purpose. Thirty years ago he gave a brief description of his historical career and a statement of his purpose, and although writers generally state their purpose better than they carry it out, I think Taylor carried it out rather better than he stated it. Be this as it may, let him speak directly in his appealing, modest way:

When I was a young man I became bent on devoting my mind and energies to the best things I could find. Not having original and creative gifts, I set myself to the study of what other men had deemed best, and had striven to attain in thought and work and conduct. I had ardently studied law, had practised a very little, and had written a book on *Private Corporations*. But the law seemed too narrow—very far from covering the whole human field; and I turned to look beyond it. Being inclined toward the humanities rather than the sciences, I soon saw that I at least should find the most humanly interesting elements in the aim and the endeavor—the forming an ideal, and the struggle through the man's years, or perhaps through the longer life of a people, to accomplish it. The accomplishment itself, if indeed it is severable from the endeavor, might be beyond the strength either of individual or of race. Achievement lies on the knees of the gods. The true human story is a story of endeavor—the endeavor for the end conceived.

So I began with the ancient world, which is the pit whence we have been digged. And I devoted the ten years that were my supreme education to writing *Ancient Ideals*. That brought my notion of the story down to the time of Christianity. I gave all my time to the book, working eight hours a day, and travelling to see some of the things and countries I was studying. I had very little money, but I used it, and at last sweated blood to pay for the publication of my work.

Then, with the advantage of this discipline of knowledge, I devoted four years to *The Classical Heritage of the Middle Ages*. During two of them, I held a lectureship at Columbia, but gave it up as interfering with my real work. Profiting by this further time of study and training, I next put ten enthusiastic years on *The Mediaeval Mind*, and, after that, six or seven years on *Thought and Expression in the Sixteenth Century*. There have been two or three smaller books, *Freedom of the Mind in History*, taking three years; and one that is now in the press bringing me to the present time.

Curiously enough I find that through all these books, if I have not been implicitly saying the same thing, I have, without intending it, been speaking with the voice of my first conviction as to the central human interest of the endeavor and the aim. Forty years, and all my mind and energy, have been put upon these books, which I mention to show the time they have taken. . . .[1]

This book seeks to describe "the freeing of the human spirit—both its intellect and its passion—from the limitations of the antique temperament and modes of thought" (p. 14). Taylor delighted in ideas, and loved to explore the recesses of the

[1] H. O. Taylor, "A Layman's View of History," *American Historical Review*, XXXIII (Jan. 1928), 247–48, from his presidential address delivered before the American Historical Association in Washington, D.C,. on December 28, 1927. Taylor was born on December 5, 1856, in New York City. He studied at Harvard (A.B., 1878) and Columbia (LL.B., 1881), and later on spent some time at the University of Leipzig. In 1905 he married Julia, daughter of William B. Isham, New York merchant and banker, for whom Isham Park in upper Manhattan is named. Through the years Taylor received many academic honors in recognition of his lifetime devotion to study and writing. He died without issue in New York City on April 13, 1941.

human mind and emotion. Most of his attention in this book is given to literature and philosophy. With skill and discernment he has analyzed for us the character of Greek and Latin classical poetry with its restraint, moderation, clarity, and proportionment, and contrasted its effect with the passionate and abandoned abasement of the Christian conscience before God: "The classic μηδὲν ἄγαν ['nothing to excess'] was abandoned; the Christian heart could not hold too much love of God" (p. 245).

Under Taylor's guidance we can trace the emotional genesis of such medieval Latin hymns as the *Dies irae* and *Stabat mater*, among the most poignant compositions in all occidental literature, bespeaking a pathos and tenderness unknown even to Vergil, who knew better perhaps than any pagan "the tears in things," *hinc lacrimae rerum*, that note of brooding pity, as John Mackail has called it, for the plight of humankind. Classical meters based upon syllabic quantity, no longer in harmony with the facts of daily speech, could not contain the wellsprings of Christian emotion; these academic meters broke down and were gradually replaced by verse forms based upon accent, in easier accord with the rhythms of living language, both Greek and Latin.

In architecture as in poetry Christian emotion was not to be restrained in its heavenward flight by the precision and grace of Doric and Ionic architecture, the embodiment of the Greek intellect. In western Europe, when the Germanic peoples had assisted in the fulfillment of Christian sentiment, Gothic architecture was evolved, a "completely Christian style" (pp. 302 ff.). As medieval Latin poetry was written in the accentual modes of living speech, so the Gothic artist "has opened his eyes and has seen living plants with living foliage" (p. 312).

We must not go too far in "the freeing of the human spirit . . . from the limitations of the antique temperament and modes of thought" (cited above), for the late G.G. Coulton is always at hand to remind us: "The idea that a medieval artist had anything like modern freedom is a delusion difficult to account for. It is possible to argue that freedom is a bad thing in art and in religious belief; but it is not permissible, in face of notorious facts, to assert that freedom existed in either field during the Middle Ages. If indeed all things are Christian in proportion to their freedom, then, in that respect, art conditions are more truly Christian today than they were during the thousand years before the Reformation." [2] Whether we agree with Coulton or not, his words supply the ground for pause and for reflection.

Taylor gives much attention to the contrast between ancient and medieval ethics and here a few introductory remarks will not be amiss. It was not until the advent of Stoicism, and more importantly of Christianity, that the ancient distinguished very clearly between ethics (relating to the individual) and politics (the state). Ethics was the politics of the individual's governance of his life as a citizen; politics was the state's ethics in the management of the lives of its citizens. A good man was a good citizen. Aristotle seems to have slight interest in moral and spiritual goodness *per se,* but only in civic goodness —a good man was good for something in the state. Goodness was external and functional; it was not the knowledge and the will to be good only as a duty to oneself. The latter attitude toward goodness seems to be an especial result of Christianity, for a man had to be good to save his soul, and so goodness became in itself a personal and spiritual thing. The ancients could, for example, condone tyrannicide. Murder was only truly wicked when it did not serve the state. Harmodius and Aristogeiton were Athenian saints.

Actually this lesson was not lost on the church fathers, who regarded pagan or heterodox emperors as tyrants, only the orthodox emperors possessing true sovereignty. Although some medieval writers, like John of Salisbury, may flirt with the concept of tyrannicide, the world of the Middle Ages nurtured different ethical ideals—"the principles of Christian ethics

---

[2] Coulton, *Art and the Reformation,* Oxford, Blackwell, 1928, pp. 133–34 (also Cambridge University Press, 1953, and Harper Torchbooks, 1958), and cf. pp. 131 ff. and Appendix 8, against the uncritical pro-medievalism of Ralph Adams Cram, *The Gothic Quest,* New York, 1907

trace their descent from the spirit of the Old Testament . . .
[p. 72]. [A] seeking unto righteousness and the love of God
through the aid of unmerited Grace, was to be the holiest inspiration of mediaeval Christianity. But it did not come altogether nor at once to Greek and Roman Christians, though
all devoted followers of Christ were touched by it. After Paul,
hardly a man is found completely possessed of these principles
and held by them, until Augustine" (p. 73). Like the latest
researchers into the earliest history of Christianity, Taylor was
well aware of the importance of the Hebrew elements in medieval civilization.

From the secular life of Pericles and Demosthenes centered
in the city-state (*polis*) to the other-worldly aspirations of St.
Antony in seclusion by the Nile and St. Benedict at Monte
Cassino is a long, long road. Everyone who reads this Introduction knows something about St. Augustine's *City of God*.
For Augustine two different loves had made two "cities" or
societies: "The love of self even to despising God made the
earthly city; the love of God even to despising self made the
heavenly" (*Civ. Dei*, XIV, 28). Augustine "eliminated pagan
ethics," says Taylor, "and substituted Christian love of God,
with the principles which it involves. . . . He prizes government and is impassioned for order. The Roman order, the *pax
Romana*, the concord of citizens, is re-set in the kingdom of
God . . ." (p. 187). In the thought-world of Christianity no
aspect of society is spared, for the other-worldliness of the faith
was all-pervasive: "The use of symbolism and allegory [in
Christian literature] indicates a greater interest in the veiled
truths of life than in life's visible facts. Conversely, this habit,
once formed, accustoms men to look everywhere and in everything for the veiled yet suggested spiritual element and to
regard that as the important, nay, as the real matter" (pp.
104–5). Augustine was not of course responsible for this point
of view, which long antedates him and was in fact the background of his own thought.

No book is perfect, including this one. Since ancient Græco-
Roman (and early Christian) culture was the product of an

urban society, Taylor should have considered, at longer length than a passing reference (p. 33), "the gradual extinction of civic life in the cities, until municipal organization becomes mere apparatus for assessment, and civic honors become burdens from which there is no escape." The question whether this municipal organization survived in western Europe from the sixth and seventh centuries into the eleventh (as Alfons Dopsch believed) or disappeared, to re-emerge in new towns in the eleventh and twelfth centuries (as Henri Pirenne believed), was a subject already causing controversy when Taylor's *Classical Heritage* was published. We can appreciate his not wishing to tie himself up in the knotty questions which the historical problem of the "origin of towns" has presented to the medieval historian of the last two or three generations, but perhaps he missed an opportunity to give further illustration of the ways in which social forces are interrelated.

As ancient clarity, definiteness, and proportion gave way, in Taylor's view, to Christian spirituality and mysticism; the classic forms and meters of literature, to Christian poetic modes which distort and misapply the ancient canons; and as "in architecture, sculpture, and painting, the Christian spirit reaches its full expression only in the Middle Ages when the classic heritage has been forgotten or abandoned" (p. 7)—so the gradual failure and decentralization of Roman government in the West, the decline of municipal life, the growth of a manorial economy, the establishment of the barbarian kingdoms, and the rise of the papal monarchy, all presaged the end of the ancient world and the beginnings of the Middle Ages. Here the political, economic, and social facts of life could have been connected more closely with religion and philosophy, art and literature, which inevitably reflect those facts of life. About the year 1200, for example, the latest point to which as a whole the *Classical Heritage* reaches (cf. pp. 66 ff.), the Gothic style begins to rise, and in architecture, handwriting, clothing, and footwear the points and angularities of Gothic taste become apparent. Thus does the style of an age inform most aspects of life.

Although Taylor deals with different topics, he seeks throughout to show how the central facts of life are related to one another, and how they all change together in the transition from antiquity to the Middle Ages. It is relatively easy to show how, with the passing of imperial authority in the West, the Theodosian Code gave way to the barbarian codes which were compounded from it. It is harder to trace, but Taylor does it well, how in the transition from paganism to Christianity the classic ideals of beauty, love, and knowledge were transformed into new values. Law and literature, the human mind and personality, were altered in this transition, but reconstructed also in different forms in preparation for the civilization of the twelfth and thirteenth centuries, all "links in the chain of eventual progress" (p. 57). In the era of transition Taylor sees sometimes decline from the higher standard of the past, sometimes liberation from the stereotypes of a moribund tradition.

Taylor was educated as a lawyer. His first publication was a legal treatise, and his admiration is quite apparent for the discipline, order, and juristic clarity of Western thought whether represented in the works of St. Augustine or the monastic organization of St. Benedict. Although he writes with perception of the early Byzantine mystic, the Pseudo-Dionysius the Areopagite, and admires the hymns of Romanus the Melode, Taylor shies away from the East, away from the "extraordinary disorder and confusion" of St. Basil's monastic precepts (p. 148), and he finds in the best examples of Byzantine hymnology and architecture a "formalism of an over-mature civilization in which the culture and principles of the great classic past had become lifeless conventions" (p. 307). Rome probably exercised as great an influence upon Greece as the latter upon Rome, "but the effect of the Roman on the Greek is of slight interest," says Taylor. "It is the influence of Greece upon Rome, and upon Italy unified under Roman dominance, that is of supreme moment" (pp. 22–23). As Horace had said, in the *Epistle* we have already referred to (II, 1, 156–57), Greece had taken her Roman captor captive, and in-

troduced the arts into rustic Latium. Since the first publication
of *The Classical Heritage*, however, almost three generations
of historians have explored the long-continued influence of
Rome upon Greece, eventuating in Byzantine civilization, an
enduring amalgam of Roman law and government, Hellenistic
culture, and Christianity. Although Taylor set out to study the
manner in which "from the third to the fifth century the
Græco-Roman world presents conditions of decadence" (p. 4),
he never quite appreciated a fact to which Ernst Kornemann
gave categorial expression a dozen years after Taylor had published this book:

The East, which had itself once brought forth the oldest cultures,
became life-dispensing twice more after its contact with Greek
culture, that "leaven of antiquity," first after the great achievement
of Alexander and his generals in the territorial monarchies of their
time, and then through the cross-fertilization of Hellenism and Irani-
anism, from which Arabian world-culture arose. Whoever will really
secure a basic understanding of the hardest of all problems, that of
the "decline of the ancient world," cannot take his point of vantage
in the west but must do so in the east of the Mediterranean, and must
draw the early Islamic world into the scope of his consideration. The
way to the understanding of the middle ages lies through the East." [3]

Like every historian Taylor looked at the past with the
spectacles of his own generation. None of us is ahead of his
time, and we are all wise after the fact. But Kornemann's
dictum was, I think, a wise caveat, at least for the historian of
medieval Rome and Italy. The Greek influence upon Italy was
not a single historic revelation. It was a continuous experience
which helped throughout the entire Middle Ages to mold the
intellectual life of the peninsula from Venice to Reggio, and
can be traced in almost unbroken continuity from Roman imperial times to the era of the Renaissance. [4] But Byzantine

[3] Kornemann, "Die römische Kaiserzeit," in Alfred Gercke and Eduard
Norden, *Einleitung in die Altertumswissenschaft,* III (Leipzig and Berlin,
1912), 296. Kornemann repeats, but softens this statement a bit in his
Römische Geschichte, 2 vols., Stuttgart, 1938–39, II, 409.

[4] K. M. Setton, *The Byzantine Background to the Italian Renaissance*
(*Proceedings of the American Philosophical Society,* vol. 100), Philadelphia, 1956.

thought and the Byzantine state were "the effect of the Roman on the Greek" (of more than "slight interest") as well as of Christianity and other Eastern influences upon Hellenistic civilization. In the reaction, then, of Byzantium upon Italy and the West, Roman ideas of law, empire, and much else returned home to help mold and diversify European culture both in the Middle Ages and the Renaissance. We are thus certainly justified in remonstrating against the conclusion of Taylor's preface: "Find what interest one may in mediaeval Byzantium, —and it is full of instruction,—still it is a tale of what had reached its zenith, of what was past its best strength, a tale of decadence postponed with skill and energy, and yet only postponed."

Byzantium endured, however, from the fourth century to the fifteenth, a great European fortress against hordes of eastern invaders whose westward advance was stopped by Byzantine military prowess and diplomatic intelligence. No measure of skill and energy could postpone decadence for eleven centuries! If some modern Byzantinists have exaggerated the fundamental values of Byzantine culture, surely Taylor has deprecated them unduly. Actually there was a greater unity to medieval civilization from the Bay of Biscay to the Bosporus than he seems to have realized—indeed, as he himself has emphasized throughout this book, the important facts of life are remarkably interrelated in every era.

The centuries of transition which Taylor has studied marked the emergence of a Christian culture distinct from that of Græco-Roman antiquity. From Origen to St. Augustine Christianity claimed champions who were the peers of Plato and Cicero, and by the fourth century almost all great minds were in the Church. How great a wrench it was for some men to abandon the Roman traditions and pagan way of life will be apparent to anyone who dips into the pages of Synesius of Cyrene, Sidonius Apollinaris, Salvian, and various of their contemporaries.

Throughout the Middle Ages there was much dispute concerning the place to be accorded the classical heritage in the life of Christian perfection, but it never seemed feasible to the intellectual leaders of Christendom to reject the legacy of antiquity altogether. The Prophets of Israel and the Sermon on the Mount did not provide all that was necessary for the elaboration of a Christian culture. Christianity needed—and wanted—to learn from Athens and Rome as well as from Jerusalem. We may safely assume that Hellenism no less than Hebraism will endure with Christianity, and that the classical heritage no less than the prophetic will never die.

To the study of this majestic theme Henry Osborn Taylor dedicated his scholarly life, and by his publications he has enabled many thousands of readers to share with him the rich experience of this study.

March, 1958

PREFACE

THE subject of this book is the transition from the Classical to the Mediæval. It seeks to follow the changes undergone by classic thought, letters, and art, on their way to form part of the intellectual development of the Middle Ages, and to show how pagan tastes and ideals gave place to the ideals of Christianity and to Christian sentiments. The argument reaches backward to classic Greece and Rome and forward into the Middle Ages; but the discussion centres in the period extending from the fourth to the seventh century. This period was strikingly transitional in Italy and the western provinces of the Roman Empire; before it had passed, the various elements of classic culture had assumed the forms in which they were to make part of the intellectual life of the Middle Ages, and Christianity had taken on a mediæval character.

In considering the antecedents of the transition period it is necessary to look to Greek as well as Roman sources, to the East as well as to the West. But the West of Europe is the province of this book, and the discussion tends always to turn from the

Hellenic East to the Western and Latin phenomena
of the transition period. These have a personal interest for us, making part of our own past. They have
also the interest of that which lived and was to grow
in life.   Find what interest one may in mediæval
Byzantium, — and it is full of instruction, — still it
is a tale of what had reached its zenith, of what was
past its best strength, a tale of decadence postponed
with skill and energy, and yet only postponed.

H. O. TAYLOR.

NEW YORK,
    January 19, 1901.

THE CLASSICAL HERITAGE OF THE MIDDLE AGES

CHAPTER I

INTRODUCTION

No date marks the passing of the ancient world and the beginning of the Middle Ages. The transition from one to the other was a process of spiritual change, during which antique characteristics gradually ceased and were replaced by much that was incipiently mediæval. There no longer existed men whose education and intellectual traits, whose moods, tastes, sentiments, and views of life were those of the time of Augustus, or Trajan, or Marcus Aurelius. The older possessors of antique culture in Italy and the provinces were transformed; within and without the Empire new races had come upon the stage; through decade and century went on a ceaseless blending of the new, the old, and the transitional.

Paganism and Christianity existed side by side in the Græco-Roman world of the fourth and fifth centuries, the one with its great steadying traditions, and the other with its power of new-found faith and its fresh moral stimulus. Christians had pagan educations, and pagans, like the emperor Julian and his friend Libanius, derived suggestions from the religion they despised. In these obviously transitional centuries, both pagan and Christian men arose who were not quite antique.[1] Some of them eclectically refashioned pagan ethics, some made useful if vapid compendiums of antique culture, some turned epics into grammars; others unconsciously remoulded primitive Christianity or produced strange creations, compounds of Christianity and paganism. Together they form the link between the earlier pagan and Christian types and the more mediæval men of the sixth and seventh centuries.

The modification of antique pagan and Christian types is one side of the change. Another is represented by the barbarian races who, often with destructive violence, were pressing into the Empire and coming under the influence of whatever existed there. They were affected by intercourse with Italians and provincials, and soon began to absorb knowledge. As their intelligence increased, through their contact with a higher civilization, they drew from the antique according to their understandings and appreciations. The old matters thus absorbed into new natures were transformed, and sometimes gained fresh life. But these barbarian men were not metamorphosed into antique persons, nor even into those pagan or Christian semi-antique types which made the Græco-Roman world of the fourth and fifth centuries. From the

[1] The word "classical" refers to the characteristics of Greek art and Greek or Roman literature at their best; "antique" refers more generally to the characteristics of Greek and Roman civilization, without special reference to period or quality; "pagan" means the same, but with the added idea of opposition to Christian thought.

beginning of the sixth century, however, the barbarians
are not to be sharply set over against Romans and
provincials; they represent all stages of civilization,
from barbarism to the best culture afforded by the
time.

These processes of overthrow, progress, and change
were complex. But it is noticeable that each succeeding generation of the mingled denizens of the Empire
is further removed from the antique type and nearer
to the mediæval. The Empire remained geographically the source of religion and culture for peoples
within it and without; and Christianity, as well as
much from the pagan classic past, was passing to the
new peoples in forms continually modified and ever
nearer to the level of the early mediæval centuries.
For example, Augustine was a Roman Christian; he
was not mediæval. One hundred and fifty years after
him comes Gregory the Great, who is partly Roman
still, yet is touched with the new ignorance, the new
barbarism. He is, however, close enough to Augustine
to appropriate his doctrines and hand them on in modes
nearer the level of the seventh and eighth centuries.
This is an example of the Christian side of the matter.
On the other hand, the classic spirit was dead before
Gregory was born, and classic literature was degraded
by the way in which it was understood. Virgil, for
instance, was no longer Virgil, but incarnate grammar
and authoritative history. Antique culture was also
undergoing desiccation in compositions of the transition centuries, whose authors took what was spiritually closest to them and made it over in accordance
with their own intelligence and character.

From the third to the fifth century the Græco-Roman world presents conditions of decadence. Military courage, civic devotion, intellectual energy, are declining. Decay shows itself in literature and art. The phenomena of this pagan decadence present analogies in the various provinces of philosophy, ethics, law, rhetoric, and grammar, as well as in art and poetry. Philosophy and ethics are eclectic: organic principles which give consistency are frequently ignored, while inconsistent sources are drawn from, and there is a tendency to summarize. In law the tendency is to conserve and compile, then to epitomize; the creative energy to make an organic system is lacking. In rhetoric, grammar, mathematics, there is merely an arranging of the old and trite examples and a summarizing. Consequently resemblances will appear throughout the decadent forms in which these various branches of culture pass over into the Middle Ages. In poetry and art there was not the same palpable summarizing of previous works; yet the failure of creative faculty appears in the mediocrity of poetic compositions, in their lack of freshness, their insipid use of borrowed phrase and trite image. The openly pagan poetry of the fourth and fifth centuries was not as current in the Middle Ages as the semi-pagan verse written by Christians. In this there was some modification of pagan elements, and it may be said generally, as to the paganism carried over into the Middle Ages in Christian writings, that the Christian spirit altered whatever it drew from paganism; and Christian modifications of borrowed pagan elements show analogies among themselves, whether the pagan element happens to be carried over in theological, ethical, or historical writings or in more strictly literary compositions. For example, the pagan matter is apt to be allegorized or treated mystically or symbolically, and novel and more spiritual meaning is given to what is taken.[1] Moreover, the later and partially decadent pagan sources are usually employed.

The fifth century concludes the course of the decadence of independent self-existent paganism. Already Christianity was showing itself a new power and inspiration in thought, letters, and art. Yet its spirit and its principles differed so essentially from those of the classical antique that some of its elements of strength corresponded with what were defects according to classical standards. Self-control, measure, limit, proportion, clarity, and definiteness were principles of the antique; the Christian spirit broke through them all. Its profound spirituality, often turning to mysticism, had not the clarity of classic limitation. It did not recognize limit. Its reach was infinite, and therefore its expressions were often affected with indefiniteness. Classic self-control meant measure, nothing in excess. Christian self-control soon came to mean the exclusion of a part of life; it knew no measure; of what it condemned it could not have too little, of what it approved it could not have enough. The higher paganism sought to weigh and proportion the elements of mortal life according to their intrinsic values and their relations to the economy of human happiness. Christianity scarcely regarded these mortal balancings. It had its own universal principle of proportionment,

[1] The myth of the Phœnix is an example, see *post*, p. 279.

—that love of God which comprehended love for all men and for self in conformity with God's love of His creatures.

Inspired by so different a spirit the creations of Christian thought and feeling could not be like the classic, and their excellence could not be the classic excellence. Classic principles of literary and artistic form and definite unity of composition could never become organic with the spirit of Christianity which overleaped the finite and the mortal.[1]   Consequently the art and literature of the transition centuries present a conflict, of which the Christian artists and authors are not always

[1] The contrast between the (late) classical and the Christian spirit may be seen in the lines on Hope attributed to Seneca: "Deceitful hope, hope sweet evil, the one solace of ills for wretched men, whereby they bear their lots. Silly thing, which no turn of fortune can put to flight, hope stays, anxious to please to the last gasp," etc. This pagan conception of *spes* is definite and unspiritualized, quite wingless, pessimistic, and void of high assurance. It lacks all that animates Christian hope and gives it wings to bear it up to God.

> Spes fallax, spes dulce malum, spes una malorum
> Solamen miseris, qua sua fata trahunt.
> Credula res, quam nulla potest fortuna fugare,
> Spes stat in extremis officiosa malis.
> Spes vetat aeterno mortis requiescere portu
> Et curas ferro rumpere sollicitas.
> Spes nescit vinci, spes pendet tota futuris;
> Mentitur, credi vult tamen illa (sibi).
> Sola tenet miseros in vita, sola moratur,
> Sola perit numquam, sed venit atque redit. . . .

—BAEHRENS, *Poetae Latini Minores*, Vol. IV, p. 65.

Compare also the *Pervigilium Veneris*, that last soft note of pagan sexual love, with Augustine's conception of the love of God (*post*, p. 129) and with the mystical love of Christ which was springing up within monasticism (*post*, p. 153).

conscious,—a conflict between the new spirit of Christianity, with its inspirations, its infinite reaches and its requirements of expression, and the antique culture, its tastes and aversions, and its definite literary and artistic rules and forms.

In the fourth and fifth centuries great works of Christian theology and polemics were produced, as well as writings more properly literary, both poetry and prose, and also works of art. The Christian authors had renounced the pagan religion, they condemned its idolatry, some of them disapproved pagan literature. But one and all were educated in standards of artistic taste and principles of literary composition which were the fruit of pagan culture. They knew no other canons to follow when they tried for literary excellence. Therefore they could not but endeavor to give their Christian writings the excellences which had distinguished the antique pagan literature and art. But these classic rules were profoundly irreconcilable with the spirit and demands of the new Christian matter, as may be readily seen in Christian poetry; antique form and metre were not suited to Christian feeling, and the Christian soul did not reach full poetic expression until it abandoned classic forms and created new ones. As for Christian art, the technical skill and principles of composition inherited from the antique were its foundations and its first source of excellence; these aided vastly more than they retarded. Nevertheless in architecture, sculpture, and painting, the Christian spirit reaches its full expression only in the Middle Ages when the classic heritage has been forgotten or abandoned.

In other respects classic knowledge deflected or embarrassed the development of Christian thought. Inconsistent elements from pagan metaphysics entered Christian theology. And pagan ethics for a time held Christian ethics from their true principles. This appears, for instance, in the ethical writings of so profound a Christian as Ambrose. On the other hand, the works of his younger contemporary, Augustine, show the casting aside of pagan ethical reasoning and the creation of a veritable Christian scheme.

If pagan form and substance thus hampered the Christian development, it may be inferred that Christian productions were ill suited to the preservation of antique elements unchanged and uncorrupted. Antique form is soon distorted in Christian literature, while the substantial elements of antique ethics and philosophy are often changed by the mixture of what is foreign to them, or are distorted through their application in schemes and to purposes alien to their nature. The larger Christian Latin poems from the time of Commodian afford examples of the distortion of antique form. Many of them, whatever may be their purpose or their topic, make an indiscriminate use of the hexameter or the elegiac metre, and disregard literary unity and pertinency at will. Examples of the misapplication of pagan substance may be found in the use of Stoical methods of reasoning as a frame for Christian ethics; also in the use of Greek philosophy for the formulation of Christian dogma, or in the manner of employing certain parts of Aristotle in the early Middle Ages. And yet the somewhat distorted manner in which classical elements were used in Christian literature represents much besides decay. For the genius of Christianity could make use of antique pagan elements only by altering and breaking them, or by misapplying them, and all this in ways that were sheer debasement, judged by any classical standard. It was through their distortion that pagan elements became part of the new growth of the human spirit coming with Christianity.

There were several ways in which the antique elements of culture passed over to the Middle Ages, or were superseded by Christian ideals. There was, of course, intercourse between the citizens of the Empire and the barbarians. One result of this may be observed in the bits of anonymous pagan opinion subsisting scattered and impersonal through the Middle Ages, and another in the magic of the great name of Rome and the deathless thought of the Roman Empire. These ideas lived in the consciousness of the people, though they were also fostered by literature. The same may be said of the Roman Law. Some popular knowledge of it survived among the inhabitants of Italy and Gaul, where it was also preserved in codes and abridgments. In England and Germany, save as an element of Canon Law, the influence of Roman Law was slight until after the rise of the Bologna school. As to the currents of literary influence, the writings of classical Latin authors still survived and were read. Antique culture was also summarized or otherwise remodelled in pagan works of the transition centuries, and so passed on in forms suited to the comprehension of the Middle Ages. Chief examples of this are the *De Nuptiis Philologiae et Mercurii* of

Martianus Capella and the *De Consolatione* of Boethius.

These pagan refashionings of the antique were not complicated by the introduction of anything foreign to paganism. But a great mass of pagan culture and philosophy passed over into the Middle Ages modified or transformed in the works of Christians of the transition centuries. In these Christian writings pagan and Christian thoughts sometimes are crudely mingled, as in the poems of Synesius. Again, the pagan and Christian elements are more closely united; instead of a mechanical mixture, as it were, there is a chemical compound, the ingredients of which are altered by their union. The writings of Pseudo-Dionysius are an example: although their inspiration was Christian, their constructive principles were drawn from Neoplatonism. Greek philosophy likewise supplied the principles for the formulation of Christian dogma, and thus passed into Christianity and on into the Middle Ages. It was afterward to have a new career, when in scholasticism it was applied to prove and systematize dogmatic Christianity. Pagan philosophy was the mediæval storehouse of reason. Finally, elements of paganism survive, sometimes as vague and sometimes as definite influences in predominantly Christian works; as, for example, the writings of the Church Fathers.

Pagan literary form survived in early Christian prose literature; but here again the transition from pagan to Christian and mediæval form is noticeable. Equally interesting is the passage of the antique forms from pagan into Christian poetry; and then most striking is their disappearance and the evolution of new Christian forms of verse as the genius of Christianity masters the art of poetry so as to express itself and the emotions of the Christian soul through this medium. Likewise in art: the genius of Christianity long follows its antique lessons, yet conquers them at last and evolves its own artistic forms in painting, sculpture, and architecture. Form is as important as substance in considering poetry and the fine arts in their transition from antiquity to the Middle Ages.

Christianity itself was changed in its passage from apostolic times to the Middle Ages. Changes sprang from the introduction of pagan elements, and other changes from its imperial triumph in becoming the religion of state. But monasticism is the great instance of the recasting of primitive Christianity by the transition centuries in the form which was to be the mediæval ideal of the Christian life. In these same centuries the primitive Christian records were superseded or changed, actually or through the way in which they were understood. Here again, as monasticism came to be the ideal Christian life, it became a factor in the transformation of the narratives of the Old and New Testaments. Under its influence Elijah and Elisha become monks, and Joseph is made a married celibate.[1] Besides the Scriptures, early Christian

---

[1] See, *e.g.*, Cassian, *Inst.* I, 1. On the other hand, the lives of the heroes of monasticism were *refacimenti* of the lives of scriptural characters, including Jesus. The scriptural characters were first refashioned to the understanding and views of the transition and mediæval centuries, as, for example, by making monks of them. The imitation of these mediævally conceived scriptural personages was then a twofold process, actual and imaginative. It was actual

writings, both Greek and Latin, needed the recasting of
the transition period to adapt them to mediæval comprehension. Justin Martyr, Minucius Felix, and the great
Tertullian were not to the mediæval taste. The works
of the Alexandrians, Clement and Origen, never became
intelligible to the Roman-minded West. Greek Christian writers of the fourth century drew largely from

in so far as the saint imitated the Biblical characters, and reproduced in his own life features of their careers; it was imaginative
as his "legend" went beyond the fact in likening his life to theirs.
The imaginative side of the process was largely occupied with the
miracles which faithful tradition readily ascribed to its hero in
making his life like that of Biblical persons. Otherwise, in this
conformation of lives of saints to the prevalent conceptions of
ancient types, it is difficult to distinguish the actual from the
imaginative.

The great mediæval instance is the life of Francis of Assisi,
which that sweetest of saints conformed so closely to the life of
his master Christ, report and tradition adding further points of
likeness. Similarly, Benedict fulfilled the precepts of Scripture,
and conformed his life to his understanding of Biblical examples.
Tradition carries out his endeavor for him, till the writer of his
legend, Gregory, consciously finds in his hero's career a catholic
inclusion of the deeds of scriptural saints. In the *Dialogues*, after
Gregory has been telling the marvellous deeds of Benedict, his in-
terlocutor, the Deacon Peter, answers and exclaims: "Wonderful
and astonishing is what you relate. For in the water brought forth
from the rock (*i.e.* by Benedict) I see Moses, in the iron which
returned from the bottom of the lake I see Elisha (2 Kings vi. 7),
in the running upon the water I see Peter, in the obedience of the
raven I see Elijah (1 Kings xvii. 6), and in his grief for his dead
enemy I see David (1 Kings i. 11). That man, as I consider him,
was full of the spirit of all the just" (Gregorius Magnus, *Dialogi*,
II, 8). The preceding chapters tell these miracles of Benedict.
The rest of the second book contains other miracles like those told
in the Bible. The life of a later saint may also follow earlier monastic types. Francis kisses the wounds of lepers, as Martin of
Tours had done. See Sulpicius Severus, *Vita S. Martini*.

them. By that time Greek was no longer generally
understood in Italy and the Latin-speaking provinces
of the Empire, and many Greek Christian writings
were translated into Latin, and usually were abridged
or otherwise modified.

Translations thus overcame the barrier of language.
Other reasons were to keep early Latin as well as
Greek Christian authors from being read in the
Middle Ages, to wit, their antique tone, and because
the circumstances under which they lived and wrote
were different from any situation that the Middle
Ages were to experience or could understand. *Non
licet esse vos* was substantially what the pagan government said to the Christians.[1] What could a later
time really know of this condition of the Church,
illicit, legally unrecognized, forbidden to exist? So
the Middle Ages, with all their cult of martyrs, did
not read the writings of a time when there was need
to defend Christianity before the pagan government
or to justify it in the eyes of the pagan people.
Another goodly part of these early writings was
directed against pagan-Christian heresies (Gnosticism) of which the Middle Ages knew nothing. One
notes with interest that Lactantius, who writes just

[1] "You are not permitted to exist" (Tertullian, *Apologeticus*).
Tertullian's writings are so difficult, his use of words is so individual, that the Middle Ages could hardly have understood him. But
his phrases seared themselves into Latin Christendom in the third
and fourth centuries, and passed into the language of dogma, and
his writings were a store for later Apologists. He also was an
influence with the important poet Prudentius (Ebert, *Allge. Ges.
der Lit. des Mittelalters*, 2d ed., I, pp. 51, 276, 287). Through these
media he is indirectly influential in the later periods, when his works
were no longer read.

as the pagan empire closes and Constantine comes to the throne, is the earliest Christian author who has any mediæval vogue. Yet he was not influential. The great Latin Christian personalities of the fourth and fifth centuries were most potent in moulding or rather in creating mediæval thought. Ambrose, Jerome, Augustine, Hilary of Poictiers, these founders of Latin Christianity, recast the Christian thought of the first centuries; and it is through these mighty powers — through Augustine, the giant of them all — that early Christian writings indirectly affect the Middle Ages.

Mention has been made of certain analogies noticeable among the various forms of decadence and change. Beyond these, there will be seen, throughout the following chapters, the freeing of the human spirit — both its intellect and its passion — from the limitations of the antique temperament and modes of thought. More especially this will characterize the transition from pagan to Christian. True, the Middle Ages will manifest less self-reliant human freedom than antiquity, and will even take on new spiritual bondage in fear of God and the fate of man's immortal soul. But they will know no bondage to any restricting principles of human finitude or to any philosophic weighings of the good and ill or even the rights and wrongs of mortal life.

The spiritual liberation, distinguishing the transition through which the antique ceased and the mediæval began, was a liberation from the inherent limits of self-reliance, and consequently from the limitations of that freedom which is established in human strength and the rational balancing of mortal considerations. It was a liberation resting upon the power of God. The human spirit, responding to the new Christ-awakened sense of the infinite and awful power of God's love, became conscious of the measureless reaches of the soul created for eternal life by an infinite and eternally loving God. The soul was lifted out of its finitude to the infinite which is its nature and its home.

This freeing of the human spirit will first appear in the modifications of the antique character and the disappearance of classic traits: the genius of Neoplatonism was beating against barriers which were burst through only by the Christian faith. Then this liberation will appear in the forms of decadence shown by pagan productions of the transition and pre-transition periods; it not only accompanies but it will seem part of the decay suffered by the strong and noble qualities of classic antiquity. It will likewise appear, often grotesquely and irrationally, in the loosing of antique pagan thoughts from their rational form and definite application when taken over into Christian compositions. Protagoras, in saying that man was the measure of all things, enunciated what had been a tacit assumption in Greek life and reflection since the time when Homer made the gods so human. Empedocles, Anaxagoras, Heraclitus, had seen principles of human nature reflected in the laws of the universe, and Greek metaphysics never ceased to entertain thoughts of a cosmic harmony having its microcosmic pattern in the temperance and proportion that made the ideal of human conduct. Manifestly,

Greek ethical reasoning could not remain undistorted when forced to hold Christian precepts; nor could Greek metaphysics escape perversion when used by the Church Fathers in the formulation of Christian dogma. A God-created world, with men God-created, God-beloved, and God-redeemed, could not be held in the categories of Greek philosophy.

Beyond the region of dogma and metaphysics, the new freedom of the human spirit will show itself with power in the freeing of the Christian ideal of love from thoughts of measure and mortality. It will show itself in the monk's dismissal of pagan proportion and comprehensiveness from his principles of life. He no longer weighs the goods and ills of earth, or seeks to make his life humanly complete. He has broken with the mortal and the finite. He knows that his soul is immortal, and can be blessed only in the everlasting love of God. The passion of this infinite love is his joy, and its measurelessness is the measure of his freedom.

Finally, very interesting is this freeing of the spirit — again often accompanied by the destruction of what had been great — in the spheres of literature and art. It is seen in the disintegration of the balanced periods of classic prose, and in the growth of new kinds of prose compositions having scant relationship with classic forms. In poetry, with emotional impulses creative in their strength, it displays itself in the abandonment of classic metres and the devising of freer forms of verse, which shall be capable of voicing the Christian soul. But sometimes it shows itself barbarously in the misapplication and abuse of those narrative and lyric forms of poetry which the classic spirit, with sure discrimination, had devised to meet the several requirements of its different moods. More slowly and, at first, less articulately than in poetry, this same freeing of the spirit will show itself in architecture, sculpture, and painting: in architecture, as, after the creation of the Byzantine dome and the tentative progress of the Romanesque, the Gothic finally attains, and the vast church lifts the worshipper to the freedom of God's infinite heaven; in sculpture, as the carver learns to cover the cathedral with the illimitable story of creation, of man's Fall and his Redemption, of human life and its devilish besettings, and of the final Judgment unto heaven or hell; in painting, as the artist learns to tell in color this boundless Christian tale and at last to depict with subtilty the beatitudes and sorrows of the Christian soul.

CHAPTER II

THE PASSING OF THE ANTIQUE MAN

WITH all the individual and racial differences among the men of the Middle Ages there were also common characteristics. The mediæval man was not spiritually self-reliant, his character was not consciously wrought by its own strength of mind and purpose. He was neither rationally self-controlled nor rationally free. Subject to bursts of unrestraint, he yet showed no intelligent desire for liberty. He relied on God or, more commonly, upon the supernatural. He also looked up to what he imagined the past to have been, and was prone to accept its authority.[1] He was crushed in the dust with a sense of sin; he was ascetic in his deeper thought. He was also emotional, and with heights and depths of emotion undreamed of by antiquity. He had no clear-eyed perception of the visible world. What he saw he looked upon as a symbol; what he heard he understood as an allegory. For him reality lay behind and beyond, in that which the symbol symbolized and the allegory veiled.

The contrast between the mediæval and the classic Greek and Roman types seems absolute. Yet it is possible to follow the change from the classic to the

[1] On the great fame of Rome in the Middle Ages, see Graf, *Roma nella memoria e nelle imaginazioni del Medio Evo*, Cap. I.

18

semi-antique or transitional types of the fourth and fifth centuries. These pass into the mediæval through gradual modifications arising from the mingled progress and decay of the succeeding centuries, during which the barbarian peoples are wrought upon and changed by the authoritative Christian religion and the awe-inspiring spectacle of the Empire. The present chapter will be devoted to the change from the classic to the transitional pagan types of the fourth century.

The Greek, as well as the Roman, was self-reliant; he looked to himself for his own strength. The gods might provide opportunity, or they might thwart men or enmesh the self-reliant doer in nets of fate. But the man himself and the quality of his accomplishment were the work of his own strength — of his ἀρετή (virtus) and πινυτή (prudentia), his valiant energies and the mind which informed and guided them. Respecting this quality of self-reliance, and the fears which come to shake it, the Greek was loftily and constructively imaginative; the Roman was practically apprehensive, and cautious with utmost fortitude. The Greek reasoned upon human limitations and man's position in the world. He coördinated these limitations in philosophies, and drew broad deductions as to Fate and the gods, conceived as favorable or untoward powers outside of man. Also the Greek imagines with his entire nature — heart and mind; from out of life's limitations he visualizes mortality, and creates epic and dramatic instances of its types or carves them in statues, and shows man's spiritual greatness in spite of Fate. The Roman has neither artistic imagination nor the gift of abstract philosophic reason ; his mind is not filled with lofty deductions, it does not create philosophies ; it guides the feet and hands of Romans on, not to the empire of the spirit, but to the empire of the world. The Roman realizes life's circumstantial difficulties; he knows that weaker power cannot withstand the stronger, and he sees the practical dangers of battle and disease. He will take all the precautions of prudence against these, and will propitiate the gods most carefully.

The Greek, as well as the Roman, was self-controlled. This with the Greek meant a self-proportionment akin to his artistic love of beauty in the visible world and in the world of spirit. His life should be fair and good, beautifully proportioned, each element cherished at its due worth. He would seek nothing excessively, nor anything excessive (μηδὲν ἄγαν), he would observe the glorious and beauty-giving principles of αἰδώς, shame at all things shameful, reverence for all things to be revered; thus rightly distinguishing between what to fear and what not to fear. So might his life and his life's close be beautified by fame.

Intimately connected with the principles guiding Greek conduct were those defining the objects of Greek desire: beauty in all things, broad and lofty knowledge not sought merely as a guide of conduct, but desired as an element of human life. There was harmony and union between the love of beauty and the love of knowledge. Due proportionment, right relation of part to whole, and of the whole to other things —this was fundamental to the thought of beauty.

Knowledge should be beautiful as well; it should pertain to noblest matters, and thus preserve the principle of proportionment in seeking the best most strenuously. Yet the love of beauty entered life's small details and trivialities; and the love of knowledge was not academic, for the Hellene had universal curiosity.

Thus gifted with clear perception, and with reason and imagination which might build systems of philosophy or present life's truths in poetry and sculpture, the Greek was a consummate artist; he could create whatever he loved. His was a happy nature, and with great faculty of joy. To him life was joyous, although mortal, and its prizes, which his intellect approved, were to be desired passionately. Artist as he was, his was the passion as well as the thought of beauty.

Men who thus keenly sought whatever they desired, and who sought ever to know better what to seek, desired liberty to direct their lives to the goal of their desire. The thoughtful, eager Greek was individualistic, seeking the complete fulfilment of his many-sided nature. Philosophers might point out that the State was the greater man, the all-embracing consummation of its citizens. And in great Greek days, citizens made this real in beautiful devotion to the city. Nevertheless, the Greek tended always to revert to the living of his own life in its most perfect fulfilment.

The Roman was undisturbed by a multiplicity of loves. Self-control was a simpler quality with him than with the Greek. It rose from practical judgment,

not from an ideal attempt toward the universal proportionment of life's contents. It was also grounded
in a sense of personal dignity. To give way to passion
was beneath a Roman. In affairs within the city,
self-control was utmost political common sense; as
to external military politics, self-control lay in daring
what might be dared, in fearing what should be feared,
and in abiding with unshakeable fortitude in whatever
was resolved. The Greeks disapproved what was unlimited or unrestrained, and conceived the principle
of this disapproval as the Romans did not. Nevertheless, actually, Roman life was limited more narrowly. Its object and scope were the honor and
aggrandizement of the State, the honor and enrichment
of the family. Without imagination, without broad
desire for knowledge, with little love of beauty, with
no stinging capacity for joy, undistracted from the
practical task in hand, the Roman was from earliest
times the grown-up man of affairs. Through his lack
of individualism, his abundant caution and conservatism, he preserved and perfected fixed types of civic
life; he was the paterfamilias, he was the citizen, he
was the citizen-soldier, he was the magistrate, and fulfilled all these functions excellently well, pursuing
whatever lay within their scope with unexampled
pertinacity and fortitude.

In the history of human development few matters
are so important as the contact between the Roman
and the Greek. Rome subjugated Greece, but the
effect of the Roman on the Greek is of slight interest.
It is the influence of Greece upon Rome, and upon
Italy unified under Roman dominance, that is of

supreme moment. An adequate presentation of this
influence would embrace the history of ancient Italian
culture and specifically the history of philosophy
and all enlightened thought at Rome, of Roman art
and Latin literature. This large and variously told
story is beyond the present purpose. Yet only a
knowledge of the great extent and many phases of
Greek influence upon Italy will yield an understanding of the general fact that by the time of Augustus
the men of Rome, while still possessing many Roman
traits of character, were Greek to the full extent of
their capacities for Hellenization. Their Hellenism,
however, is not pure Greek, and the Roman traits are
also modified. Much of the Roman fortitude abides,
and Roman dignity, likewise Roman energy, although
the Empire closed many of the political needs and
opportunities which had made the lives of the men
of the Republic. The Roman is still a practical man
of affairs, though the better regulation of imperial
taxation no longer permits stupendous private enrichment out of the subject provincials. The great matter
is that he has tasted the tree of knowledge of good
and evil, and is enlightened for better and for worse.
His practical intelligence, energy, and valor have given
him the mastery of the Mediterranean world. His
Greek enlightenment has enabled him to realize that
this wide power is Empire, and the consciousness of
this fact widens and clears his vision. While the
work of diplomacy and conquest went on, the Roman
was absorbed in deeds. Now the Empire is fixed;
Deus Terminus will advance no further, but the god's
strength not to recede is ample. The civil wars are

over. There is now more leisure to consider all things
and contemplate man. But the manner of this contemplation is still shaped by Roman traits. There is
no disinterested quest of knowledge, no full philosophy. Since Aristotle, that had hardly thriven even
with the Greeks. Philosophy had tended to narrow
to a guide of life. The Roman had never any com-
pleter thought of it. He had asked always from his
Greek tutors for its practical teachings, by which to
conduct his life more satisfactorily. He desired to
know for that purpose. Yet in these great imperial
times, he wished to know life's full enlightenment in
order to conduct it well, if, indeed, not beautifully.
He would have the ἀγαθόν, though he never quite felt
or knew the καλόν. Life still presented itself to the
Roman in modes of doing rather than in modes of
being.

The Greek-enlightened Roman was still self-reliant
and self-controlled. But now these qualities were as
much the result of philosophic consideration as of
native strength of character. He was now self-reliant
because his philosophy taught him that the human
soul must rely on its own strength. He had not yet
conceived that there might be an inner spiritual aid
which was not the man himself. He was now self-
controlled because philosophy taught him the misery
entailed by any other state. He was rational and still
relied on reason. Yet incidentally he was superstitious,
and reverent still with great force of conservatism.

To the close of the Republic the Romans were
provincials. In Cicero's time their stiff provincial
dignity turned to dignified urbanity, as was natural

with those who dwelt in a city which was becoming the world's centre of artistic and literary life, besides being the fountain-head of political power. Rome set the fashion for at least the Latin world, and men of Africa and Spain and Gaul were influenced by the urbane character of Romans whose power held the world, and whose speech and literature were becoming the speech and literature of the world's western half. And all these peoples who affected Roman fashions, read Latin literature, and used the Latin tongue, were becoming Roman-minded, stamped with the genius of Rome; their natures took the impress of Rome's chief intellectual attainments, especially of her oratory and her law. The Roman Law, that most distinctive original creation of the Roman people, was an ever working influence upon the personalities of its creators. The Roman was always a legal-minded man, one whose conceptions naturally framed themselves in categories of the law. The quality of legal-mindedness passes into the entire Latin world, just as much as the rhetorical study of Latin literature. It will show itself in the works of Christian Fathers as markedly as in pagan writings.

Thus, despite the influence of Hellenism, many distinctive traits of Roman character remained; its dignity, its stanchness, and its legal-mindedness, its love of order, of civic concordia which was the true Roman analogue of the more philosophic Greek conception of ἁρμονία.

The Greeks themselves were also undergoing change. The classic strenuousness had gradually passed from the Greek intellect and character. The great qualities of intellect and temper which had made Greeks Greeks, and had given the distinctive and preëminent qualities to the creations of the Greek genius, were waning among the people, and were not strenuously adhered to and insisted upon in literature or philosophy. These Greek qualities had, for instance, shown themselves clearly in form, the perfect way in which the veritable subject matter was presented, without impertinences or distractions, as in the tragic drama, or Phidian sculpture. From the Alexandrian times, distractions and impertinences were admitted readily; the forms of literary productions lost their purity; the matter was less noble, and less strictly presented. Likewise the subjects of sculpture were less nobly treated, and that art declined from its classic purity, for instance, borrowing picturesque elements from painting. Philosophy ceased to hold the grand unity of life, wherein knowledge was a noble element. It became mere ethics, yet first with strenuous reason, as among early Stoics and Epicureans; then that too relaxed, till with Plutarch there comes a hospitable harboring of popular superstitions and a genial attempt to justify and systematize them.

The fact that the Greeks in the fourth century before Christ were ceasing to be themselves as greatly as they had been, made the career of Philip possible. Thereupon, the career of Alexander made Greek civic freedom a thing of past reality, and abolished barriers, if not distinctions, between Hellas and the East. The life of a pliant cosmopolitan was now open to the Greek. As the cleverest man of all the Mediterranean and Asiatic world, he could use whatever circumstances he found himself in. And as his strenuous insistence on his own great distinctive qualities and loves was passing from him, there was no reason why he should not adapt himself to circumstances, and also adopt whatever element or view of life seemed agreeable or expedient. His mind was open to novelty, his taste was less exclusive, his reason less exacting. So he accepted the East — many of its ways of thought or foolishness, and whatever of its emotion and ecstasy he could bring himself to feel or imagine. He amused himself with hoary dreams in Egypt, with more luxurious emotion in Syria, and with Phrygian orgies All this told upon Greek character; and was to give an oriental color to Greek thought of the coming centuries. It naturally affected the Greek influence on Rome, whose expanding rule was also bringing many Greek-enlightened Romans to the East.

The modifications of the Greek and Roman characters already mentioned appear as distinctly intellectual. But during the last centuries before Christ another change had been going on, first among Greeks and then with greater fulness of promise among the Romans. This was the development of the emotional side of the human spirit. The Greeks of Homer had ready emotions, and of many kinds, — a full and fair foundation for a catholic growth of the human soul. Emotions intensify with the lyric poets; each lyrist represents some form of feeling more intensely, or at least in clearer consciousness, than in the Epics. Archilochus' poems most consciously breathe hatred; those of Alcæus, the ardor of high-born defiance of the crowd; Mimnermus and Theognis are filled with bitter or sad feeling; Pindar feels fame; and Sappho pours forth the passion of the vision of beauty. The emotions expressed by these poets are direct and personal, springing from their own desires and relating primarily to the immediate satisfying of them. They are not broad or altruistic; they do not rise from souls touched by the sadness of others' lives.

The intellect predominates in Greek tragedy. With Æschylus and Sophocles the feeling which is expressed is intellectually related to life's ethical proportionment. The inheritor of their fame, the supplanter of their popularity, Euripides, certainly understands and perhaps feels human emotion in its varied range and bitterness. After the great period of tragedy, those men whose names make up the roll of Alexandrian literature had personalities too petty for broad feeling, though some of them could express personal passion. The dominance of the intellect is no longer impressive, as with Æschylus and Sophocles, yet no dominance of great emotion succeeds it, but only an uncompensated decline from the power and loftiness of earlier Greek poetry.

The story of Sculpture is analogous. Formal strength predominates with Polycletus, the living power of animal life with Miron, intellectuality with Phidias, and all things physical in harmony therewith. The later artists, Scopas and Praxiteles, and many lesser sculptors after them, express more clearly life's subtile passions. But it was not theirs to realize the breadth of life. The development of human capacity for emotion was continuing; but a greater age was needed, with greater men; an age which should hold

the sum of its spiritual antecedents, and whose sons
should greatly show the heart's growth of which they
were the last result. Such an age could not come to
Greece, irrevocably declining; but, through Greece,
such an age was to come to Rome in the fulness of
her spiritual strength. And it was a Latin that should
voice the saddened grandeur of the pagan heart.

Virgil had Roman forerunners. Catullus' nature
quivered at near pain; and perhaps no Greek had felt
the round of human woe as deeply as Lucretius. The
emotional capacities of these two were modulated and
beautified as well as coördinated with life's aspirations,
in Virgil. His nature held pity for life's pitifulness,
sympathy for its sadness, love for its loveliness, and
proud hope for all the happiness and power that the
imperial era had in store. During the later centuries
of the Empire, further elements were to enter the
antique personality. They may have been elements
of weakness, due to the senescence of the Greek and
Latin races. They were at all events to prove elements
of disintegration, because of their inconsistency with
the rational self-reliance and control which constituted
the strength of the antique man whether Roman or
Greek.

Reading Horace, one is impressed with the sadness
that Epicureanism was resulting in; and the reader
notices that Horace seeks to strengthen his latter years
with the teachings of the Porch. Yet still this self-
poised man looks to his own strength for peace;
Jove may furnish opportunity; he possesses in himself the strength of will to use it or to let it pass.
When Horace was no more, the hesitating thought of

seeking spiritual aid through prayer came to the last
great representatives of Stoicism — to Epictetus and
to Marcus; perhaps God or the gods may help the
soul to resolve more firmly. Stoicism, however, was
losing its power to cheer; with many, the system was
becoming a matter of devitalized phrases. True Stoics
needed self-reliance and self-sufficiency, qualities which
were ceasing to be general. Humanity was a little
weary of its self-poised rationalism. In the second
century, there sprang up a new spirit of religiousness,
showing itself in a craving to learn the future from
the supernatural powers and to gain their aid through
prayers or sacrifices or magic rites. This was not a
crude, strong mode of religion, capable of purification.
Rather it represented the weakness of men consciously
turning from their best strength and highest thoughts
to seek aid or stupefaction by means which those best
thoughts had not approved. A loftier phase of the
new religiousness lay in a yearning for communion
with the divine. The soul, its self-reliance outworn,
its reason found empty, was seeking to renew its life
through ecstatic union with God. This yearning was
to create philosophies or at least remould old thoughts.
The greatest of these new forms of philosophy was
Neo-platonism, a system which sought in dialectic
mode to outsoar reason and attain the super-rational.
Its goal was that ecstatic vision in which sense as well
as reason falls away, leaving the soul enraptured with
the immediacy of God.

Neo-platonism was Hellenic in structure, but touched
with oriental influences which entered through the
eclectic moods of the Hellenic temperament of the

third century. It passed to Rome, and found many
natures open to it among Hellenized Romans. The
goal of Neo-platonism, like the yearning whence it
sprang, was a state of metaphysical ultra-emotionalism.
Might not this philosophy complement the human
feelings which Virgil voiced and which touched
Juvenal with a sense of tears? Would not such a
union make a great and complete personality? It
was impossible. That final Virgilian compass of feeling was real love and pity. Neo-platonic ecstasy was
dialectic mysticism, which had uncertain share in the
heart's realities. Its higher modes scorned them, its
low modes debased them. Virgilian feeling could not
unite with such phantasy or such debasement. Virgil's
tenderness for all life might have made part with the
Christian love of God. But, unhappily for this consummation, the later pagan philosophy devitalized and
mystified such love of God as paganism seemed to
touch. And, on the other hand, there had come on
Christianity a monastic asceticism which set on one
side the love of God and against it, as a devil's snare,
the love of all things human. The round of noble
human feeling could not include itself under such love
of God, any more than it could unite with the Neo-
platonic ecstasy.

The apparent portentous fact was this: with the
Augustan era the final catholic development of the
Hellenized Latin man was reached. The elements
of the pagan personality might severally make some
special advance. There might be a weary, but complete, reliance on reason in Marcus Aurelius, a conscious sense of pity in Juvenal, a general kindliness

in the younger Pliny, a comprehensive stately view of human affairs in Tacitus; and the Coptic Greek Plotinus might create a final dialectic structure, the rational foundations of which were crowned with a super-rational ecstasy. But there was not sufficient strength in latter-day paganism to make a living unity out of these elements.

CHAPTER III

PHASES OF PAGAN DECADENCE

THE fact that Christianity drew into its currents
much of the intellectual strength of the fourth century may have checked any distinctive pagan progress.
On the other hand, the Greek and Latin races, apart
from the Christian inspiration which was about to
touch them, were in a state of decadence. Evidence
of this appears on every hand. For instance, it was
necessary continually to recruit the Roman army with
new barbarian strength. At the fall of the Western
Empire (476) the army had become so completely
barbarian that its revolt appears as a barbarian invasion. Odoakar was but the chief barbarian in the
Roman army, till he chose to have no more imperial
shadows in Ravenna or Rome. Further symptoms of
decay may be seen in the gradual extinction of civic
life in the cities, until municipal organization becomes
mere apparatus for assessment, and civic honors become
burdens from which there is no escape. Still more con-
clusive evidence is afforded by the diminishing population of Italy and the older provinces. Very striking
also is the decay of art; and, lastly, the decadence of
the Greek and Latin pagan personality appears in the
decline of literary faculty and literary taste.

In general this literary decline was a decline from

relevancy of treatment of subjects having real interest to irrelevancy of treatment of subjects having no real interest; from setting forth veritable features of human life to devising preposterous fictions; from large delineation of human character to the absence of any veritable and distinctive characterization of persons real or imaginary; from setting forth the course of human life according to its most truly considered laws to setting it forth in ways of happening and accident, which bear no true relation to character and situation. These decadent traits do not all appear in any one class of compositions; but those writings which exhibit them most strikingly are those which also show characteristics of mediæval literature. Among these are works which continued in vogue through the Middle Ages, or served as the originals from which by translation and adaptation were constructed some of the most popular mediæval compositions. Thus these latter-day Græco-Roman writings illustrate how the classical, or rather the Græco-Roman, or Hellenized Roman personality, was intellectually declining to the level of the men of the early mediæval times, whether barbarians by birth or native denizens of the Empire.

Rhetorical studies, and compositions of a rhetorical character, illustrate the indiscriminate use of subjects void of real interest, as well as the irrelevancy of treatment even of the subject chosen. Roman rhetoric had been a great civilizer and Romanizer of conquered provinces. The rhetorician followed hard on the army to teach the new provincials the Roman Latin literature, and in a way which fostered oratory and the faculty of turning off rhetorically proper Latin phrases. But under the Empire, oratory, whether practised at Rome or in the provinces, was emptied of its genuine purpose, which is to express opinions held upon public matters in order to influence the action of free fellow-citizens. Outside the business of the law, oratory became empty and insincere. It had its apt preparation in the schools of rhetoric, where the rounding of grammatical periods in prose or verse was everything, while pertinency to anything real in life was nothing. Subjects of study and discourse rhetorically selected in order to cultivate cleverness of expression, do not bind the writer or speaker to pertinency to the matter in hand. Education by such means may become an education in irrelevancy for the youth of a society which is becoming more and more dilettante as it loses power to shape its destinies.

The result of this rhetorical fostering of irrelevancy is seen in compositions written for an occasion, as a panegyric on an emperor. These are flatteries, if not lies. They may, however, be pertinent. But in declining times the deeds of the great man dwindle, and the orator is tempted to fill out his speech with pretty matters not quite pertinent. At last these panegyrics became models of irrelevancy. The man praised is fulsomely addressed and flattered, and great deeds are heaped on him. Then the orator may pass to regions of mythology — safe topic ! — nor return. This is one mark of intellectual decline ; for pertinency of treatment is as indicative of intellect as is the character of the subject treated and the reality of its relationship to life. It marks one phase of Roman decline that great numbers of such panegyrics were composed, delivered, and immensely admired. They gave Symmachus his reputation; and Sidonius Apollinaris was made *præfectus urbi* as a reward for one addressed to the shadow emperor Anthemius.[1]

In the antique world a large part of education was education in literary taste. This was so even in the times of the great Greek lyric and dramatic poetry, when form corresponded perfectly to substance. In the Augustan period, and previously, the Latins sedulously studied the form and metres of approved Greek compositions. Their best writers — Catullus, Lucretius, Cicero, Virgil, Horace, Ovid — are learned. Nevertheless, in the good literary periods there was noble substance to express, and the study of form

---

[1] 468 A.D.   A like emptiness had before this characterized Greek rhetoric, or sophistic, as it came to be called. It, likewise, had no practical purpose to subserve; it ceased, even in form, to be forensic; it became a matter of glittering discourse on any literary subject likely to interest an audience. Then it drew from ethics and philosophy, and its discourses became beautiful pagan sermons. Some sophists had great reputations, and their discourses brought them riches and honor. See C. Martha, " La predication morale populaire," in *Les moralistes sous l'empire romain;* Hatch, *Hibbert Lectures,* 1888, pp. 86–104; Croiset, *Hist. de la littérature Grecque,* Vol. V, 466 et seq. The best of them was Dio, a native of Prusa in Bithynia (H. von Arnim, *Leben und Werke des Dio von Prusa*). Throughout the Hellenic East, as well as the Latin West, people delighted in such setting together of brilliant phrases in beautiful form. They were thought admirable literary creations, though there were not lacking sincere protests (Epictetus, *Discourses,* III, 23) against the vain and mercenary character of the men and the shallowness of their discourses. Rhetoric also infected the Greek romances, and produced such a rhetorician's biographical romance as the *Life of Apollonius of Tyana,* by Philostratus.

occupied its proper secondary place as a study of how most fittingly to express the substance.

After the death of Juvenal and Tacitus, the Latin power of literary creation waned rapidly, just as substance and sincerity passed from oratory. Yet there was increased ardor for grammar which taught correctness of expression, and for rhetoric which sought to teach the higher virtues of style. So, both in prose and verse, the study of form went on while substance diminished. Latin education became more and more education in literary form. But form deteriorates when cultivated exclusively, since it can be good only in relation to the substance which it should express. And as the substance dwindles, the tendency develops to treat it in lofty language. Thus poetry and oratory became rhetorical and in the end bombastic. The latter-day pagan world illustrates the common rule, that literary taste, cultivated for its own sake in a period of waning creative power, becomes vapid; and bad taste arising in this way is an evidence of general decline — of decadent humanity.

An interesting illustration of this is the decline in the literary appreciation of the greatest work of Rome's greatest poet. As decade followed decade, and century followed century, there was no falling off in the study of the Æneid. Virgil's fame towered, his authority became absolute. But how? In what respect? As a supreme master of grammatical correctness and rhetorical excellence and of all learning. With increasing emptiness of soul, the grammarians — the "Virgils" — of the succeeding centuries put the great poet to ever baser uses. Here the decadent

Imperial period joins hands with the Middle Ages. Even before the fifth century, Virgil was regarded with superstitious veneration. As early as Hadrian's time the habit had arisen of finding one's future lot indicated in a line of Virgil chosen at random — the "sortes Virgilianae." His commentator Macrobius, a contemporary of Jerome and Augustine, holds him to be infallible in every branch of learning. Hence, he is an authority respecting everything as to which an opinion can be elicited from the real or imagined meaning of his language. This is a point of joinder with the Middle Ages; for the mediæval man who read old Latin authors regarded them primarily as authorities upon whatever branch of fact they seemed to treat; their statements were accepted as true.

When Latin poetry culminated in Virgil, there was no greatness left in Greek literature, which, however, was still to show some small excellences from time to time. Plutarch, for example, catches the illustrative pertinence of the incidents he tells. His narratives bring out the characters of his worthies; and he sees a relation between a man's character and his fortunes. But even in Plutarch's time writings were coming into vogue which had lost all sense of ordered causal sequence of events, as well as of anecdotical pertinence; and, lacking all perception of character, they failed to preserve any proper relation of fortune to the personality of the hero, or rather to the personality of him to whom the incidents of the story happen.

A typical example is the *Life and Deeds of Alexander the Great*, by the pseudo-Callisthenes. This work probably was written in Egypt not later than

the year 100 A.D.[1] Its most apparent motive was to
give an Egyptian parentage to the great conqueror.
Though the narrative is utterly unhistorical, it is not
an original romance invented by its author; for
it appears to have been put together from popular Græco-oriental myths respecting the conqueror's
career. Some of these stories originally may have
had no connection with Alexander, but were gradually
attached to him, just as the French *chansons de
geste* ascribe to Charlemagne and his peers many
deeds of former heroes whose fame was absorbed in
the epic effulgence of the greatest of mediæval emperors. But whatever its source, this collection of
fantastic, impossible stories exhibits all manner of
literary decline. In place of deeds which some hero
might have done, there is a succession of preposterous
occurrences having no related sequence; nothing of
real human significance takes place; there is no relation of fortune to character; and no character to
which one lot rather than another might properly
have fallen.

Adaptations of this work — in some of them Alexander is a propagator of the Christian faith — in many
languages filled the East; it was turned into Latin,
and Latin versions of it in the West were the chief
source of that vast company of versified vernacular
romances which, while they fed the mediæval passion
for the remote and marvellous, also satisfied the historic and literary sense of the Middle Ages with

[1] It is interesting to note that it is not later than the time of
Arrian, who wrote the most sober historical account of Alexander
that we possess.

respect to the great conqueror. Perhaps no other work so illustrates the juncture of the Middle Ages with antiquity on a common level of degeneracy and barbarism — unless it be the *Tale of Troy*. This appears to pass over into the popular literature of the Middle Ages through the medium of writings pseudonymously ascribed to " Dares the Phrygian " and " Dictys the Cretan." The extant " Dares " is in Latin, and evidently is neither an original composition nor a proper translation. Its date is hardly prior to the sixth century. It is an epitome of some other work, and thus bears analogy to the forms in which so much of classic culture passed over to the Middle Ages. The sources of " Dares " are lost. Probably there was a Greek original, written by some one well acquainted with the old cyclic and tragic poets. This would seem to have been turned into Latin, and from this Latin version our extant " Dares " was compiled by some degenerate. It lacks style and form, and is utterly wanting in proportion ; vital events are told in a few bald sentences, while matters antecedent and irrelevant are retained and given at considerable length. Its mechanical monotony precludes the possibility of its being an original composition — the maker of such a work could not have invented anything. We also notice that it foreshadows the mediæval epic way of prefacing the main story with the fortunes of the ancestors or typical forerunners of the heroes.[1] The extant " Dictys " is a similar though less miserable composition. It is fairly written, and the narrative

---

[1] As in the *Kudrun*, in Gotfried's *Tristan*, or Wolfram's *Parzival*.

has some proportion. It seems to have been translated from a Greek original.[1]

In the twelfth century the *Tale of Troy* received its grandiose mediæval telling, in thirty thousand lines, by Benoît de Sainte-More. He gives the story as its threads exist in the extant "Dares" and "Dictys," and appears to observe the authority of the former to line 24301, and then the story of "Dictys" to the end. But probably Benoît followed a lengthier Latin version than the extant "Dares," possibly the very one of which that is the epitome. He may also have been acquainted with a lengthier "Dictys" version.

Further illustration of the degeneracy of Greek literature is afforded by the Greek love-romances, as, for example, the *Ethiopica* of Heliodorus and the *Leucippe and Clitiphon* of Achilles Tatius, both of whom lived in the third or fourth century after Christ. Their delineation of character is poor, and there is scant relation of character and fortune. They elaborate themes which first became prominent literary motives in Alexandrian literature. They are stories of pairs of lovers, to whom all kinds of unexpected ill-chance happen. The man's life and the girl's life and chastity are preserved through it all, and a happy marriage ends the tale. The gods often interpose to avert death or ruin; but their interpositions and all the ups and downs of fortune coming to the lovers show that the only real power in these romances is

---

[1] See E. Patzig, "Dictys Cretensis," *Byzantinische Zeitschrift*, 1892, pp. 131-152, also p. 590. The Greek versions of Trojan legends in the *Heroicos* of Philostratus (author of the *Life of Apollonius of Tyana*) of the second century may be compared with the Dares and Dictys narratives.

chance — τύχη. Chance, stringing itself out in a
succession of unexpected happenings, cannot make
a plot to satisfy an intelligent person. Such a plot
would have been abominable to Æschylus or Sophocles or Aristotle or to Homer; for the adventures
which befall Odysseus in the *Odyssey* serve to bring
out that hero's greatness of character, and are accomplished by him as only he could have accomplished them.
But the hero and heroine in these Greek romances are
characterless puppets, to whom nothing happens in
accordance with any law of life or fate. Yet we may
bear in mind that in the Greek romances fantasy is
dominant, and hence there is no rationally constructed
sequence of occurrences; and also that in the Old Comedy the plot was far less rigorous than in tragedy. But
Aristophanes was a wilful giant, rollicking in imagin-
ings which no chains of reason could hold. He could
also revere the greatness of Æschylus. The imagination
of the Greek romances consists mostly in failure to appreciate causality in fiction, and to grasp the laws of life.

These stories also are rhetorical, the writers loving their polished, conventional, and often borrowed
phrases. There are lengthy descriptions of the countries to which the lovers come, and the customs of the
people. The poems of the Alexandrian poets, Theocritus and Moschus, were pictorial, and contained
charming pictures of the deeds or situations of their
heroes. Achilles Tatius seeks to outdo these real
poets with elaborate descriptions of actual paintings
which his lovers' eyes chance to rest on.[1]

[1] The *Leucippe and Clitiphon* opens with a long description of
a picture of Europa and the Bull, seen by Clitiphon in a temple at

These romances have another unmistakable trait of decadence. Although love stories, they express lubricity rather than passion. The passion of love had been sung by Sappho; it had been made pastoral by Theocritus. Again, utter coarseness, life unveiled amid loud laughter, wanton animal exuberance, had also existed in literature, as with Aristophanes; yet these traits did not indicate a polluted mind. The interest lay in the fun, which might seize on any subject, and quite readily on what was obscene. But the Greek romances, like their forerunner, Lucian's *Ass*, contain neither overmastering passion nor the indiscriminate laughter which may take one subject as readily as another. They contain much that touches only sexual desire, which they seem intended to arouse. Sometimes shameless details are told, showing what the author and his public really cared for. Passion has been always part of human strength. But there is no surer sign of decadence than the dwelling of the mind on such matters as are prominent in the Greek romances.

Sidon. In Book III pictures of Andromeda and of Prometheus are described, and near the beginning of Book V a picture of Philomela and Tereus.

CHAPTER IV

THE ANTIQUE CULTURE

I. *The Transmission of Letters*

THE influence of Greek models upon the development of Latin literature under the Republic and during the first years of the Empire was quite different from the Greek literary fashions, which afterward set in at Rome and reached their height when a Roman emperor wrote his *Thoughts* in Greek. A blank literary period followed, and then Latin literature reasserted itself, and even spread geographically. From the fourth century the Greek tongue and literature were no longer at home in Italy, while the knowledge of Greek became more and more scanty in those lands which had been, or still were, the western provinces of the Empire. In the sixth and seventh centuries the Irish were well nigh the only western Greek scholars. Ireland had been spared the torrential barbarian invasions, and now its scholars spread culture in Gaul and northern Italy, and kept the knowledge of Greek from extinction. Nevertheless Greek works almost ceased to be read.

Latin had become universal in the West, and was to be for centuries the common speech of educated men and serve as their literary vehicle. The Latin

literature passed over into the Middle Ages in its
classic writings, and also in the summarizing and
remodelling works of the transition centuries.

For the preservation of the classics in the period
of barbarian wars, no man deserves equal glory with
Cassiodorus, the Roman-minded minister of Theodoric
the Ostrogoth. As an old man, in the year 540, he
founded the cloister of Vivarium in the extreme south
of Italy. There he first incited monks to study the
classics and copy the manuscripts. The example was
followed in the rapidly increasing monasteries of the
Benedictines. Of great importance also were the
labors of the Irish, of Columbanus above all, who,
in 615, founded that home of letters, the cloister
of Bobbio, in the north of Italy. Then the Anglo-
Saxons, eagerly learning from the Irish, take up the
good work, — and the famous names are Aldhelm
(d. 709), Bede (d. 735), Bonifacius-Winfried (d. 755),
and Alcuin, Charlemagne's minister of education.[1]
These men were monks, and to monks, generally
speaking, was due the preservation of the classics.
Not that they had any special love for the classics,[2]
which they often erased in order to write the lives
of saints on the profane parchment. Nor was the
church altogether friendly to pagan literature. The

[1] See Ebert, *op. cit.*, under these names: Norden, *Antike Kunstprosa*, pp. 665–669; Ozanam, *Civ. Chrét. chez les Francs*, Chaps. IV,
V, and IX.

[2] The rules of Isidore of Seville and of some other monastic legis-
lators forbade the reading of pagan writings without special permission. See Comparetti, *Virgil in the Middle Ages*, p. 85; Graf,
Roma nella memoria e nelle imaginazioni del Medio Evo, II, p. 161;
Specht, *Geschichte des Unterrichtswesens in Deutschland*, pp. 40–57.

classics could be preserved only by men who could write, and such men lived in cloisters, which also afforded leisure for the labor and safekeeping for its result.

Thus classic literature reached the Middle Ages through the same agents that brought the authoritative Roman-Christian religion. The classic writings were received as the works of a greater time; they were accepted as authorities upon whatever topic they treated or could be interpreted into treating.[1] There was little literary appreciation of them, and scanty severing of legend and fiction from history and science. The utmost human knowledge was ascribed to the authors. It also fell in with the temper of the Middle Ages to interpret the classics, like the Scriptures, allegorically. As Virgil was the supreme Latin author, the strangest examples of allegorical interpretation are connected with his writings.[2] Finally, the

[1] It is characteristic of the mediæval use of ancient literature that it is taken as authoritative. What was a work of art or fanciful literature may be taken as *praecepta*, e.g., *Praecepta Ovidii doctoris egregii*, as in the beginning of the *Romaricimontis Concilius* of the early twelfth (or eleventh) century. See Langlois, *Sources de la Roman de la Rose* (Vol. 57 École Francais of Rome, p. 7, etc.). The manner in which the Middle Ages accept matters on authority is still shown in Dante. In *Conv.* III, 5, he says that Aristotle — "that glorious philosopher to whom above all others Nature disclosed her secrets" — has proved that the earth is immovable; he adds that he will not repeat Aristotle's arguments because "it is enough for all people that I address to know *per la sua grande autorità*," that this earth is fixed and does not revolve. Cf. Moore, *Scripture and Classics in Dante*, p. 9.

[2] An extraordinary example is the *De Continentia Vergiliana* of Fulgentius, written not later than the sixth century. See Comparetti, *op. cit.*, Chap. VIII, Ebert, *op. cit.*, I, p. 480.

ignorance and fantastic spirit of the Middle Ages ascribed magic powers and marvellous careers to the classic authors.

Many monks regarded the classics as a source of sinful pleasure, save when used for some educational purpose according with the views of the times. If that purpose could be attained in a shorter way, why read the classic authors? Mediæval education was comprised in the trivium and quadrivium, the seven liberal arts of Grammar, Dialectic, Rhetoric, Geometry, Arithmetic, Astronomy, and Music. These had been held by the ancients to be preparatory to the study of philosophy. The Christian Alexandrians, Clement and Origen, accepted this view and went a step farther. For they held that philosophy and all its preparatory studies were preparation for an understanding of Christian theology. In a narrower and barbaric way the Middle Ages held that liberal studies were the handmaids of theology.[1] The seven arts included all that was necessary as a preparation for theology, and could most conveniently be studied in compendia. Hence it seemed useless to read the authors themselves. This view tended to discourage

[1] See Norden, *Antike Kunstprosa*, pp. 680 et seq., where passages are collected and quoted bearing on this subject; *i.e.* Ennodius, ep. IX, 9; Carolus Magnus, *Epist. de literis colendis, Mon. Germ. leg.* sect. II, tom. I, p. 79; Alcuinus, *Grammatica*, Migne, *Patr. Lat.*, Vol. 101, col. 853; Notker Labeo, in a letter, ed. by P. Piper, *Die Schriften Notker's*, pp. 859 ff.; Honorius Augustodunensis, *de artibus*, ed. Pez, *Thes. anec. noviss.*, II (1721), 227 ff.; Abelard, *Introductio ad theologiam*, opera ed. Cousin, Vol. II, pp. 67 ff.; Hugo de St. Victor, *Erudit. didasc.*, 1, III, c. 3 (Migne, tom. 176, col. 768); John of Salisbury, *Entheticus*, V, 373 f. (Vol. V, p. 250, ed. Giles).

the reading of the classics; but there was great diversity of individual taste and opinion and practice. The general statement may be made that, as century after century men grew in humanity, there came a deeper literary appreciation of the classics, forming a transition to the poetic and literary reverence in which they were to be held by Boccaccio and Petrarch.

Men use what they have need of and appreciate what is nearest to their temper and intellectual level. The works of the Latin commentators and grammarians — Servius, Donatus, Macrobius, Priscianus — were needed when they were written, as well as afterwards, in order to preserve some knowledge of the structure of the Latin language. They were fundamental in the studies prosecuted in the schools of mediæval education.[1] Besides these grammarians, there were other men of the transition centuries who wrote compendia of the seven liberal arts, and still others who summarized pagan ethics or philosophy. Such transition works remained widely popular; some of them became standard text-books in the schools; and through them the men of the Middle Ages received their profane education and the larger part of their classical knowledge. They were true works of the transition period, gathering and selecting from the classic past, recasting and presenting the antique substance in forms suited to the tastes and capacities of their own and the following centuries. We may

[1] See as to these works, which were mainly based on Virgil, Comparetti, *op. cit.*, Chap. V; Teuffel-Schwabe, *Geschichte der Röm. Lit.*, II, §§ 409, 431, 444, 481. How much Priscianus (sixth century) was used may be inferred from the fact that there are extant nearly a thousand manuscripts of his grammar, Teuffel, *op. cit.*, II, § 481.

outline the contents of the two most famous of them, the one a compendium of the seven liberal arts, the other a final presentation of the ethics of pagan philosophy.

Perhaps the most widely used school book of the Middle Ages was the *De Nuptiis Philologiae et Mercurii* by Martianus Capella, an African Neo-platonist, who wrote in the first part of the fifth century.[1] It is a work in nine books. The first two are devoted to the allegorical narrative of the marriage of Mercury with the polymath virgin Philology. Mercury[2] seeks a bride; he cannot have Sophia or Mantice or Psyche; Virtus counsels him to ask Apollo's advice, and Apollo advises him to wed Philology. Under the joyful convoy of the Muses and enzephyred by the music of the spheres, Virtus, Apollo, and the bridegroom fly to Jove's palace to ask his consent. A council of the gods is summoned; a favorable decision is reached; the bride shall be raised to divine rank. With the second book she appears, desiring the marriage, but fearful at the greatness of the honor. Her mother, Phronesis, adorns her for the wedding; four noble matrons, the cardinal virtues, greet her, and the Graces, with three mystic kisses, give her courage. Athanasia, daughter of Apotheosis, comes to lead her to Heaven, but first commands her to deliver that with which her bosom is seen to swell; at this she vomits forth many rolls

[1] On the date of Capella, see H. Parker, "The Seven Liberal Arts," *English Historical Review*, 1890.

[2] Mercury — or Hermes — is, according to Plotinus, the λόγος; hence the propriety of his marriage with Philology (φίλειν-λόγον). Zeller, *Phil. der Griechen*, III, 2, p. 561; Ebert, *op. cit.*, I, p. 483, note.

of papyrus and of linen, which are gathered up by the Virgin Artes and Disciplinae, Urania and Calliope helping. The bride now drains the goblet of immortality, and rises to heaven, where Juno Pronuba meets her with offerings. Under the guidance of Juno, she traverses the circles of the planets and reaches the Milky Way, where Jove's palace is. There all the gods and beings known to Latin mythology assemble, with here and there a deity from Egypt, besides the guards of the elements (*elementorum praesides*) and a most beauteous company of the angelic folk and souls of blessed ancients. Now the bride's prudent mother demands a reading of the tables of dower and the *lex Papia Poppaeaque*, regarding the property rights of married women. Thereupon Phœbus rises and leads forward, to place with the bridal gifts, seven maid-servants from his brother's household; these are the seven Artes — Ars Grammatica; Ars Dialectica, "a little paler;" Rhetorica; Geometria;[1] Arithmetica; Astronomia; Harmonia. Each one, as Phœbus leads her forward, tells her parentage, and then expounds the substance of her art, most dryly, all virginal allegory laid aside. They have a book apiece, and make up the tale of the nine books of Capella.

This work became the "standard" school book of the Middle Ages. Its form and character anticipates mediæval taste, upon which it was to be so influential. It is written in prose and verse, the *chantefable* form;[2]

[1] Which includes geography.

[2] As with Boethius' *De Consolatione Philosophiae*. Properly speaking, the origin of this is the Roman *Satura Menippea*.

though the song-element is unimportant in the last seven books. These are strictly instructive, and sapless as the rods of mediæval schoolmasters. The allegory of the first two books is pleasingly pedantic and the whole work presents the sterile union of fantasy with pedantry, so dear to the closing years of pagan scholarship, when the old straw was thrashed, re-tied in queer-shaped bundles, and then thrashed again. The process produced *pabulum* for coming generations.[1]

The *De Nuptiis Philologiae* shows its author to have been a desiccated person, one who in his leisure might have enjoyed the romances of Achilles Tatius. We have a more living phenomenon in the personality of Anicius Boethius, who summarized pagan logic and ethics for the Middle Ages, as Capella summarized other sides of pagan culture. In somewhat adaptive mode Boethius translated Aristotle's *Categories*, with more elaboration, he translated and commented upon the philosopher's περὶ ἑρμηνείας, *De interpretatione*. He composed two versions of the latter work, one for

[1] St. Isidor of Seville, who wrote in the latter part of the sixth century, was an important personage of the transition, handing down not only Christian doctrine, but pagan learning also. In his Etymologies (*Etymologiarum libri XX*) he includes the whole range of knowledge constituting early mediæval culture. The first book is entitled "De Grammatica"; the second, "De Rhetorica et Dialectica"; the third, "De quatuor disciplinis mathematicis, arithmetica, geometria, musica, astronomia"; the fourth, "De medicina"; the fifth, "De legibus et temporibus." The dryness of this work and its poverty of thought are outdone only by the absurdity of its etymologies. Another work, kin in its saplessness, is the *Mythologiarum libri* of Fulgentius (480–550 A.D.), for which see Teuffel-Schwabe, *op. cit.*, II, § 480; Ebert, *op. cit.*, I, 476–480; also cf. Comparetti, *op. cit.*, Chap. VIII.

beginners, the other for advanced students. He translated and commented on Porphyry's Ἐισαγωγή, or Introduction to the *Categories* of Aristotle. This work is likewise executed in two editions, one comprising two dialogues, the other, five books of greater length. These works are the foundation of mediæval logic, and lie at the basis of mediæval scholastic disputations as to realism and nominalism.[1] They were scholastic interpretations of another's thought. The writer was himself interested in the question of the real existence of universals. His methods of exposition even in his more constructive works point to the methods of scholasticism, as may be observed by glancing through his treatises on arithmetic and music.[2] His influence was very weighty in establishing the trivium and quadrivium.

So far the writings of Boethius appear merely learned and impersonal. It is otherwise with his *De Consolatione Philosophiae*. This final work of pagan eclecticism discloses an extraordinary situation. The author, a man of noble birth, apparently lofty character, wide learning, and enlightened thought, occupying a preëminent official position, is in prison under condemnation of death on a charge of treasonable conduct. And the monarch who has permitted or commanded this, and will permit or command the execution of this noble philosopher, is the most just and enlightened ruler as yet arisen from the Teutonic

[1] Cf. Haureau, *Hist. de la philosophie scholastique*, Vol. I, Chap. IV and VI. They were superseded by the complete translations of Aristotle's works in the twelfth and thirteenth century.

[2] Migne, *Patr. Lat.*, Vol. 63. Cf. Maurice, *Mediæval Philosophy*, pp. 4–14.

races, a king indeed, the Ostrogoth Theodoric. This king is great in reality, and is to have in minstrel story a fabled name [1] and fame equal to the philosopher's repute of him who was once his trusted friend, but is now his condemned prisoner.

The wherefore of all this may never be known. We do not know what may have led Boethius to contemplate or feebly attempt the impracticable. It is not certain that he was connected with any scheme prejudicial to the king. [2] That open-minded monarch was sometimes a barbarian. He was an old man now, and perhaps had become suspicious. Probably the doctrinaire philosopher had laid himself open to suspicion. With less real cause, though perhaps with more irritating provocation, Vespasian put to death Helvidius. The deaths of Boethius and Symmachus, his noble father-in-law, blot Theodoric's fame; but for the philosopher, the evil condemnation was to be posthumous good. It led him to compose a book which was to be read and prized by great and noble men.

No pagan-minded scholar whose manhood saw the year five hundred could be other than a transmitter of the greater past. Not only would his thoughts have come to him from the past, his character also would be moulded by his mighty heritage. So it was with Boethius. The contents of his mind came from the past, which also largely made his personality.

[1] Dietrich of Berne (Verona).

[2] Boethius, *De Con. Phil.*, I, prosa 4, says that he was accused of hindering an informer from producing evidence to prove the Senate guilty of treason. Hodgkin, *Italy and her Invaders*, Vol. III, Bk. IV, Chap. 12, discusses the whole matter.

He himself, the man Boethius, was mostly the product of antecedent pagan thought. But he was also a man of rhetorically ardent feeling and literary gifts; and when in final sorrow he sought the solace of his life-long studies, his thoughts and character fused themselves into a veritable literary creation. In the manner of that decadent time, the work summarized much ethical pagan thought, and presented it with surface consistency. But the book was more than a summary. Having a unity of feeling inspired by the situation, it offers its contents and its writer in a most appealing way, and speaks to the reader as the author's self.

The *Consolation of Philosophy* is not a Christian work.[1] But its author undoubtedly conformed to Christian worship, and was not unlearned in Christian teachings.[2] He presents Pagan ethics from the standpoint of one impressed by the problems which Christianity had made prominent, for instance, that of the compatibility of human free will and God's foreknowledge.

The allegorical opening — Philosophy appearing in a garb adorned with symbols — suited the taste of the time and of the Middle Ages. The romantic pathos of the author's situation proved most appealing to all men touched by life's vicissitudes;[3] and this prison-writing is optimistic in its teaching, seeing only good

---

[1] See *Das System des Boethius*, by Nitzsch, pp. 42–92; also the work itself.

[2] He probably was the author of the *Christian Theological Tracts* attributed to him. See Hildebrand, *Boethius und seine Stellung zum Christenthum;* also *Boethius, an Essay*, by H. F. Stewart.

[3] As, *e.g.*, Alfred the Great, one of the many translators of the work.

in ill: so it might be an encouragement to all unfortunates.

In easy, attractive modes of statement, the *Consolation of Philosophy* sets forth ordinary, universally valid thoughts upon the uncertainty of fortune and the emptiness of its favors. Any man can think in its words. Moreover, there was in it much that Christians could interpret in a Christian way. For example, the *amor* of which the author speaks is not in reality Christian love, but the great concordant energy of the universe inspired by the Creator, making for harmony and perfection. This *coelo imperitans amor*, this bond of all nature's concords, is the physico-philosophic conception coming down from Empedocles: —

> O felix hominum genus
> Si vestros animos amor,
> Quo coelum regitur, regat !¹

Its proper yet transformed self reappears in Dante's

> L'amor che move il sole e l'altre stelle.

Christian conceptions could be read into it. In the beautiful metre nine of Liber III, which was in fact an adaptation of a passage from Plato's *Timaeus*, the Christian heart could find echo: —

> te cernere finis,
> Principium, vector, dux, semita, terminus idem.

Here the Christian might see the "I am the way, the truth, and the life." Again, with what responsive feelings might Christians read of the happy region where the *dominus regum* holds the sceptre, from

¹ *Con. Phil.*, Lib. II, metre 8.

which tyrants are exiles — haec patria est mihi![1]
And, finally, the writer argues that blessedness and
God are the *summum bonum* and are one and the same;
man gets blessedness by gaining *divinitas*. A Christian heart might feel in this the emotion of the opening of Augustine's *Confessions:* "Thou hast made us
towards thee, and unquiet are our hearts till they find
rest in thee."

All of these reasons conduced to give the *Consolation* its great future. It presented the spirit of pagan
ethics to the Middle Ages: and its office may be compared with that of the *Imitatio Christi*. That work
also, in more beautiful and simple language, was a compendium, and likewise had its unity, its selfhood, in
the author's intense feeling, which fused the thoughts
and emotions of the saintly past into a devotional
outpour of one Christian soul.

II. *Transmission of the Roman Law*

The passage of the Roman law over into the Middle Ages, the modifications and corruptions suffered
by it, and the manner of its appropriation by the Celtic and Germanic peoples, present analogies with the
fortunes of other elements of classic culture. These
races came in touch with Roman law when the great
periods of its development were past. In the provinces

---

[1] Lib. IV, metre 1. Lib. III, metre 12, sings the lyric tale of
Orpheus and Eurydice, to teach that he who once sees the bright
fount (*fontem lucidum*) and looks back, is lost, — a pagan story,
but having its analogy with him who, putting his hand to the plough
and looking back, is not fit for the kingdom of heaven.

it was adapting itself to the needs of imperfectly Romanized provincials; at the centres of Roman government and affairs it was entering upon a stage of codification. The changes which the law was undergoing in Spain and Gaul were corruptions, in that they represented the adaptation of a developed and intellectual system to the demands of peoples whose mental vision was not broadened to the range of metropolitan life. Yet they were also links in the chain of eventual progress; for they represented the process of appropriation of the Roman law by races who were to develop these modified legal rules as their own law. The result might be, as in the south of France, a Romanesque law presenting in its growth an analogy to the development of the Romance tongues and literatures out of the Vulgar Latin speech.

The people of the provinces had some acquaintance with this provincialized law; but only lawyers or officials were likely to have the larger knowledge of the Roman law as it then existed in imperial codifications and collections. For the emperors were grouping their edicts into codes and were endeavoring to preserve and protect with their authority the legal attainment of the past. The legislation of Theodosius and Justinian did not arrest the development of Roman law; rather it preserved the law in a form suited to the understanding of the fourth, fifth, and sixth centuries. It cannot even be said that Valentinian's famous "Law of Citations"[1] or Justinian's prohibition of

---

[1] *Theod. Cod.*, I, IV, 426 A.D. See Muirhead, *Hist. Introd. to the Law of Rome*, § 78, for a translation of this enactment, which accorded equal authority to the writings of Papinian, Paulus, Gaius,

interpretation[1] had the effect of checking the development of the law. The first was a declaration that the
legal principles and rules evolved by the past should
be accepted without question; it tended to prevent
their loss or corruption. It was anticipatory of the
general attitude of deference of the mediæval centuries toward what had come down from antiquity.
The men who labored at the command of Theodosius
or Justinian could not add to the legal science of
Paulus and Papinian any more than Capella could add
to the contents of the seven liberal arts, of which his
De Nuptiis Philologiae et Mercurii afforded a compendium. Codes did not impede the development of a
law which the men of the time had not the faculty to
advance; rather they tended to preserve the law from
corruption and oblivion.[2] The Theodosian code and

Ulpian, and Modestinus, and provided that in case of divergent
dicta the party having the greater number on his side should prevail, save where the authorities were equally divided, and then he
having Papinian on his side should prevail.

[1] *L. 12 Cod. de leg.*, I, 14. See Windscheid, *Pandektenrecht*,
Bd. I, § 25.

[2] The principal collections or codifications of Roman law within
the Roman Empire were: The Codes of Gregorianus and Hermogenianus, made at the end of the third century; these were collections of imperial rescripts and were the work of private persons,
but they received statutory recognition from Theodosius and Valentinian. The Codex Theodosianus and the *novellae constitutiones*,
published subsequently by Theodosius and by his successors. This
emperor's plan was to enact a single comprehensive code drawn
from writings of the jurists, from the Gregorian and Hermogenian
collections of rescripts, and from the edicts of prior emperors. The
Codex was first published at Constantinople in the year 438, and the
next year went into force in the West. Legislation of Justinian:
The Codex (529 A.D.), a collection of statutes, intended to be the
sole repertory of statutory law; the Digesta or Pandectae (533 A.D.),

other legislation before Justinian formed the chief
sources of the codes of Roman law enacted by barbarian kings.[1]

The old Germanic principle, that a people carries
its own law with it, was a principle natural to peoples
potentially or actually migratory, for whom blood,
rather than territory, constituted the test of racehood
and tribal unity.   The ready recognition by the Ger-

an authoritative compilation of jurisprudential law in fifty books,
drawn from the writings of jurists whose authority had been recognized by Justinian's imperial predecessors; the Institutes (533 A.D.),
based on the Institutes of Gaius, a well-known school text-book;
the Novels, the *novellae constitutiones post codicem*, published from
time to time during Justinian's reign.

[1] These comprised the following: *Edictum Theodorici*, promulgated by the great king of the Ostrogoths. It constituted a code of
law for both Goths and Romans — *Barbari Romanique*. Its sources
were not Gothic law, but Roman law, statutory (*leges*) and jurisprudential (*jus*); to wit, the Code and Novels of Theodosius, the
Codes of Gregorianus and Hermogenianus, the writings of Paulus
and Ulpian. The incapacity of its authors to enunciate clearly principles of law appears in the unskilful use they made of their sources.
Lex Romana Visigothorum, or *Breviarium Alaricianum*, commonly called the Breviarium, compiled at the command of Alaric II,
king of the Visigoths, shortly before the year 507, when the Visigoths were driven from the northern parts of their dominion by the
Franks. The compilers selected their material, *leges* and *jus*,
without altering the text save by omissions, and in some instances
by qualifying or limiting it by their accompanying *interpretatio*.
The sources were practically the same as those of Theodoric's Edict.
This Code, which regulated the rights of Roman subjects of the
Visigothic king, became the most widely used source of Roman law
in the west of Europe. *Lex Romana Burgundionum* (cir. 510 A.D.),
called "Papianus," an edict for the Roman subjects in the kingdom
of the Burgundians. Its sources of Roman law were substantially
the same as those of the Breviarium. It was not free from the influence of the popular provincial Roman law, and contains traces of
the influence of the Burgundian code for Burgundians.

manic kingdoms of the Roman law as valid for their new subjects was incidental to what they esteemed of far greater importance, the preservation of their own Germanic law for themselves.   As in the Visigothic and Burgundian kingdoms, so in the kingdom of the Franks the Roman provincials retained their own private law.   But the Franks found the Breviarium of Alaric in force and had no need to issue another code for Roman provincials.   So, at a later period, the Lombards did not need to issue a code for their Roman subjects in Italy where they found the Justinian legislation in force.

Before the fifth century, the Roman law as applied among provincials, in Gaul for example, had to some extent recognized local custom.   It is also to be borne in mind how pronounced, not to say dominant, the Germanic element in the Roman army and government became in this, the last century of the Western Empire.   In the next century Germanic ideas and institutions obviously affected the law of the Roman population of Burgundy, France, and Lombardy.   For example, in the Visigothic Breviarium, the *interpretationes* accompanying the selected texts show traces of Germanic influence.

Conversely, the Roman law affected the codes formulated under the direction of Germanic kings for their own peoples, and some effect of Roman culture may also be observed.   In the first place, it was the example of the Romans that led to the formulation of these barbarian codes as codes.   The attempt to state and to group laws together in a written code marks a stage in the history of barbaric law.   Secondly, the Germanic codes were written in Latin, which could not fail to affect their substance.

Besides these marks of Roman influence, even the *Lex Salica*, the earliest and purest of the Germanic codes, shows some slight traces of Roman law.[1] The same is true of the *Lex Ribuaria*, which was in large part a working-over of the *Lex Salica*. In the *Lex Burgundionum* of Gondobada, the king of the Burgundians, and in the Visigothic codes, the influence of Roman provincial law is still more obvious. In revisions of the Visigothic codes references to eloquence and philosophy show the effect of Roman culture, and the participation of the Roman clergy in their composition is also apparent. The Lombards appear to have kept their early codes the freest from Roman legal notions.[2]

There was still another great current by which Roman law was transmitted to the Middle Ages. After the establishment of Germanic kingdoms the clergy continued to live under Roman law as their personal law,[3] in France using mainly the Breviarium, and in Italy portions of the legislation of Justinian. The principle that the clergy should be judged by a personal law of their own endured long after the law of the person as applied to other men had made way for the principle of the law of the land. This law of the person for the clergy became the Canon law.

---

[1] The first redaction of the Salic law was made in the reign of Clovis, before his conversion (496 A.D.).

[2] These are the Codes of Rothari (643 A.D.) and of Luitprand (713 A.D.). See Savigny, *Gesch.*, I, pp. 123, 124, 129; II, p. 219; Brunner, *Deutsche Rges.*, Bd. I, § 53. Cf. Hodgkin, *Italy and her Invaders*, Vol. VI, Bk. VII, Chaps. 5 and 10.

[3] Ecclesia vivit lege Romana, *Lex Ribuaria*, 58.

The Western Church had grown, lived, and expanded in Roman or Romanized lands and under the rules of Roman law. Naturally, when the administration of its affairs, temporal and spiritual, had been fully accorded to it under the Christian emperors, it drew upon the Roman law for the rules under which its members should live and its property and their property be governed. Though the Church may never have formally admitted that the Roman law formed part of its law (*i.e.* of the Canon law), such always has been the fact, a fact, however, which has undergone modifications according to the varying political and ecclesiastical conditions of the different centuries of the Church's existence. For example, the Constitutions of the Roman emperors from Constantine's time, so far as they affected the Church, formed an integral part of its law down to the destruction of the Western Roman Empire. In other periods the Church drew from such sources of Roman law as were in use at the time.[1] It may be remembered that Gratianus, whose work for the Canon law was epoch-making, as the work of the Bologna school was for the Roman, lived in the twelfth century while the Bologna school was flourishing, and was himself a monk at the convent of St. Felix in Bologna. Jealousy of Roman law — of the law that regarded emperors rather than popes as om-

[1] See Conrat (Cohn), *op. cit.*, pp. 5–30, for references by the clergy to the Roman law, or passages showing a knowledge of it, from the sixth to the eleventh century, as, *e.g.*, in the letters of Gregory I (590–604). Also, for compilations of Roman law for ecclesiastical use in Italy (*Lex Romana canonice compta*, etc.), see Conrat, *op. cit.*, pp. 205–218, and in France, *ib.*, pp. 252 et seq.

nipotent — first awoke during the struggle between the Empire and the Papacy.

Rules drawn from a system of law developed under paganism were not likely to remain unmodified when applied by the Church. But the effect of Christianity on the development of Roman law does not become apparent before Constantine. From his time enactments begin in favor of the Church and its property and its privileges as legatee, as well as enactments conferring the supervision of charities upon the bishops and a power of interference in guardianships, and others recognizing the validity of acts done in the presence of priests, and imposing certain disabilities upon heretics. Of still greater importance was the institution of the bishop's court,[1] the penalties imposed upon divorce, and the repeal of the *lex Papia Poppaeaque* discouraging celibacy.

These enactments show the opposition between the Christian ideal and the Roman. The bishop's court was the realization of the desire of the early Church to rule itself and its members and to keep free from secular trammels; pagan Rome had known nothing analogous. In the restrictions on divorce, the Christian ideal of the sanctity of marriage struggles to assert itself. The provisions of the Roman law encouraging fruitful marriages and imposing penalties on celibacy fell prostrate before monasticism, which was coming to be recognized as the perfect Christian life. The emperors, with a view to civic order, endeavored to control the conduct of the hordes of monks.[2] But

---

[1] *E.g.*, *Novellae Valentinian III*, Tit. **XXXV**.
[2] See, *e.g.*, *Cod. Theod.*, Lib. **XVI**, Tit. **III**.

never did a Christian emperor enact a law contravening
the universal recognition of the Christian Church that
the virgin state was the state of preëminent Christian
merit and holiness. These novel Christian views embodied in imperial edicts did not touch the principles
of the Roman law ; its mode of reasoning, its legal
conceptions, and the general rules of contract law
were not affected.

As has been seen, the pre-Justinian codes with bits
of the old jurisprudential law were the sources of the
barbarian codes of Roman law current to the north
and west of Italy. In Italy, however, the Roman law
as applied was drawn from the legislation of Justinian, and indeed from his legislation proper — Codex,
Novels, Institutes — rather than from his compilation
of jurisprudential law, the Digest. Some knowledge
of Roman law always existed in Italy and other parts
of Western Europe ; and to some extent Roman law
continued to be applied in the courts of the Romance
countries. But from the seventh to the end of the
eleventh century the Roman law as a whole was not
known and understood in a scientific and intelligent
manner. During this period there appear to have been
no schools of law, properly speaking, nor any original
writing upon jurisprudence.[1]

---

[1] This is substantially the view of Savigny, *Gesch.*, I, Cap. VI,
and Bd. III, p. 83, and of Flach, *Études Critiques*, etc. See, also,
Conrat, *op. cit.*, pp. 96 et seq.; Muirhead, *op. cit.*, § 90; S. Amos,
Civil Law of Rome, p. 414, etc. It is opposed by Fitting, who
maintains that Roman law was taught at all times in the Middle
Ages in schools of law, mostly connected with the Church; that it
was also taught in connection with the Trivium; that at all periods
there was a juristic literature, and law was treated scientifically.

The decadent or barbaric use of a highly developed system of law seems to be marked by the composition and use of epitomes and compilations of extracts. This is analogous to the way in which decadent and barbaric periods adapt to their use the culture of the past. The Theodosian code and the legislation of Justinian compiled and codified the existing law, which the fifth and sixth centuries found difficulty in understanding and applying.[1] It is noteworthy how these compilations were used by the barbarians and in the succeeding semi-barbarous centuries. The *Breviarium* of Alaric II was practically an epitome or compilation of excerpts from the Theodosian code. But the *Breviarium* was itself the code which maintained its preëminence as the vehicle of Roman law in France and elsewhere. It likewise was abridged and was used in epitomes more than in its original form.[2] The legislation of Justinian was also chiefly used, from the seventh to the eleventh centuries, through epitomes and compilations of extracts. In France, where it was never promulgated, and where it therefore remained foreign law, it was well-nigh exclusively known and used in these abbreviated forms, and even in Italy the use of such works was more general than the use of the original texts.[3]

[1] Of course, this is the usual function of codification. The spirit and ability with which the particular codification is accomplished determines whether it is to be regarded as a work of decadence from the standard of previous legal attainment. A code may in itself be an advance.

[2] See for these epitomes, Conrat (Cohn), *op. cit.*, pp. 222–240.

[3] Among these compilations and epitomes, the *Summa Perusina*, the *Brachylogus*, and the *Petri exceptiones legum Romanorum* may be mentioned as in use in both France and Italy.

The fresh and springing life of the Lombard cities at the beginning of the twelfth century stimulated the more thorough and scientific study of Roman law which a better stage of intelligence rendered possible, and which, in fact, had begun at Bologna under Irnerius and others of the Bologna school. There resulted a practical re-discovery and revival of Justinian's Digest, that great collection of jurisprudential law which had been beyond the needs and the comprehension of the preceding centuries. And it was from Bologna that currents of the new and larger knowledge of Roman law went forth through France, England, and Germany.

In France in the course of the ninth, tenth, and eleventh centuries the old Germanic principle of the personality of the law, that is, of law as applicable to persons according to their race, had given way to the principle of territoriality, that is, of law as valid within a certain country. The application of the principle of personality had become impracticable; it would have been necessary to determine the race of the defendant, and then to know the text of the *lex* or capitulary applying to him and to the case. But the races were mingling, and an increasing illiteracy made it difficult to understand the written law. The principle of personality had to be abandoned, and often the text of the *lex* was ignored. In each province a customary law applying to all inhabitants was forming, its rules being usually drawn from the older *lex* applicable to the race there dominant; but that older *lex* was no longer actually applied. The full change therefore was from *lex* applied according to the racehood of the parties, to customary law valid for all within a certain territory. In the eleventh century the last traces of the former system disappeared. The renewal of the study of the Roman law in the twelfth century was fruitful of results through France. That law could now serve as a model for jurists. In some provinces it was accepted as actual law, written and authoritative. Accordingly, in the south of France, where the people lived under a customary law derived from Roman law, the Roman law proper now regained validity. In the middle and north of France, where there was less Roman law in the customary law, Roman law was not accepted in bulk or as authoritative in itself; but it influenced the customary law. Thus a line was drawn between the *pays de coutumes* and the *pays de droit ecrit*, and this division endured from the thirteenth century to the French Revolution; roughly, it was the same line that separated the *pays de langue d'oc* from the *pays de langue d'oil*.

The law prevailing in England before the Norman conquest was in the main pure Germanic law, which came with the English conquests of Britain. A distinct Scandinavian strain entered with the Danish invasion; and the Norman law of William the Conqueror may have included Scandinavian elements; but it brought a far more important contribution of Frankish ideas and customs. Possibly some apparently English institutions may be related, through the customs of Normandy, with some of the institutions of the last centuries of the Roman government. But the new, direct, and certain influence of Roman law begins with Lanfranc as William the Conqueror's adviser, and in the twelfth century the full current sets in from Bologna.   Evidently, this was not a survival of Roman or Romanic law in institutions and customs, but a revival of the Law of Justinian.

In the twelfth century a close relation existed between Roman and Canon law in England, the Canonist frequently citing the *leges*.   The Roman and Canon laws entered England together.   In ecclesiastical courts the latter gained wide jurisdiction.   But the Roman law proper was without a court and was chiefly used by the Canonists in the practice of Canon law.   Some knowledge of it appears to have endured. The author of the *Tractatus de legibus*, attributed to Glanville, Henry II's Chief Justiciar, is versed in it; and at least the opening chapters of Justinian's *Institutes* were well known in the time of Henry III. Bracton's *Note Book*, written between 1250 and 1258, has been styled "Romanesque in form, English in substance."   He absorbed much from the Corpus Juris Civilis, and may represent the climax of the study of Roman law in mediæval England, which again appears to wane in the reign of Edward I. But all lawyers know the great debt which the English law in its later development owes to the jurisprudential law of Rome, to which in the main it owes its Equity Jurisprudence, its Law of Admiralty, and much of its Law Merchant.

In Germany, as in France, from the close of the ninth century the personal law gives way to the territorial.   And in the establishment of a territorial law, a *landesrecht* proper, one strain of Germanic law tri-

umphs over its kindred and for the time over Roman
law as well. This was the Frankish law, the *Lex
Salica* as supplemented by the Capitularies of the
Frankish monarchs.[1] But in Germany the Roman law
was to reassert itself with power, and that, too, the
Roman law as known and reëstablished in its higher
forms by the labors of the Bologna school. A portion
of this knowledge may have reached Germany in the
twelfth century from the law schools of Italy. But
the practical "reception" of the Roman law, that is,
its application in the courts, begins with the fifteenth
century.

Clearly the appropriation of Roman law in Germany, England, and France, under the inspiration of
Bologna, was essentially different from the survival of
Roman law in Italy and the early Germanic kingdoms.
Through the sixth and immediately following centuries, the Roman law, modified, barbarized, dispersed
in scattered influences upon Germanic codes, belittled
and debased by unreasoning abstracts and epitomes,
was understood and applied as a decadent and semi-
barbaric period would naturally understand and apply
it. The centuries went on. The races of Western
Europe grew in all the elements of humanity. They
became capable of a better understanding of the
Roman law, while the exigencies of an increasing

---

[1] See Sohm. "Fränkisches Recht und Römisches Recht," *Zeitschrift für R. gesch. Savigny-Stift.*, Bd. I (1880), pp. 1–84. Or,
perhaps, one should say that it was the Frankish *Lex Ribuaria;*
recognizing, however, that the latter was derived from the *Lex
Salica.* Brunner, *op. cit.*, § 33 (Bd. I, pp. 257–258) ; Schröder, *op. cit.*,
52, and *ib.*, "Die Franken und ihr Recht," *Zeitschrift für R. gesch.
Savigny-Stift.*, Bd. II (1881), Germ. Abtheilung, pp. 1–82.

commerce demanded the application of legal principles such as only the Roman law contained. So a more thorough and intelligent study began in Bologna and the cities of Lombardy, which were centres of the new growth of trade and had preserved the strongest traditions of Roman law. A new stage in the knowledge of Roman law was reached, and this higher knowledge crossed the Alps to France, England, and Germany. In those countries there were men fit to receive the gift, and the Roman law henceforth was appropriated and applied in the new spirit of a larger time, a spirit which in its rationality and comprehensiveness drew nearer to the spirit of the classic jurists.

CHAPTER V

The Life and Deeds of Alexander, the Trojan History, and the Greek Romances afford illustrations of the manner in which classical narrative and imagination sank to the level of mediæval taste. The works of Capella and Boethius show the forms in which classical culture and philosophy were rendered congenial to the coming centuries. The barbarized abridgments of the Roman Law show how that was brought within the comprehension and adapted to the circumstances of the transitional and early mediæval periods, while the codification of Justinian remained above the needs and understanding of men until a later time. So far the antique elements remained clearly pagan. Quite as important were those which in the medium of their transmission were clothed in Christian phrase, or were more deeply altered in their combination with Christian thought or feeling. Certain writings of Ambrose illustrate the use of stoical reasoning as a basis of Christian ethics. Synesius of Cyrene is an example of a man in whose mental composition pagan and Christian elements are mixed together yet do not unite; in his writings Neo-platonism has scarcely donned Christianity. Dionysius the

Areopagite shows the more organic union of Christianity and Neo-platonism.

I. *Ethics*

Generally speaking, excellence and right in every school of pagan ethics was a matter of the rational and strenuous endeavor of the enlightened man. When he acted wrongly, he had his passion or ignorance to blame; when he acted aright, he might congratulate himself. A pagan is neither tempted of the devil, nor very definitely helped by God. Right conduct, that is, conduct most conducive to the actor's welfare, is whatever human experience and reason have approved. Approval by the best human reason based on the widest human knowledge was the standard. There was no thought of divinely revealed righteousness, nor any clear conception of a God whose ways with men and whose commands set the standard for man's conduct. God was not the pattern of human righteousness in Greece and Rome, although divinities might be conceived in accordance with ideals which men could reach wherever mortality was not a bar.

But the principles of Christian ethics trace their descent from the spirit of the Old Testament, — from the great note of the Pentateuch, " And Abraham believed God, and it was accounted unto him for righteousness; " from the psalmist's cry, " Against thee only have I sinned " — " In thy sight shall no man be justified; " from the note of Proverbs, " The fear of Jehovah is the beginning of wisdom," — to love what

Jehovah loves, to hate what He hates and as He loves and hates, is righteousness, is wisdom, is long life and length of days. In the Old Testament the ethical and religious standard was God's power and love; the means to righteousness was His aid and comfort given to those who seek His ways; and the unapproachable pattern of all human righteousness was God Himself, and His ways with men.

"Good Master! Why callest thou me good? There is none good but God" — "Be ye perfect, even as your Father in heaven is perfect" — "Thy faith hath saved thee" — "If ye love me, ye will keep my commandments." All these words of Christ accord with Old Testament thought, develop it, fulfil it. And Christianity in progressive development of the religious ethics of the Old Testament, was faith in God, and prayer, and love of Him; a turning always unto Him for guidance and strength; an utter humbling of self, a sense of insurmountable sinfulness, of failure to be like Christ; a sense of righteousness never reached, but always to be striven for in the love and grace of God. This seeking unto righteousness and the love of God through the aid of unmerited Grace, was to be the holiest inspiration of mediæval Christianity. But it did not come altogether nor at once to Greek and Roman Christians, though all devoted followers of Christ were touched by it. After Paul, hardly a man is found completely possessed of these principles and held by them, until Augustine. That father of mediæval Christianity, in his warfare with Pelagianism, was combating a survival in Christianity of the general spirit of pagan ethics, self-reliant, unappreciative of the absolute need of God.

The ethics of Ambrose may be contrasted with those of Augustine. The great archbishop was a Christian, a father of Christian song and chant, an exponent of Christian feeling. But the reasoning of his *De Officiis Ministrorum* is pagan. In plan the work follows Cicero's *De Officiis*. Cicero addressed his work to his son, and began with remarks on the propriety of writing for him a treatise on duties. So Ambrose declares that he will write to inform his sons (the clergy), since grace as well as nature impels to love (I, 24); and he justifies himself as a bishop in speaking on the subject. He then says (I, 27) that philosophers thought that *officia* were derived from the good (*honestum*) and useful (*utile*), and he repeats Cicero's statement of the matter (*De Off.*, I, iii, sec. 9 and 10). But, continues Ambrose (I, 28), we regard only the good, and that with respect to the future life, and we deem useful only what helps thereto. They reckon (I, 29) secular advantages among goods (*in bonis*), we hold them the contrary.

Ambrose (I, 30) refers to what Cicero says as to the seemly (*decorum, De Off.*, I, xxvii, sec. 93); and then follows him (I, 36) in saying that every *officium* is either *medium* or *perfectum* (*De Off.*, I, iii, sec. 8). Nothing escapes God's notice; He rewards and punishes; the account is made up in the life to come; in the blessedness of that life lies the sanction of righteousness. Ambrose then speaks of the duties to be observed throughout life (I, 65; Cic. *De Off.*, I, xxxiv, sec. 122); and lengthily inculcates modesty

(*verecundia*) and warns against anger (*iracundia*).
Through all of this, Cicero's treatise is in his mind
and often quoted.

Again, Ambrose (I, 105, following *De Off.*, I, xxix,
141) shows how his mode of regarding virtue is sometimes the Ciceronian, *i.e.* the pagan stoico-eclectic.
In acting, says Cicero, and Ambrose after him, three
things are to be considered; first, that *appetitus* should
obey reason; secondly, that we should bestow pains in
proportion to the weight of the matter; and, thirdly,
that we should observe the fitness of times and places.
Ambrose agrees with Cicero that the first is the most
important. These were the principles of pagan ethics.
Ambrose might apply them somewhat differently from
Cicero, and nevertheless be reasoning in a pagan way.
A man who regarded the future life as all-important
would apply these principles differently from one to
whom the present life was the main matter. Ambrose
continues, pointing out (I, 107-114) how Abraham
and Jacob and Joseph observed these principles; and
then argues that their conduct exhibited the four cardinal virtues, *prudentia, justitia, fortitudo,* and *tempe-
rantia.* He discusses these virtues as constituent
parts of good conduct. *Primus officii fons prudentia
est,* says Ambrose, a phrase which hardly represents a
Christian point of view (I, 126; cf. *De Off.*, I, v, sec.
15). The discussion of the virtue of *fortitudo,* which
follows (I, 175, et seq.), is stoical in tone.

Likewise Ambrose follows Cicero closely in the treatment of the seemly, *decorum* (I, 221, et seq., *De Off.*, I,
xxvii, 96-98), even to the point of saying, — what is
sheer stoicism, — *decorum est secundum naturam vivere*

(I, 222); *quod ita naturae consentaneum sit,* is Cicero's phrase (*De Off.,* I, xxvii, 98). To be sure, in this first book of the *De Officiis Ministrorum,* he occasionally contradicts rules of pagan ethics, for example, as to vengeance, the permissibility of which he does not admit (I, 131; but see 139; cf. *De Off.,* I, vii, 23).

At the beginning of the second book Ambrose considers what constitutes blessed life (*vita beata*). The riches of this world do not bring this blessedness, but rather bar the path — woe unto ye rich! *Certum est solum et summum bonum esse virtutem, eamque abundare solam ad vitae fructum beatae : nec externis aut corporis bonis, sed virtute sola vitam praestari beatam, per quam vita aeterna acquiritur. Vita enim beata fructus praesentium : vita autem aeterna spes futurorum est* (II, 18). Like the Stoics, Ambrose sees no blessedness in riches; virtue alone produces blessed life, through which eternal life is reached. For Ambrose the ultimate blessedness lies in life eternal, which is the fruit of virtue, while the Stoics find it rather in virtue itself, with whatever may come therefrom here or hereafter. He adds : *Scriptura autem divina vitam aeternam in cognitione posuit divinitatis, et fructu bonae operationis* (II, 5, citing John xvii. 3, and Matt. xix. 29). Here is a Christian statement which, however, Ambrose has not found inconsistent with a stoical way of reasoning.

Having spoken thus generally as to what constitutes a blessed life, Ambrose proceeds to discuss the useful (*utile*), thus returning to Cicero's arrangement. *Superiore libro ita divisionem fecimus, ut primo loco esset honestum et decorum, a quo officia ducerentur, secundo loco quid utile* (II, 22; cf. Cic. *De Off.* II, iii, 9).

Utility lies in gaining piety, not money (II, 23). What is useful is also just; *justum est ut serviamus Christo qui nos redemit* (II, 24). This is a Christian turn of the argument, which none the less continues to accord with the stoical view in finding the *utile* to be the *honestum*, and *vice versa*. Ambrose now enters upon a practical discussion of the details of conduct according to the desirable virtues of love, charity, justice, and prudence.

In the third book it is said that there can be no conflict between the *honestum* and the *utile*, since nothing can be *honestum* (morally good) that is not useful, and *vice versa*, wherein he follows Cicero (III, 9; *De Off*. III, iii, 11). And in his concluding exposition of right Christian conduct, as in the discussion contained in the second book, Ambrose is not out of accord with Cicero and the Stoics, though his rules of Christian morality may go further than any pagan ethics demanded.

In fine, although some precepts of Ambrose's treatise contravene pagan ethics, and although his opinions may be such as Augustine would have approved, nevertheless in tone and spirit the *De Officiis Ministrorum* is separated by great gulfs from the Christian cry, with which Augustine's *Confessions* open, a cry prophetic of the mediæval soul: *Fecisti nos ad te, et inquietum est cor nostrum, donec requiescat in te*. A man might follow the guidance of Ambrose's precepts, and still be of the company of those not yet *salubriter prostati et elisi a te, Deus meus*.[1] Utter humility before God, man's helplessness without His grace and love,

---

[1] *Conf.*, IV, 1.

finds voice in Augustine. Despite all the antique elements of his personality, which made him still a Roman man of the transition epoch, these Christian sentiments proclaim him the true continuer of the spirit of the Old Testament through Christ, and make him the most completely Christian man since the Apostolic time, and the great father of mediæval Christianity.

II. *Synesius of Cyrene*

Synesius, a native of Cyrene, an ancient but decayed Greek city of the Libyan Pentapolis, was a live Hellenic personality of the end of the fourth and beginning of the fifth century. His writings were not to be of great influence in Western Europe, but they show the mingling of Hellenic-pagan and Christian elements in a man of the transition epoch. He was honest, brave, lovable. Before his adoption of Christianity he was a Neo-platonist, and a devoted admirer of Hypatia, the Neo-platonist woman-philosopher of Alexandria, where Synesius spent some happy years. He loved study and cultured ease, as well as hunting and the agricultural occupations of a country gentleman. He hated public affairs; but the misfortunes of his province forced military and then episcopal leadership upon him, as he was the only man brave enough to quell marauding Libyans and oppose tyrannous officials. His countrymen compelled him to be ordained Bishop of Ptolemais; and a troubled episcopal career brought him prematurely to his grave. Hellenic Africa had its woes when Rome fell before

Alaric. Synesius was made bishop in the year of that catastrophe (A.D. 410), and died four years afterwards.

When Synesius has something important to communicate, he can say it bravely and directly, whether in a speech[1] or in letters. Otherwise, his letters show the affectations of fourth-century pagan epistolary literature. He can also amuse himself by composing elaborate rhetorical trifles, like his Eulogy on Baldness, in which he sought to rival Dio's discourse upon Long Hair. He mentions a curious habit of his, when reading, of closing the book, and then devising an ending for the work, in order to compare his ending with the writer's. Just as he wrote poems in imitation of any author that struck his fancy, so he was utterly eclectic in his thinking. Naturally, like all antiquity, Synesius believed in divination and dreams. But it was characteristic of the academically superstitious age in which he lived, that he wrote a work on Dreams, and advised keeping a systematic record of them, that their significance and warnings might be compared.

Synesius' Neo-platonism shows Christian influence. For instance, the so-called Neo-platonic trinity of the One, the Nous — perfected universal Mind — and the Soul, has become in his hymns Father, Spirit, Son. These hymns also draw near to Christian feeling. Christianity was in the air, and Synesius breathed it. His gentle conversion suggests no spiritual con-

---

[1] As in his famous address to Arcadius, on the duties of kings, when he had been sent to plead his city's cause before the court at Constantinople.

flict. While still a pagan, he wrote a hymn referring to the time of his stay in Constantinople: "To all Thy temples, Lord, built for Thy holy rites, I went, and falling headlong as a suppliant bathed the pavement with my tears. That my journey might not be in vain, I prayed to all the gods, Thy ministers, who rule the fertile plain of Thrace, and those who on the opposite continent protect the lands of Chalcedon, whom Thou hast crowned with angelic rays, Thy holy servants. They, the blessed ones, helped me in my prayers; they helped me to bear the burden of many troubles." These "temples" were Christian churches;[1] and this hymn shows how the syncretistic religious philosophy of Synesius could embrace the Christian cult. The hymn indicates that yearning for inner divine aid and comfort, which no pagan cult could more than tantalize. In the troubles of his life, Synesius' mood gradually becomes Christian. As a pagan, he had prayed fruitlessly for freedom from cares; next he begins to feel their pertinency to the soul's progress; and at last the Incarnation, that great stumbling-block to pagan thoughts of the divine dignity, presents itself as the dearest comfort to his much-tried soul. The hymn marking his adoption of Christianity is addressed to Christ as the son of the Holy Virgin. Christ's attributes are described in nearly the same terms as those which characterize the "Son" in Synesius' Neo-platonic hymns. A hymn on the Descent into Hell shows some of the pagan ideas which mingled with Synesius' acceptance of Christianity: "Thou wentest down to Tartarus,

[1] There were no heathen temples in Constantinople.

where death held the countless races of mankind.
The old man Hades feared Thee, the devouring dog
(Cerberus) fled from the portal; but, having released
the souls of the righteous from suffering, Thou didst
offer, with a holy worship, hymns of thanksgiving to
the Father. As Thou wentest up on high, the dæmons,
powers of the air, were affrighted. But Æther, wise
parent of harmony, sang with joy to his sevenfold
lyre a hymn of triumph. The morning star, day's
harbinger, and the golden star of evening, the planet
Venus, smiled on Thee. Before Thee went the horned
moon, decked with fresh light, leading the gods of
night. Beneath Thy feet, Titan spread his flowing
locks of light. He recognized the Son of God, the
creative intelligence, the source of his own flames.
But Thou didst fly on outstretched wings beyond the
vaulted sky, alighting on the spheres of pure intelligence, where is the fountain of goodness, the heaven
enveloped in silence. There time, deep-flowing and
unwearied time, is not; there disease, the reckless and
prolific offspring of matter, is not. But eternity, ever
young and ever old, rules the abiding habitation of the
gods."

Such was Synesius, the guardian bishop of his people, whose manhood would excommunicate the tyrant
governor, but would not give up that wife given him
by " God and the law and the sacred hand of The-
ophilus." [1] When a pagan, he was not averse to
Christianity; when a bishop, he did not give up

---

[1] Patriarch of Alexandria. The celibacy of the clergy was an
issue in Synesius' time. There is no evidence that Synesius lived
with his wife after he became bishop.

Neo-platonism.   His last letter was one of respectful
devotion to Hypatia; his last prayer was to Christ;
"O Christ, Son of God most high, have mercy on Thy
servant, a miserable sinner who wrote these hymns.
Release me from the sins which have grown up in my
heart, which are implanted in my polluted soul.   O
Saviour Jesus, grant that hereafter I may behold Thy
divine glory."   The man's hope flickers upward toward
the last and most adorable figure of his pantheon.

III. *Dionysius the Areopagite*

The thought and opinions, even the moods of Synesius show a crude mixture of Christianity and the
higher paganism.   The pagan elements were scarcely
modified by their new association.   But in the writings of Pseudo-Dionysius,[1] there is a union of Christian and pagan, Greek, oriental and Jewish, a union
wherein the nature of each ingredient is changed.
Theological philosophic fantasy has never built up
anything more remarkable.   It was a very proper
product of its time; a construction lofty and systematized, apparently complete, comparable to the

[1] It would require a volume to tell the history of the controversy
regarding the authorship of the famous *Celestial Hierarchy* and
other writings purporting to be the works of Dionysius the Areopagite, who heard Paul preach (Acts xvii. 34).   That contention is,
of course, untenable.   These writings were probably the product
of Græco-oriental Christianity of the fourth or fifth century.   See,
for a statement of the present status of the Pseudo-Dionysius or
Pseudo-Areopagite question, the article on Dionysius in the *Dictionary of Christian Biography*, and Harnack's *Dogmengeschichte*,
Vol. II, p. 426, note.

Enneads of Plotinus which formed part of its materials. Indeed, materials for it abounded in the minds and temperaments of the mystic, yet still dialectically constructive, Syro-Judaic, Hellenic, Christianized personalities of Alexandria. They offered themselves temptingly to the hand strong enough to build with them. There was all that had entered into Neoplatonism, both in its more severely dialectic modes as established by Plotinus, and in its magic-mystic pagan foolishness as left by Iamblichus. There was the Jewish angel lore, and the encroaching Eastern mood and fancy mingling with it, and there was Christianity, — what did not that include as understood or felt by high and low, by shouting rabble or angry dogmatist, by the semi-pagan or by him who was all turned to Christ; by men and women, by dreamers, mystics, rhetoricians, soldiers, sycophants, and tyrants, Greeks, Syrians, Copts, hot-hearted African Latins, Italians, Romans, and all the sheer or semi-Hellenized or Romanized barbarians who thronged the Empire? There had been and still were great builders who had taken their materials from this mass of "Christian" beliefs. From it materials were drawn for formula and creed; also the principles of liturgic and sacramental doctrine and corresponding sacerdotal function. A great man like Augustine, his heart filled, not with vapors, but with real love of God, and having a mind of universal power, might from out of this same mass mould vital truths of Christ to a juristic scheme of sin and grace. But other portions made a potent part of faith for more men than would understand Augustine. These included the popular beliefs regarding the intermediate superhuman beings who seemed nearer to men than any member of the Trinity. Such beliefs, held not only by the driven crowd, but by its guides and drivers, demanded systematizing, that they might be tabulated as a part of the hierarchically authorized religion.

By what means could this be accomplished? The materials were everywhere, huge, unformed, wavering. Whence should come the schematic principle? Was it to be juristic, like the Roman, Pauline, legalistic work of Augustine? That was too austere and intolerant. Latin Christianity had already taken its metaphysics from the Hellenic East. In the sphere of transcendental reason and fantasy, Hellenism always held adaptable constructive principles. Its last great creation, Neo-platonism, was potent to gather and arrange within itself the manifold elements of latter-day paganism. The Neo-platonic categories might be altered in name and import, and yet the scheme remain a scheme. And its constructive principle of the transmission of life and power from the ultimate divine Source downward through orders of mediating beings unto men, might readily be adapted to the Christian God and His ministering angels. The dogmatic formulation of Christianity set God and the Mediator, Christ, beyond the reach of man's imagination and man's heart, both of which needed intermediate conceptions, as of angelic and saintly mediators. God's removal was so great there must even be a series of these. The needed scheme would naturally spring from Hellenism in its latest and most readily adaptive system, which was also nearest to the moods of

the time.   And a schematic principle drawn from the
most all-embracing syncretistic pagan system would
not narrowly exclude matters lying beyond the sacred
writings or the decrees of councils.   Finally, was not
the prevailing allegorism there, to alter whatever in
literal sense was stubborn, and to adorn the structure?

There was thus abundance of material and a tool
of marvellous constructive potency.   There was also a
man, whoever he was, who could use the tool.

"Dionysius," our great pseudonymous unknown, was
a transcendental mystic pantheist.   These terms, if
contradictory, are at least inclusive.   He had a grand
conception, sprung from Neo-platonic and Christian
metaphysics, of the sublime transcendence of the ultimate divine Source.   This Source, however, was not
severed, remote, inert; but a veritable Source from
which abundant life should stream to all lower orders;
in part directly into all beings, in part indirectly, as
power and guidance, through the higher orders to the
lower.   With Plotinus, the One overflows into the
Nous, the perfected universal Mind, and that into
the World-Soul and the souls of men.   With Dionysius, life, creation, every good gift, is from God
directly; but His flaming ministers also intervene,
and guide and aid the life of man, which comes not
from them; and the life, which, through love, floods
forth from God, thereby creating the beings in which
it manifests itself, has its mighty counterflow whereby
it draws its own creations to itself.   God is at once
absolutely transcendent and universally immanent.
To live is to be united with God; evil is the non-
existent, that is, severance from God.   All that is, is

part of the forth-flowing divine life, part of the creative saving process, which ever purifies, enlightens, and
perfects, and so draws back unto the Source.

Such is the inner principle of Dionysius' scheme.
It was, however, the mode of carrying out the scheme,
which was to hold the imagination if not the faith of
men to our own day. The transcendent Source, as
well as the Universal Immanence, is the Tri-une God.
Between that and men are ranged the three triads
of the Celestial Hierarchy: the Seraphim, Cherubim,
and Thrones; the Dominations, Virtues, Powers; the
Principalities, Archangels, Angels. Collectively, their
general office is to raise mankind to God through purification, illumination, and perfection; and to all of
them the term angel may be applied. More particularly the highest triad, which is nearest God, contem-
plates the divine effulgence and reflects it onward
to the second; while the third, the more specifically
angelic triad, immediately ministers to men. The
sources of these names are evident; Seraphim and
Cherubim are vague but mighty forms in the Old
Testament; later Jewish writings, possibly under
Persian influence, gave names and classification to
archangels and angels,[1] who also fill important functions in the New Testament. The other names were
well derived from two great mystic passages in Paul's
Epistles;[2] but neither in the writings of the Areopagite nor in the mediæval centuries, did they acquire
definite attribute and personality. Rather, Seraph and
Cherub, Angel and Archangel, with sometimes inter-

---

[1] See, e.g., Daniel viii. 16; ix. 21; x. 21; xii. 1; Enoch ix. 1;
Tobit xii. 15.   [2] Eph. i. 21; Col. i. 16.

changeable but always vivid personalities, were to form the flaming host of divine ministrants and guardians of men.

The works of the Areopagite may not have been widely read in the West before they were translated in the ninth century by Erigena. But from that time the *Celestial Hierarchy* constituted the canon of angelic lore, authoritative for the religion and religious art of the Middle Ages.[1] Its closing fifteenth chapter was more especially the canon of angelic symbolism for literature and art. There the author explains in what respect theology attributes to angels the qualities of fire, why the Thrones are said to be fiery ($\pi\nu\rho\ell\nu\nu\nu$); why the quality of fire is attributed to the Seraphim, who are burning ($\epsilon\mu\pi\rho\eta\sigma\tau\dot{\alpha}\varsigma$), as their name signifies. " It is' the fiery form which signifies, with Celestial Intelligences, likeness to God ; " and then he speaks of fire's marvellous subtile qualities. Again, he explains the significance of the human form, — erect, rational, contemplative of the heavens — and of the parts of the human body, when ascribed to celestial beings ; for example, feet are ascribed to angels to denote their unceasing movement on the divine business ; and theology declares that their feet are winged ($\upsilon\pi\sigma\pi\tau\dot{\epsilon}\rho\sigma\nu\varsigma$) to denote their celerity.[2] Further, he

[1] Of course, there is plenty of mention of angels among the Latin fathers ; *e.g.*, Augustine, *Civ. Dei*, VIII, 24, speaks of angels, whether they be Sedes, Dominationes, Principatus sive Potestates. In *Civ. Dei*, XI, 29 sqq., he discusses the knowledge of God possessed by the angels, and says that the angels, also, have the joy of rest, — *requiescendi felicitatio*.

[2] This seems to be a bit of symbolism taken direct from the pagan form of Hermes.

explains the symbolism of the garments and attributes, such as wands and axes, which are given them,
and why angels are called winds,[1] and are given the
appearance of clouds; then the significance of brass
and gold and of many-colored stones, when joined to
celestial beings; and then the symbolic significance
of the forms of lion, ox, eagle, and horse; and what is
denoted by rivers, wheels, or by a chariot, when such
are furnished to celestials.[2]

In the works of the Areopagite, the *Celestial Hierarchy* is followed by the *Ecclesiastical Hierarchy*, its
counterpart on earth.   What the primal tri-une
Godhead is to the former, Jesus is to the latter.
The Ecclesiastical Hierarchy is likewise composed of
three triads.   The first includes the great symbolic
sacraments : Baptism, Communion, Consecration of
the Holy Chrism, which last most directly represents
Christ, the Anointed One.   Baptism signifies purification; Communion signifies enlightening; and the
Holy Chrism signifies perfecting.   The second triad
is made up of the three orders of Bishops, Presbyters,
and Deacons; or rather, to use the Areopagite's mys-

---

[1] Much of this symbolism is drawn from Biblical phrases: *e.g.*,
as to the symbol of *winds*, see Daniel vii. 2 and *passim* that chapter; also Psalm xviii. 10; and the Areopagite, Chap. XV, § 6, quotes
John iii. 8: "Thou canst not tell whence it cometh nor whither it
goeth."

[2] With Chap. XV of *Celestial Hierarchy* compare Epistle IX of
the Areopagite to Titus, "The order of the visible universe sets
forth the invisible things of Almighty God, as says Paul and the
infallible Word" (§ 2).   See also Epist. VIII, § 6, of the Areopagite
on a vision of the mouth of Hell.   Also compare the opening of the
Byzantine Manual of Painting (on which see *post*, p. 344), for its
reference to Dionysius.

tic terms: Hierarchs (ἱεράρχων τάξις), Light-bearers (φωταγωγικὴ τάξις), Servitors (λειτουργῶν τάξις); to wit, the consummate interpreters of the Sacraments, the light-bringers who administer them in Communion, and the purifiers who prepare them. The third and lowest triad consists of the monks, who are in a state or process of perfection, the initiated laity, who are in a state of illumination, and the catechumens, who are in a probationary state of purification. This treatise finds in all worship a celebration of holy mysteries, and many of its terms suggest the pagan mysteries. It was a systematic presentation of the symbolical significance of all acts of worship.

Perhaps the noblest of the Areopagite's work is that on the Divine Names, which follows the Ecclesiastical Hierarchy. It is a discussion of the qualities which may be predicated of God, according to the warrant of the terms applied to Him in Scripture. This work, however, was not unique, like the Celestial Hierarchy. It was occupied with a Neo-platonized Christian discussion of the Divine Nature. In such fields the Areopagite had many rivals.

The fourth and least of the Areopagite's main works is that on Mystic Theology; in which is explained the function of symbols, and how he who would know God truly must rise above them and above all conceptions of God drawn from sensible things; for all these things are not He.[1]

The work of the Areopagite was a representative

---

[1] There exist also ten letters ascribed to the Areopagite; and the extant writings refer to other works which either are lost or never existed.

product of its time, and suited to the tastes of the
coming mediæval centuries; suited to their mystic
fancies, and suited to their need of concrete superhuman beings who, closer at hand than God and the
homöousian Christ, should aid men in their combats
with each other and with the besetting swarms of
devils.[1]

IV. *Mysteries, Symbolism, and Allegorical Interpretation*

The word "mystery" has had many meanings. It
has always meant something hidden, beyond common
knowledge or even human capacity for knowing. But
the hidden "mysteries" might differ greatly; and
there might be a difference in the mode of conceiving

[1] The Areopagite becomes a power in the Western Middle Ages
after the translation of his works by Erigena and the definite
form given to his legend in the *Vita Dionysii* by Hilduin, abbot
of St. Denis in the time of Louis the Pious. This *Vita* identifies
the Areopagite with St. Denis, a fact unquestioned until Abelard.
See also *Mystère des actes des Apôtres*, Didron's *Annales Archéolo-
giques*, XIII and XIV. The Areopagite frequently appears in mediæval art; his decapitation is rendered in the tympanum of the north
portal of the Abbey of St. Denis; he appears in the Spanish Chapel
of St. Maria Novella in Florence. In the Louvre there is a painting of the last communion and martyrdom of St. Denis, of the
latter part of the fourteenth century. W. Preger, *Geschichte der
deutschen Mystik im Mittelalter*, Vol. I, pp. 283–291, speaks of mystical teachings in the German tongue, and gives a German rhymed
poem of the thirteenth century containing doctrines of the Areopagite. For his influence on Meister Eckhart, see Preger, *op. cit.*,
under "Eckhart." Also in Hildebrand, *Didaktik aus der Zeit der
Kreuzzüge* (Deutsche National Literatur), pp. 38–49. For Dante's
debt to Dionysius see Edmund Gardner, *Dante's Ten Heavens*, also
article "Dionisio" in Toynbee's *Dante Dictionary*.

the fact and reason of their being "mysteries." When Christ spoke of the "mysteries of the Kingdom of Heaven," He spoke of what was beyond mortal comprehension — even as there is for man the necessary mystery of God. But men are surrounded by the common things of daily life, which are not mysteries to the ordinary human consciousness. Such, for example, is the food of man, like bread and wine. Only a thoughtful or poetic nature would see any mystery here; common men are scarcely conscious even that there lies a mystery in the growth of wheat or of the vine. Likewise, the function of food is known to all, — man must eat to live. But when some one says, this bread before us has received strange properties, whereby eating it shall have a marvellous effect, then a mystery has been added. This mystery is factitious, introduced into a common thing, and the human act, through which mysterious qualities have been imparted to a common thing, is an act of magic. But there is no magic in the mystery of God, or in the mystery of whatever is naturally recognized by men as beyond their comprehension. Here lies the difference between mystery and mystery.

Furthermore, a material object may readily be regarded as the symbol of a spiritual fact; a material object or a physical human act may be taken as a symbol of the action of God working a spiritual change in man. To conceive an object or a fact to be a symbol of something else is different from conceiving it to embody, or to effect, or *be*, that something else. The difference is plain; how could any one ignore it ? Yet a considerable part of the intellectual and religious, as

well as the artistic and literary, history of the first
fifteen centuries of the Christian era is a history of the
many ways in which this difference has been ignored,
and of the many ways in which the magic mystery has
been confused and made equal with the mystery which
exists by reason of the limitation of human knowledge.
Moreover, this confusion must be regarded as wilful.
It was not that germinal mental chaos which exists in
savages and barbarians who have not developed the
faculty of perceiving clear distinctions; it was rather
a confusion to which human beings abandoned themselves after periods of clear thinking among their
ancestors, Roman, Greek, and Hebrew.

There is a further related phase of intellectual history; the perverse and wilful use of allegory, or rather
the ascribing to ancient writings and myths an allegorical significance which they did not have. Christ
made abundant use of allegory and image in parables
which should suggest the character of what was beyond his hearers' comprehension : "the Kingdom of
Heaven is like unto" many situations and factors of
common life. These parables were meant as allegories. But between understanding as an allegory that
which was meant as an allegory, and interpreting as
an allegory that which was stated as a fact, there lies
a difference analogous to that between treating the
symbol as a symbol and treating it as if it were what
it symbolizes, or between the magic mystery and the
mystery of the Kingdom of Heaven.

These are three elements of surpassing importance
in the history of man during the opening Christian
centuries : the magic-mystery, the symbol taken for

the fact symbolized, allegorical interpretation. These mental processes are of dominant moulding influence upon the personalities of those with whom they constitute usual modes of thinking; and they are very representative of at least one side of the personalities of the men of the Empire from the fourth century, and of the mediæval personality in general, and of the difference between it and the classic personality. They do not, however, originate with Christianity, but have their roots in the Hellenism and Judaism and Orientalism of the later pre-Christian centuries.

Before noticing the course of these three mental processes, recall for an instant the reasoning of the Areopagite. The *Celestial Hierarchy* was an attempt to set forth something of the mysteries of the Kingdom of Heaven, that is, of the mystery of God and His relations to mankind. The Ecclesiastical Hierarchy was the symbol on earth of the Celestial Hierarchy. But the Ecclesiastical Hierarchy, in every branch, is more than symbol; it is mystery, and magic-mystery, and represents a magically wrought manifestation of the Celestial Hierarchy on Earth, a magically wrought presence of the divine and spiritual within material objects and human acts. The three sacraments embody and produce the effect of the divine and spiritual; from symbols they have magically become that which they symbolize. And, of course, the Areopagite uses allegorical interpretation of Scripture wherever it suits his purpose. All this makes his work so representative and so influential.

The secret of the Eleusinian and other pagan mysteries has been kept so well that there have been doubts as to its existence. Probably the object of those mysteries was to insure a happy lot to the initiated in the life beyond the grave. This purpose may never have been a secret. The secret lay rather in the rites which worked so potently upon the mood of the participants. In general, these consisted in purification, initiation, and ἐποπτεία, the highest degree of participation.

With the renewed religiousness of the second century after Christ, a renewed life came to the various pagan mysteries, which were necessarily influenced by the aims and moods inspiring the last phases of pagan philosophy. Probably in the mysteries men were seeking σωτηρία, salvation from the pains and fate of mortality; and to this desire was joined a yearning for purification from sin and for reconcilement with the Divine. There was a connection between pagan mysteries and the initiations and doctrines of Gnosticism. Here the details are obscure, as is obscure any connection that there may have been between Gnosticism and the growth of mysteries in the Catholic Church. The terminology of the pagan mysteries certainly passed into these last : yet it does not follow that the development of the Christian mysteries was connected with any ancient pagan rites. The growth of " Mysteries " was proceeding vigorously in both Christian and pagan circles ; and Christian rites were rapidly becoming a celebration of mysteries. There was in the rites the element of secrecy, in that they were celebrated in the presence only of those who, after formal instruction, renunciation, and profession, were duly admitted. And a mystical power was ascribed to the material substances and physical acts by which the rites were accomplished. Catechumens were instructed plainly as to the meaning and effect of baptism only when they were about to be baptized; they were forbidden to divulge the teaching save to other catechumens preparing for baptism, and only the baptized were admitted to the celebration of the Eucharist. This point of resemblance to the heathen mysteries is not to be unduly pressed. Christ had said, "Cast not your pearls before swine," and had explained His parables only to His disciples. And, as Cyril of Jerusalem says, there was fitness in not divulging matters to the unworthy, who would not understand. Moreover, the early situation of the churches furnished practical reasons for wariness as to strangers.[1]

The other element of *Mystery* is of greater import. Writing near the middle of the fourth century, Cyril of Jerusalem, in the Introduction to his lectures to catechumens preparing for baptism, maintains, as the Catholic Church always maintained, the spiritual significance of the rite; he distinguishes between the external rite of Baptism and the change of heart, without which Baptism profits not. Yet the magic-mystery element is strong with Cyril, as with all the men of his time both East and West. He calls the candidates partakers of the mysteries, and invites them to come to the mystical seal, εἰς τὴν μυστικὴν σφραγῖδα.[2] Instruction and preparation render the

---

[1] The *Didaché of the Apostles*, which gives the earliest non-canonic picture of the Christian community, shows (Chap. XII) the care exercised in receiving strangers professing to be Christians.

[2] *Catecheses*, I, 2.

catechumens "competent" for the divine and life-
giving baptism (θείου καὶ ζωοποιοῦ βαπτίσματος); [1] and
just before the rite is performed they are formally
exorcised to purify their souls from evil,[2] whereupon,
in answer, they with equal solemnity "renounce the
devil and all his works." As to the baptismal water,
says Cyril, just as meats, simple in their nature, are
polluted (μεμολύσμενα) by the invocation of idols, so
the simple water, by invocation of Father, Son, and
Holy Spirit, acquires a power of holiness (δύναμιν
ἁγιότητος). The magic-mystery lies in the novel
property imparted to water through a human act.

So much for the element of magic-mystery in the
rite of Baptism. The far mightier tale of how Christian worship came to be summed up in the mystical
sacrifice of the Eucharist need not be entered on.
With Ignatius, in the early part of the second century, the bread and wine have become φάρμακον
ἀθανασίας,[3] the drug of immortality; with Cyril of
Jerusalem, the seeming bread is not bread, but the
body of Christ, the wine is not wine, but the blood
of Christ.[4] This transformation of Christ's commemo-
rative supper, this ceaseless priest-wrought reincarna-
tion of our blessed Lord, is the supreme instance of
the development of the magic-mystery element in the
Christian Church.

It is clear that the development of the magic-mystery in Baptism and the Eucharist was related in
many ways to the confusion of the symbol with the

---

[1] Cyril, *Mystagogica*, I, 1.
[2] See Gregory Nazianzen, *Or.* 40.
[3] Epistle to Ephesians, xxi.
[4] *Mystagogica*, IV, 9.

fact symbolized. Such magic and such confusion were no part of Christ's teachings; but they had always been part of the religions of heathen peoples from India to Rome. The treatment of these two chief acts of Christian worship as magic-mysteries, by all the authoritative leaders of the churches, opened the door to many other pagan elements which more slowly gained authoritative sanction. As the baptismal water and the bread of the Eucharist have magic virtue, so other material objects, to wit, the bones and relics of the saints and martyrs, acquire magic power. And despite some feeble protests and qualifications by the Fathers,[1] many ideas and practices from polytheism passed into the beliefs and practices of Christianity — only with saints and angels and the Virgin Mary substituted for heroes and gods and goddesses. All of this, important as it is for the transition centuries and for the Middle Ages, calls for no special mention here.[2] But the relation of magic-mystery and confused symbolism to allegorical interpretation may be noticed,[3] and something said regarding the last.

Allegorical interpretation represents that conservative religious progress which avoids a breach with the past and clings to the statements of ancient seers. This was a fundamental reason for allegorical interpretation with Greeks, with Jews, and with Christians.

Homer and Hesiod made the gods; their writings

---

[1] Augustine, for example, *Civ. Dei*, VIII, 27.

[2] Cf. Harnack, *Dogmengeschichte*, 2d Ed., II, 413–462.

[3] Many of the rites of the pagan mysteries were intended as allegories.

were authoritative for the traditional religion of
Greece. Only the overbold philosopher-moralist Xenophanes would denounce their tales of divine doings,
or the clear-eyed idealist Plato refuse to admit those
poets to his commonwealth, or one great ethical poet,
Pindar, might adjure men to repeat only worthy tales
of the gods. Usually the conservative spirit of Greek
religious progress insisted upon the truth of the time-
honored poets. That truth lay, however, not in the
literal sense of their words, but in the meaning
therein veiled; that is to say, these tales were allegories. Allegorical interpretations became current
in the fifth century before Christ. In spite of Plato,
Homeric stories of the gods were held by the learned
to be representations of natural phenomena; books
were written on the allegorical significance of Homer,
"whose words would be impious were they not allegories." The religious conservatism of the Stoics
caused that large and respected school to adopt the
system. By the time of Augustus, the habit of finding an allegory everywhere had become so universal
that learned men deemed that no great writer would
write save in allegories.[1]

It was the same with the Jews. Philo of Alexandria[2] was not the first to apply allegorical interpretation
to the Pentateuch; but he is the great example of a
Hellenized Jew, by this means, reading into the sacred
writings all the best that he had drawn from philosophy. This universal eclectic is still a Jew; he deems

[1] See, for examples, Hatch, *Hibbert Lectures*, 1888, pp. 50–65.
[2] Born between 20 and 10 B.C. He took part in the embassy to
Caligula, 40 A.D.

the Pentateuch to be inspired truth, and thinks that
the Greeks drew their wisdom from the works of
Moses. The Christian Fathers took many scriptural
interpretations from Philo's writings.[1]

The Old Testament abounds in images; the later
prophets, Ezekiel and Daniel, construct elaborate allegories. Likewise the earliest Christian writings. The
synoptic gospels have the parables; John's gospel, its
images; the Book of Revelation is the culmination of
Hebrew allegorical apocalyptic literature; and the
"Shepherd of Hermas," one of the earliest and most
popular of the extra-canonical writings, is allegory
from beginning to end. Thus image and allegory
were native with Christianity's forerunner, and sprang
to renewed life with Christian beginnings. The Gen-

---

[1] For example, in Philo, *Allegories of the Sacred Laws*, I, 19, the
four rivers of Eden represent the four virtues, prudence, temperance, courage, justice: the main stream, out of which they separate, is generic virtue, the Wisdom of God. This interpretation is
retained by the Fathers.

Philo's chief works were: (1) Ζητήματα καὶ λύσεις, *Questiones et
solutiones*, on the Pentateuch; this work gives the literal meaning
as well as the allegorical significance; it was used by the Fathers,
especially by Ambrose; (2) Νόμων ἱερῶν ἀλληγορίαι, the large allegorical commentary devoted entirely to the allegorical meaning. Schürer
(*Jewish People*, etc., III, 330) says that its "fundamental thought
is that the history of mankind as related in Genesis is in reality
nothing else than a system of psychology and ethic. The different
individuals, who here make their appearance, denote the different
states of soul (τρόποι τῆς ψυχῆς) which occur among men. To analyze these in their variety and their relations both to each other
and to the Deity and the world of sense, and then to deduce moral
doctrines, is the special aim of this great allegorical commentary."

Turning Biblical thought into Greek affects Philo's style, and
makes him a literary precursor of the Greek Fathers. Cf. Croiset,
Hist. de la lit. Grecque, V, pp. 430–434.

tile churches were to wage mighty battles with Gnostics, Manicheans, and all their kin, and with professed heathens too, upon the character of the Old Testament, its inspired truth or diabolic falsity, and its relation to Christianity.　Much in the Old Testament could not but shock the Greek consciousness, whether Christianized or still pagan.　Yet its divine authority was not to be denied in the religion whose Founder proclaimed Himself the final Messianic fulfilment of Scripture.　Among all educated people, the habit of allegorical interpretation was so strong that the Old Testament, whatever its character, was certain to be read allegorically by Christians, who would not be slow to tread in Philo's steps.　This system offered itself as the natural means to explain the harsh deeds and the anthropomorphic crudities in the conception of divine action recorded in the Sacred Writings. Thus allegorical interpretation found again in Christianity its primary apologetic function; and thereupon this great defence of the inspired truth of Hebrew Scripture was used as the sword of the Gospel against Jew as well as heathen.　With many a subtle turn and flash of unexpected meaning it was made to prove that the life and death and resurrection of Christ were predicted by prophecy and spiritually prefigured in the entire contents of the Old Testament.

Thus, first applied to the Old Testament and then to the New, allegorical interpretation pervades Christian literature, and becomes the authoritative system of interpretation.　It begins openly with Paul's "And that rock was Christ,"[1] and with the same apostle's

[1] 1 Cor. x. 4.

equally wonderful interpretation of the twenty-first chapter of Genesis.[1]   Not many decades later, in the Epistle of Barnabas, the goat cast forth with the sins of the people is a type of Christ;[2] so is Moses; so is the brazen serpent which he set up;[3] and the numbers, ten and eight and three hundred, of men circumcised by Abraham show symbolically that the patriarch looked forward to the crucified Messiah.[4]   A Greek philosopher Christian like Justin might refrain from allegorical interpretation in an apology where there was slight reference to the Hebrew Scriptures; or might employ it pertinently in arguments with a Jew,[5] even as the great African-Latin Christian advocate, Tertullian, used it against the gnostic Marcion.[6]   But the perfecters of the system, as applied to explain the Old Testament and harmonize it with the New, and thus make it prophetic and prefigurative of Christ, are the Alexandrians Clement and Origen.   With them it is also used to correct literal interpretation of the New Testament.

The Alexandrian Fathers do not stop with this. Every symbol is symbolical of something which it apparently is not; every allegory veils in its stated facts a deeper meaning.   So every allegory may suggest that the real and spiritual essence and truth of things is not according to their sensible appearance, but lies in their symbolical analogy with the unseen

[1] Gal. iv. 22; v. 1.   Cf. Heb. vi–x.
[2] *Ep. of Barnabas*, Chap. 7.
[3] *Ib.*, 12.
[4] I=10; H=8; and the cross T=300.
[5] See *Dialogue with Trypho*, 40, 41, 42, 91, 113, 126, 134, 138.
[6] *E.g.*, *Contra Marcion*, III, 16 and 18; also in *De Baptismo.*

workings of the Divine.[1] In all allegory there is mystery, and in all allegory mysticism, with its inherent spirit of contradiction and paradox, is implicit. Thus allegory serves not only to set forth mystery, but to develop mysticism. So it was in the Christian Church. The first great mystical interpretation of Scripture was Origen's allegorical commentary on the Song of Songs, which, according to him, is an Epithalamium; but the bride is the Church and the bridegroom Christ, or the bride is the soul and the bridegroom is the Word of God.[2]

Origen is the first to systematize allegorical interpretation. For him all Scripture has a spiritual meaning; while not all of it has a bodily, *i.e.* a literal, meaning; for a passage cannot be taken to have a literal meaning when such meaning would be absurd; and he instances certain statements in Genesis as to the Garden of Eden, and the story of the Devil taking Christ up into a high mountain and showing him all the kingdoms of the earth; also the Saviour's command, " If thy right eye offend thee, pluck it out." [3] But these have a spiritual meaning, as those have which are also literally true. Likewise many scriptural commands are useful, literally taken, though they may be more spiritually interpreted. Or, again, according to many passages in Origen, Scripture may

[1] *E.g.*, see Origen, *De Principiis*, Introd. Sec. 8.
[2] Lib. I, *Origen in Canticum Canticorum*, in Rufinus' Latin translation. The Queen of Sheba coming to Solomon is the Church of the Gentiles coming to Christ, *ib.* Origen, *Homilia*, II, 1, on Song of Songs, refers to Col. iii. 9, " Husbands, love your wives, as Christ loved the Church."
[3] *De Prin.* IV, I, 16, 18.

be said to have three senses, the literal, the moral, and
the spiritual: as "The grain of mustard is first the
actual seed, then faith, then the Kingdom of Heaven.
So again, the little foxes of the Song of Songs are
typical, in the second sense, of sins affecting the individual, in the third, of heresies distracting the Church.
The moral embraces all that touches the single soul
in this life, in its relation to the law of right, or to
God; the spiritual includes all 'mysteries,' all the
moments in the history of the community, the Church,
in time, and still more in eternity." [1]

There was opposition to allegorical interpretation.
Some Christian writers [2] opposed it altogether, as Plato
had done; or, again, pagans objected to the validity of its
application to the Old Testament,[3] and Christians said
it could not be used to veil the vileness of pagan mythology.   But there was no checking a system universally
in use, and which alone seemed capable of drawing forth
the essential meaning of Scripture.   In its application
to both Old and New Testaments, the writings of Hilary
of Poictiers,[4] of Ambrose,[5] and of Augustine [6] authori-

---

[1] Bigg, *Christian Platonists*, p. 136.

[2] See Hatch, *Hibbert Lectures*, 1888, pp. 79–82.   St. Basil in *Hom.*
III, 31, in Hexæmeron (Migne, *Patr. Gr.*, 29, col. 74), condemns the
interpretation of the division of the waters, which makes them signify δυνάμεις πνευματικάς (*virtutes spirituales*), etc.   See also *Hom.*
IX, in Hexæmeron, fol. 80 (Migne, 29, col. 188).

[3] *E.g.*, Celsus, in Origen, *Contra Celsum*, IV, 48.

[4] Hilarius, *Commentarius in Matthaeum*, *e.g.*, Cap. 7, 10.   The
foxes (false prophets) have holes, and the birds of the air (demons)
have nests, etc.

[5] See Ebert, *All. Ges.* (2d Ed.), I, 147–155.

[6] See *e.g.*, *Reply to Faustus the Manichæan*, XII, 25–31, and XXII;
Sermons on Gospel of John, XVII, 8; XXIV; XLVIII, 5; CXVIII,
4; CXXII, 7, 8; *Civ. Dei*, XIII, 21; XV, 27. Cassian, *Conlatio*,

tatively made it part of the Latin Church forever.
Perhaps in fantastic — incipiently barbaric — extravagance of interpretation, no Greek Christian writer had
ever equalled the Commentary on Job by him who
rightly was called Gregory the Great.[1]

In the writings of these great Fathers of the Latin
Church, whose personalities are so deeply representative of the transition from the antique to the mediæval, are to be found those myriad mystical allegorical
interpretations of Scripture which were to dominate
the literature and inspire the art of the Middle Ages.
Some they invented, some they took from Philo or the
Christian Alexandrians. A study of these matters
shows how the human spirit may be moulded by the
instruments and forms which the tendencies of some
epoch of its development have created. We have seen
how the system of allegorical interpretation came into
Christian use after it had been used by Jews and
heathens. Christianity was a supremely spiritual
religion; it had a foundation in an historical antecedent, the spirituality of which was cruder. It adopted
the system of allegorical interpretation in order to
harmonize its antecedent with itself, and also as a fitting medium through which to express itself. The
use of symbolism and allegory indicates a greater
interest in the veiled truths of life than in life's
visible facts. Conversely, this habit, once formed,

XIV, 8, having spoken of πρακτική and θεωρητική *scientia*, says that
the latter is divided into *historica interpretatio* and *intellegentia
spiritalis*, "spiritalis autem scientiae genera sunt tria, tropologia,
allegoria, anagogia." Cf. *Conlatio*, XIV, 11.

[1] In thirty-five books. This work is usually called the *Moralia*.

accustoms men to look everywhere and in everything
for the veiled yet suggested spiritual element and to
regard that as the important, nay, as the real matter.
To Christians, far more than to Jews or pagans, the
spiritual life, as foretaste and determinant of life eternal, was the important and the veritably real.   They
should be always seeking it and its hidden traces.
Material objects spread before the eyes, or narrated
facts, were in themselves transient and distracting.
Their real interest, indeed their reality, lay in their
symbolism, in the allegory which the spiritually
minded man might draw.   The barren physical thing
or fact was as the "letter which killeth"; it had no
salvation in it.   That lay in the spiritual significance
which the fact shadowed forth.   Herein was the veritable essence, the real fact.   Reality lies not in the veil,
but in what the eye of the spirit sees beneath the veil.

These transcendental interests and assumptions,
which are promoted by allegorism, were, in the time
of deepening ignorance, to open wide the door to all
miracles, — the mysterious work of God and his ministers.   They were intimately connected with the universal desire for miracles, a desire so expectant that
to those possessed by it the miraculous occurrence
is the occurrence to be looked for.   For the miracle
was the fact which directly disclosed the will of God,
and so was a manifestation of the unseen power which
other facts could but suggest symbolically.   Alone
among facts, the miracle even in itself was not the
"letter which killeth," but an instance of the "spirit
which maketh to live," a veritable instance of salvation.   In miracles, the fact, the symbol, was identical

with what was symbolized. Habits of allegorical interpretation disposed learned men toward the miraculous; while the ignorant, universally superstitious crowd expected miracles everywhere.

These interests and assumptions were also to be potent in moulding literature and art. Under their influence the artist's imagination will not be busied with creations which represent facts as they visibly occur; but will evolve such facts and series of facts as most fittingly symbolize the unseen. In painting, in sculpture, and finally in architecture, the artist will endeavor to shadow forth in symbols things of the spirit; his work shall be a work of love for truths veiled in their symbols. And likewise in literature, the interest, the truth, the reality of the poem shall lie in its mystic meaning. The full new blood of the young northern peoples will wrestle mightily against this tendency; will produce tales of wonderful adventure, of unimaginable bravery and strife, of earthly love quite sufficiently animal. But time and again, and in most typical productions, this tendency shall triumph both in the earthly interests of human life and in humanity's sublimer spiritual strainings. It will produce at last, on one hand, the *Roman de la Rose*, and on the other, the *Divina Commedia ;* while, as it were between these two, swing and waver or circle like starlings strange tales of sinful love and holy striving, whereof Arthur's knights shall be the heroes, and wherein across the stage pass on to final purity Lancelot and Guinevere as well as Galahad and Parcival.

CHAPTER VI

THE IDEALS OF KNOWLEDGE, BEAUTY, LOVE

THE genius of Greece evolved and gave the world two principles of life, the love of knowledge and the love of beauty. They appear in Homer; they were perfected in the classic Greek age. Through the Alexandrian and later Hellenistic periods of mingled decadence and spiritual growth, these principles were active; and then they were as leaven to the Latin race, though always changing with the times. The Christian Fathers, with other classically educated men, recognized them. And the manner in which they were modified in great Christian personalities, especially in those of the transition epoch, is of importance in tracing the juncture of antiquity with the Middle Ages.

In the transition from the antique to the mediæval, the changes in the ideals of beauty, love, and knowledge are involved in the religious change from paganism to Christianity. No sharp lines can be drawn between the degrees of modification undergone by various elements of antique culture in their passage to the Middle Ages, or between the transmission of pagan elements and the partial or complete substitution of Christian principles. Yet the preceding chapters have been gradually passing from the consideration of pagan elements subsisting scarcely modified in Christian writings to the consideration of those which were more deeply Christianized; and in this and the following chapters topics are considered wherein pagan elements have been either transformed or discarded. From the antique to the mediæval attitude toward love and other emotions the change is fundamental; while in the rise of monasticism there is a complete elimination of pagan principles and the evolution of a Christian system.

I. *Philosophy and Dogma*

With Christians, the love of knowledge would bear relation to their views of literature and philosophy. Deep aversion might be felt toward the sinful and idolatrous pagan literature; yet the impossibility of forbidding it was evident, when Christianity was spreading among educated men. There was no other means of getting that education which distinguished a Roman from a barbarian. In their conflict with the heathen world, Christians could not condemn themselves to inferiority in intellectual equipment.[1] The Fathers lamented that pagan literature was the only means of culture; yet the fact remained. And cultured Christian taste recognized the unfitness of Christian writings for use as models in the place of Cicero and Virgil. Even Tertullian had to admit the necessity of studying pagan literature,[2] yet he would forbid

[1] Cf. Augustine, *De doctrina Christiana*, IV, 2, 3.

[2] See, *e.g.*, *De Idolatria*, 10. An interesting account of modes of education in the Roman Empire, and of Christian difficulties in this regard, is given in Boissier, *Fin du Paganisme*, Vol. I, Livres 2 and 3.

Christians teaching it in public schools when that involved recognition of the imperial religion. But the Church refused to follow him, and subsequently none of Julian's covert attempts against Christianity aroused more anger than his edict prohibiting Christian professors from teaching the classics.

Yet there always remained qualms which disturbed cultured Christians just because they felt how dear to them was all the beautiful pagan literature, the friend and educator of their youth. Augustine was troubled; but his disquietude was slight compared with the sense of sinfulness which love of the classics roused in Jerome. Never could he forget them, never could he cease to love them. But what concord has Christ with Belial? What has Horace to do with the Psalter, Virgil with the Gospels, Cicero with Paul? And Jerome tells the dream of his stung conscience, how, appearing before the judgment seat of Christ, he heard the words, "Thou a Christian! Thou art a Ciceronian! Where the heart is, there is its treasure."[1]

Likewise with Greek philosophy. In spite of the early Christian distrust of it,[2] the tendency to reason and define, and the necessity of reasoning in ways known to the reasoners, was sure to bring philosophy into the church. The attitude of individual Christians depended largely on temperament and race and on the influences under which they had been educated. There would be difference here between the East and West, the Greek and Roman. For the Hellenic mind

[1] Jerome, *Epist. XXII ad Eustochium*, Par. 29, 30. Jerome's dream deeply impressed the Middle Ages.
[2] As with Paul, 1 Cor. et seq. and Col. ii. 18.

could never cease to philosophize and confide itself to philosophy, while the Roman temper was less curious and was averse to speculation. The Roman-minded, legally educated Tertullian is an example of the Roman temperament. To him philosophy is a source of heresies and a rash interpreter of the nature and ways of God. "What in common have Athens and Jerusalem? The Academy and the Church? Heretics and Christians? Let them see to it who teach a stoical and Platonic and dialectic Christianity! We find no need of curiosity reaching beyond Christ Jesus, nor of inquiry beyond the gospel. When we believe, we need nothing further than to believe. Search that you may believe; then stop." [1]

Somewhat on the other side is Justin, who often speaks of Christianity as a philosophy, and realizes that through Platonism he reached Christian truth.[2] But more explicitly the Alexandrians, Clement and Origen, intrenched their Christianity in philosophy, and apprehended it in modes of Platonic thought. With them Christianity is the culmination of philosophy, and includes all truth; philosophy is the preparatory study. Clement devotes the opening chapter of his *Stromata* to the vindication of this position: "Before the advent of Christianity," says he, "philosophy was needful to the Greeks for righteousness (δικαιοσύνη). Now it is useful to piety for those who attain faith through demonstration. Philosophy was a schoolmaster to the Greeks, as the law was to the

---

[1] Tertullian, *De Praescriptionibus adversus Hereticos*, VII, x. See also Irenæus, *Contra Haer.*, II, 26, 27.

[2] *Trypho*, II, etc.

Hebrews, preparing the way for those who are perfected by Christ."[1] The one and only God was known by the Greeks in a Gentile way, by the Jews Judaistically, but is known to us Christians in a new and spiritual way. The God who gave both covenants, gave Greek philosophy.[2] Likewise with Origen Christianity is the sum of knowledge; his life's endeavor was to bring all knowledge into the scheme of salvation through Christ. "If we see some admirable work of human art, we are at once eager to investigate the nature, the manner, the end of its production; and the contemplation of the works of God stirs us with an incomparably greater longing to learn the principles, the method, the purpose of creation. This desire, this passion, has without doubt been implanted in us by God. And as the eye seeks light, as our body craves food, so our mind is impressed with the characteristic and natural desire of knowing the truth of God and the causes of what we observe."[3]

Gregory Thaumaturgus, in his panegyric on his master, says that Origen, wishing to gain him and others as pupils, praised the lovers of philosophy, declaring that only those live a life worthy of reasonable creatures who aim at living an upright life, and seek to know first themselves, and then what is good and what man ought to strive for, and what is evil and what man ought to flee. Thus he reproved ignorance. He asserted that there could be no genuine piety toward God in the man who despised the gift of

[1] *Stromata*, I, 5. See the rest of this interesting passage.
[2] *Strom.*, VI, 5.
[3] Origen, *De Principiis*, II, 11, 4, Westcott's translation.

philosophy; that no one could be truly pious who did
not philosophize. But beyond this, Origen's benevo-
lent mind inspired us with the love of the Word and
of our teacher himself. Afterwards he assailed us in
the Socratic fashion, purged us by argumentations,
then sowed the good seed. He taught us also physics,
geometry, and astronomy, and ethics not only by word
but by deed, and constrained us to practise righteousness. He had us study all philosophers, except the
atheists, that we might not attribute undue importance
to one doctrine through ignorance of the rest. But
above all he taught us to devote ourselves to the
teaching of God and the prophets in Scripture.

Christianity gave to Christian students of philosophy a definite purpose and a point of view. Thus
Origen writes to Gregory: "Good natural parts help
one toward any end, and yours might make you a
good Roman lawyer or a Greek philosopher. But I
advise you to use the strength of your natural parts
with Christianity as an end (τελικῶς εἰς Χριστιανίσμον)
and to seek from Greek philosophy what may serve
as preparation for Christianity, and from geometry
and astronomy what may serve to explain the Holy
Scriptures, so that, as students of philosophy speak of
geometry, music, grammar, rhetoric, and astronomy as
fellow-helpers to philosophy, we may speak of philosophy itself in relation to Christianity."[1]

Irenæus had said: "True knowledge, γνῶσις ἀληθής,
which is opposed to the fallacies of the Gnostics, is
the doctrine of the apostles, the constitution of the
Church according to the succession of bishops, and

[1] *Epistola ad Gregorium.*

its exposition of the Scriptures unfalsified by forg-
eries, but read plainly and in the gift of love (*munus
delectionis*)." [1] This statement might seem to Clement
and Origen to beg the real question: What is the doctrine of the apostles? How shall it be understood and
stated? To an understanding of the Gospel as contained in the Scriptures, that is to say, to the ascer-
tainment and statement of the true Christian γνῶσις,
a training in preparatory modes of knowledge, *i.e.* in
Greek philosophy, was essential.[2] If so, the unlearned
could not have knowledge of Christianity. Clement
and Origen recognized two classes of Christians, those
who had simple faith, and those who with fuller
knowledge were the true knowers, γνωστικοί.[3] The
first, however, had the saving faith, which must also
underlie the further perfections of the latter.[4] Indeed,
Clement would trace all demonstration back to its
basis in undemonstrable faith.[5] Nevertheless the
view of gnosis as higher than faith tended to destroy
the unity of the Christian ideal of life, which is faith,
love, and knowledge of the truth, and also to break
the unity of the saving work of Christ. Says Origen:
"The Redeemer becomes many things, perhaps even
all things, according to the necessities of the whole
creation capable of being redeemed by him. . . .
Happy are they who have advanced so far as to need
the Son of God no longer as a healing physician, no

---

[1] Irenæus, *Contra Haer.*, IV, xxxiii, 8.

[2] Clement, *Strom.*, I, 7, 8, 9.

[3] These true γνωστικοί are not to be confused with the Gnostics.

[4] *Strom.*, II, 12; IV, 21, 22, etc.; V, 1, 13. Cf. Bigg, *Christian
Platonists of Alexandria*, p. 84, etc.

[5] *Strom.*, VIII, 3. See *Strom.*, II, 2, 4, 6.

longer as a shepherd, no longer as the Redemption; but who need him only as the Truth, the Word, the Sanctification, and in whatever other relation he stands to those whose maturity enables them to comprehend what is most glorious in his character." [1]

From a consideration of the necessity of philosophy to a complete understanding of Christianity, Clement often passes to the inculcation of some definite philosophical doctrine, and introduces it into his Christian system.[2] For example, the readiness coming from previous training helps in the perception of essential matters. Demonstrations secure faith, so that the learner cannot conceive of what is demonstrated as being different. In such studies the soul is purged of sensible things and enabled to perceive the truth; without letters, a man may be a believer ($\pi\iota\sigma\tau\acute{o}\varsigma$), but cannot understand the faith.[3] Here a thought foreign to Christianity is introduced from Greek philosophy, that by speculation the mind is purged of attachments to things of sense. Again he says: Abstraction from the body and its passions is the sacrifice acceptable to God. If, making such abstraction, we cast ourselves into the greatness of Christ, and then advance into immunity by holiness, we may reach toward some conception of what God is.[4] The Saviour Himself said, "Watch"; which is to say, study how to live, and endeavor to separate the soul from the body.[5] Christ

---

[1] *Origen in Joann.*, T. I, Sec. 22 (from Neander); Migne, *Pat. Gr.*, 14, col. 56.

[2] Clement was himself an influence affecting Plotinus' Neoplatonism.   [3] *Strom.*, I, 6.   [4] *Strom.*, V, 12.

[5] *Strom.*, V, 14. Clement elsewhere says that the Logos (Christ) cures the passions of the soul.

was completely ἀπαθής (passionless, without suffering, unmoved, insensible). The true γνωστικός is free from emotion and passion; he is not courageous, because he fears nothing, and nothing can sever him from his love of God; he has no common affections, but loves the Creator in His creations.[1] Thus Clement's philosophy causes him to apply the term ἀπαθής to Him who was moved to indignation, who wept at Lazarus' grave, whose soul was exceeding sorrowful in Gethsemane.

The Alexandrians approached the gospel through philosophy. Whatever their shortcomings, they presented the thought to the Christian world, that Christ's gospel was the sum of knowledge, and all true knowledge could not but conduce to a fuller understanding of it. This principle was recognized by Augustine. More strongly than Clement or Origen, he felt the limitations of human rational cognition;[2] while he, as well as they, saw that whatever human knowledge might comprehend could be included in the compass of Christ's revelation. Augustine had found in his own case that reason did not reach to the proving of the truth of Christ, and in the end he believed through faith. But it was along the paths of human knowledge, *in libris saecularis sapientiae*, that he had approached Christianity.[3] He had been a lover of wisdom, a philosopher; now he raised his love toward wisdom's self: "If God through whom all things are

---

[1] *Strom.*, VI, 9.

[2] For example, he says, *Confessions*, IV, 29, that he had found little help to the understanding of God from studying Aristotle's Ten Categories; for within them one cannot conceive God.

[3] See *Confessions*, V, 6, 8, 9.

made is Wisdom, as the divine truth declares, the true philosopher is a lover of God." [1]   Augustine's Christianity does not exclude profane knowledge, rather has scope for all knowledge.   But woe unto that knowledge, or seeming knowledge, which leads from knowing God: "Wretched that man who knows all philosophies, and knows not Thee; blessed is he who knows Thee, though ignorant of all those matters." [2]

The apostolic period was scarcely passed when the need came upon the Christian communities to define their faith in terms suited to the understandings of the multitude of intelligent men who were, or might become, Christians.   This involved a formulation of its teachings in prevalent ways of thinking.   Such a formulation was in itself a process of reasoning; it proceeded from the needs of man as a being who must reason and apprehend through reason; it involved a statement of the grounds of its own validity; it was stimulated and forced onward by the necessity of sustaining the gospel against pagan arguments and of suppressing religious error among Christians.

Men can reason only with the knowledge and conceptions they possess.   Hellenic philosophy held the sum of knowledge in the Empire, in the Latin West as well as the Hellenic East.   From no other source could come the elements of knowledge constituting the categories of rational apprehension in which Christianity could be formulated.   There was, however, another terminology wherein men might reason, which had its basis in the Roman temperament and its chief

[1] *Civ. Dei*, VIII, 1; citing "Wisdom," vii. 24–27; Heb. i. 2, 3.
[2] *Confessions*, V, 7; cf. *ib.*, X, 54–57.

expression in the Roman law.   Accordingly, in the formulation of Christian teachings the substantial knowledge and rational basis was of necessity Greek philosophy, while the methods of reasoning might be those of philosophy or consist of the terminology and conceptions of the Roman law.   The choice of Christian theologians would be determined by their nationality and education, and by the language which they used ; the Latin temperament, education, and language being rather legal than philosophical, the Greek being the reverse.

Although Greek philosophy alone could furnish knowledge, the fact that Roman ethical conceptions were fundamentally legal influenced the mode in which Christianity was apprehended by the Roman mind.   There were analogies between Roman and Hebrew ways of conceiving justice and righteousness. Both races had a strong sense of the responsibility which rises from covenant, a sense of the absolute obligation of persons to fulfil their solemn promises. Among the Hebrews, righteousness and justice had their source in the archetypal covenant between Jehovah and Israel, and Hebrew ethical conceptions progressed along the lines of its requirements.   Through his part in the covenant with Jehovah the Hebrew owed his duties to his brethren.   With Paul righteousness is still primarily a quality which justifies man before God.   The Romans saw the matter directly from the side of covenant relations between citizens ; yet these depended on the State's superior power, and the Roman legal *sanctio* was connected with fear of divine vengeance, and so was partly religious.

Roman conceptions of justice and right kept their legal form because the sense of legal responsibility made up so much of the Roman temperament. Tertullian's writings are an example. He had been a lawyer, and his legal education gave him command over a terminology suited to express juristic thoughts of righteousness and religion. But the cause of his legal modes of reasoning lay deeper; for, beneath his education, he was a Latin, a Roman-minded man, like Augustine, who also reasons juridically although his education was chiefly in rhetoric and philosophy.

On the other hand, legal conceptions were absent from Greek thoughts of right and justice; for the Greeks reached their ethical conceptions in part through philosophical speculation as to the universe and man and God, matter and mind, and in part through their sense and understanding of the beautiful, that is, through the æsthetic and artistic side of their nature, which sought everywhere harmony, fitness, and proportion. So the Greek would formulate Christian doctrine in terms of cosmological speculation and of the beautiful and fit; while the Roman would proceed rather with juristic thoughts, yet would have to take the data of his knowledge from Greek philosophy. The Roman legal spirit, as well as Greek philosophy, sought to define, and so was part of the general tendency to dogmatize the Christian faith. But in that great process of formulation, ending say in the Council of Chalcedon (451 A.D.), Greek philosophy was the overwhelmingly important factor, not only because it furnished the elements of knowledge, but because the majority of early Christian theolo-

gians were Hellenic in spirit and wrote Greek; while
the Latin Fathers reset in Latin and juristic phrase
the definitions which the East had evolved.   An illustration is afforded by the Latin juristic word *persona*,
which represents — it does not translate — the Greek
word ὑπόστασις. The Latins had to render the three
ὑποστάσεις of the Greeks; and "three somethings,"
tria quaedam, was too loose, as Augustine says.
Hence, the legal word *persona* was employed, although its unfitness was recognized.[1]   Of course
it received new meaning from its use in the Creed.

   The loose beliefs of paganism felt no need to
formulate themselves, except externally in cults.   But
Greek philosophy from its beginning was formulation
of knowledge and opinion, and might discard whatever religious belief it deviated from.   Christ's gospel was definite revelation; the Christian faith was
too strong to surrender its elements whenever they
seemed inconsistent with the knowledge of the time.
It could only advance to further definiteness, using
human knowledge and reason to promote and sub-
stantiate definitions of itself.   Unquestionably the
Catholic formulation operated to preserve Christianity from errors and corruptions;[2] and if it veiled,

---

[1] See Augustine, *De Trin.*, VII, Sec. 7–12.   ὑπόστασις, literally, is
substantia, the word used by the Latins to represent the Greek
οὐσία, of which the equivalent would have been *essentia*, had that
word been in use.

[2] Athanasius shows how Arianism tended to pagan polytheism;
see, *e.g.*, *Discourses against the Arians*, III, xxv, 16.   There was
pagan pride, as well as Gnostic tendencies, in Arianism; see, *e.g.*,
the Fragments of Arius' *Thalia*, and cf. Athanasius, *Discourses*,
etc., II, xvii, 24–26.

it did not exclude the realities of Christ's gospel. Through the storm of his life, Athanasius stood on the rock of the reality of the salvation which Christ brought mankind.[1]

Nevertheless, the formulation of Christianity in dogma was Hellenic and metaphysical, and a departure alike from the Hebraic spirit of the Old Testament and from the nature of Jesus' teachings. If we follow the gradual revelation in the Old Testament of Jehovah as a great personality with a definite character, and if we then pass to the synoptic gospels, and see how Jesus sets forth, phase by phase, the relationship of God to man, the loving ways of God the Father, and finally, if we observe in the fourth gospel how in modes deeply analogous to his way in the synoptics, Jesus sets forth teachings which pass man's understanding, yet are real to the mind and give to the heart's realities a further range, then we shall find throughout a common trait, the absence of definition and formulation — the absence of any formulation of what, when formulated, the human mind cannot grasp and realize.[2]

[1] Athanasius, in his *Discourses against the Arians* and other writings (see, *e.g.*, *De Incarnatione Verbi Dei*), founds his Christology on his Soteriology; *i.e.* on the principle that Christ must have been God to effect a real reconciliation between men and God — to be a Redeemer. See also Harnack, *Dogmengeschichte*, II (2d Ed.), p. 157, etc.

[2] It would be interesting to point out how the formulation of belief, when pushed beyond the range of man's inner experience and external observation, becomes unreal, and in becoming unreal tends to evoke formalism complemented by superstition. Christianity has been affected by two apparently opposite kinds of superstition, which nevertheless present analogies, and are not unrelated

The preceding remarks upon the formulation of the Christian faith apply primarily to the Eastern or Hellenic portion of the process, which was mainly concerned with the divine metaphysics of Christianity, that is, with defining the nature of Christ. The Latin West approved the results of this formulation, but for its own part, caring less for metaphysics than for life, it felt itself more earnestly concerned with the sinfulness of man and the relation of the human will to God's grace and foreknowledge. Here the moulder of men's thoughts was Augustine.[1]

In the formulation of dogma, Greek philosophy passes into Christianity. Although the course of this

in source. The one regards the magic-mystical effect of the outward act, eating of bread, or baptism, or penance done — a superstition opposed to the spiritual regeneration set forth by Christ. The other attaches a quasi-magical efficiency to the mind's accurate acceptance and the mouth's correct enunciation of metaphysical propositions. Its source lay in the process, if not in the spirit, of doctrinal formulation. Equally with the first error, it ignores the actual condition and the needful spiritual regeneration of the soul. Moreover, the dogmatic definition of Christ's nature tended to lift him above the people's hearts, and caused them to set between themselves and the heartless Christ the interceding mother-love of Mary and the mediatorship of all the saints.

[1] Whatever one may think of these Pauline-Augustinian questions, it must be admitted that as Nicene formulation held fast to the reality of Christ's mediating salvation, so Augustine's reasoning held fast to man's need thereof; while Pelagianism threatened man's need of Christ, just as Arianism threatened the reality of Christ's redeeming function. Such views as Augustine's, dark as they were, promoted among higher minds the passionate love of Christ, of God; and perhaps promoted also devotion to all the mediating means and instruments — saints, martyrs, Virgin Mary, and the rest — by which the lowering intelligence of man was for some centuries to link itself to the Kingdom of Heaven.

formulation lay largely in progressive disclaimer and condemnation of opinions pronounced erroneous, it was also a creative process resulting in the establishment of original propositions. Besides eclectically modified Stoicism, the Greek system chiefly used in this formulation was Neo-platonism, the dominant pagan philosophy in the fourth century. Dogma grew from Hellenic reasoning upon gospel data, and was itself in turn to form the subject of further processes of reasoning based on Greek philosophy. After its first and creative Christian career, Greek philosophy, from the ninth century onward, runs its second Christian course in scholasticism. With the schoolmen, philosophy was not to be entirely uncreative; yet was chiefly to consist in a systematizing of dogma and a new endeavor to place it upon a basis of reason and knowledge. The Greek system employed was Aristotelianism, a philosophy in its nature more systematizing and less creative than Platonism.

During the first Christian career of Greek philosophy the classic sources were open to the Christian world, which, however, made chief use of those closest to Christianity in spirit and in time. For the second Christian career of Greek philosophy the sources had to be gradually redisclosed. Boethius' Aristotelian translations[1] represent the knowledge of Greek philosophy in the West in the seventh and eighth centuries. In the ninth, the first great schoolman, John Scotus Erigena, translated the works of Dionysius the Areopagite, and in the centuries following the tenth there gradually came a larger knowledge of Aristotle, till

[1] See *ante*, Chap. IV.

by the thirteenth his works were fully known:[1] *prœ-cursor Christi in naturalibus sicut Joannes Baptista in gratuitis.*

II. *Beauty and Love*

As the Christians abominated the idols of the heathen, it was natural that their aversion should extend to all images.[2] Moreover, such beauty as commonly was sought by the plastic art of the Empire was meretricious in the eyes of Christians[3] who sometimes refer to it in order to illustrate by contrast their own conceptions of true beauty. An early trend of Christian thought is seen in the common application to Christ's person of Isaiah's words, "He hath no form or comeliness."[4] For Christians the beauty of the body consisted in those physical qualities which suggested moral or spiritual qualities according with

---

[1] Cf. Erdmann, Hist. etc., I, §§ 133, 146, 153, 191, 192, 203, 205; Überweg, *History of Philosophy*, I, pp. 260 et seq.; Maurice, *Mediæval Philosophy*; Haureau, *Histoire de la philosophie scholastique*; Jourdain, *Récherches critiques sur l'age et langue des traductions latines d'Aristote* (1843); L. Stein, "Das Princip der Entwickelung in der Geistesgeschichte," *Deutsche Rundschau*, June, 1895; *ib.*, "Das Erste Aufstanden der Griech. Phil. unter den Arabern," *Archiv für Gesch. der Philos.*, Bd. VII, p. 351 (1894), and *ib.*, in *Archiv*, etc., Bd. IX, p. 225 (1896).

[2] See, *e.g.*, Origen, *Contra Celsum*, IV, 31; Tertullian, *De Idolatria, passim.*

[3] On the other hand, it was an age when pictorial decoration was a matter of course. This habit the Christians generally continued, as is shown by the well-known Christian house on the Aventine and the earliest catacombs. See *post*, p. 316.

[4] Yet many Fathers maintained that Jesus was noble and beautiful in person.

the Christian ideal.[1] Says Clement of Alexandria:
He who in chaste love (ἀγάπην ἀγνήν) looks on beauty,
thinks not that the flesh is beautiful, but the spirit,
admiring the body as a statue (ἀνδριάντα) through
whose beauty he transports himself to the artist and
the true beauty.[2]

Augustine's early manhood is known to all. Too
passionately had he loved the beauty of the flesh; yet
it was beauty that he loved, and would be often saying
to his friends, "*Num amamus aliquid nisi pulchrum?*"[3]
"But I saw not yet the essential matter in thy art,
Almighty One, who alone makest marvellous things;
and my soul was travelling through corporeal forms;
and I was defining and distinguishing what was beautiful in itself, what was fit, and what should be adapted
to something; and I was finding corporeal illustrations. Also I turned to the nature of the soul; and
the false view I held of things spiritual did not permit me to perceive the truth."[4] But as Augustine
found his way more surely to Christianity, these
thoughts changed with him, till he knew that outward

[1] Clement praises a spiritual beauty, rather than any beauty of
an embellished body. The true beauty is of that man with whom
dwells the Word; for he then has the form of the Word, and is
made like God; and another beauty of men is love. Love vaunteth
not itself, seeketh not what is not its own and God's, so does not
behave itself unseemly; all of which would be opposed to the true
spiritual beauty, as of Christ, who had neither form nor comeliness.
—*Paedagogus*, III, 1. Ambrose says, speaking of the Virgin: "ut
ipsa corporis species simulacrum fuerit mentis, figura probitatis,"
De Virginibus, II, 2; Migne, *Patr. Lat.*, 16, col. 209.

[2] *Strom.*, IV, 18.

[3] *Confessions*, IV, 20. At the age of twenty-seven he wrote the
De Pulchro et Apto.

[4] *Confessions*, IV, Sec. 24. The Latin is somewhat obscure.

beauties were but human fashionings of the beauty whence they come, for which his soul now yearns day and night.[1]

Of all philosophies, Platonism seemed to Augustine nearest to Christian truth.[2] But Platonism as he understood it was largely Neo-platonism. Gregory of Nyssa, however, is an interesting example of a Christian Father taking thoughts of beauty directly from Plato, and endeavoring to give them Christian hue. In his treatise on "Virginity" he argues that the only way to escape the bondage of low desire is to turn one's life to the contemplation of the Father of all beauty, and so beautify the lines of one's own character from imitation of the source of beauty; herein is virginity a helper. What words can express the greatness of the loss in falling away from real goodness? If a man has kept the eye of his heart so clear that he can in a way behold the promise of our Lord's beatitudes realized, he will condemn all human utterance as powerless to express what he has apprehended. But when passion like a film has spread over the clear vision of the soul, expression is wasted on that man;

---

[1] *Confessions*, X, Sec. 53. From his rhetorical occupations Augustine evolves an extraordinary argument as to the ways of God: God would have made no man or angel whom He foreknew would be evil had He not known that that being would be of use for good. Thus would God embellish the succession of the ages as a beautiful poem (*carmen*), by antithesis, as it were: Antitheta enim quae appellantur in ornamentis elocutionis sunt decentissima, quae latine appellantur opposita. . . . Sicut ergo ista contraria contrariis opposita sermonis pulchritudinem reddunt; ita quadam, non verborum, sed rerum eloquentia contrariorum oppositione saeculi pulchritudo componitur. *Civ. Dei*, XI, 18.

[2] See, *e.g.*, *Civ. Dei*, VIII, 5.

he cannot perceive, as one born blind cannot see the splendor of sunlight. To see the beauty of the true and intellectual light, each man has need of eyes of his own; and he who by gift of divine inspiration can see it, retains his ecstasy unexpressed, while he who sees it not cannot be made to know the greatness of his loss. How should he? For this good is inexpressible, we have not learned the language to tell this beauty. Well may one exclaim in the psalmist's words, "All men are liars!" not because hating the truth, but because of human feebleness to express in language the ineffable light. How can language tell of the invisible and formless Beauty which is destitute of qualities perceptible to sense? Not that we are to despair of winning it, but, as it is so very great, we must lift our thoughts, fearful of losing share in that Good which we always run the risk of losing because of its height and mystery. Yet we must pass to the unseen Beauty by means of data of sense. One with clear vision sees that visible beauties are but the elements on which the form [1] of beauty works; to him they will be but the ladder by which he climbs to the prospect of that intellectual Beauty from which other beauties derive their existence. He who turns from all grosser thoughts and longings after what seems, and explores the nature of beauty which is simple, immaterial, and formless, is in the path leading to its discovery; he will leave behind and below him all other objects; he will lift up his powers to heights the senses cannot reach, beyond the beauty of the heavens, to the Beauty whose glory the heavens and firmament declare and

---

[1] The Platonic idea.

whose secret the whole creation sings. To this he can mount only by the self-made image of the Dove, which is the Holy Spirit, within himself. With this alone may the mind of man soar above this murky world to the true Purity, that atmosphere of light, where the soul itself becomes a Light, according to our Lord's promise that the righteous shall shine forth as the Sun. And so shall we become as the Light in our nearness to Christ's true light, if the true Light that shineth in the darkness comes down even to us, unless there is any foulness of sin spreading over our hearts. Thus may we be changed to something better than ourselves; and this union of the soul with the incorruptible deity can only be attained by her reaching the virgin state of utmost purity; a state which being like God will grasp what is like, while she places herself as a mirror under the purity of God, and moulds her own beauty at the touch and sight of all beauty's archetype. A character strong enough to turn from all that is human, will feel as a lover only toward that Beauty which has no source but itself, and is not beauty relative or particular, or changing, or waxing, or waning. To such a soul, by virtue of her innocence, comes the power of apprehending that light. And real virginity has no other goal than the power thereby of seeing God, the only absolute and primal Beauty and Goodness.[1]

The same Platonic Christian elsewhere says that the speculative and critical faculty is the property of the soul's godlike part, for by this we grasp the deity also.

[1] *On Virginity*, Chaps. X, XI. Cf. Plato, *Phaedrus* and *Symposium*.

When the soul by purgation becomes free from emotional relation to the brute creation, there will be nothing to impede its contemplation of the beautiful. The only habit of the soul, which will remain, is love; and that clings by natural affinity to beauty. "The life of the Supreme Being is love, seeing that the Beautiful is necessarily lovable to those who recognize it, and the Deity does recognize it, and so this recognition becomes love, that which he recognizes being essentially beautiful. The insolence of satiety cannot touch this true Beauty."[1] This is Platonism set in Christian phrase.

Augustine's yearning for the beauty of God, and Gregory of Nyssa's adaptation of Plato's fantasy which held so much ideal reality, accord with much of the deeper and more devotional feeling for beauty in Christian art through the Middle Ages, and harmonize with the spirit of Christian allegorism. The visible form is valid only as suggestion of the spirit; let it suggest beauties, not blemishes; holiness, rather than fleshly incitement; purity, rather than lust; the power of the spirit, rather than the soul's temptations.

"Love is of the beautiful," said Plato. Do we love anything except the beautiful? asked Augustine, as his soul was wandering deviously on.[2] With Plato love was desire and motive; for Christians, besides being desire and motive, love was itself to be fulfilment, a reaching God, a bringing unto Him of all the elements of the individual's life, thereby perfected in

[1] Gregory of Nyssa, *On the Soul and the Resurrection.*
[2] *Ante,* p. 124.

eternal truth. Such love is the synthesis of all elements of life, wherein no noble element is lost, wherein desire of knowledge in itself and beauty in itself gain further sanction as true modes of life's completion.

Augustine knew the whole nature of love, its final object, and its true proportionings and directings of itself thereto. Man can be at one with himself only in God. Augustine had proved this in the restlessness of his early manhood: "Thou hast made us toward Thee, and unquiet is our heart until it rests in Thee."[1] This was true of Augustine, a representative man; likewise it was true of the yearning of those centuries which produced Neo-platonism, as well as turned to Christ. Augustine was athirst for God; his heart was stricken, bathed, healed, and given peace and joy, with the love of God. "Not with doubting but certain consciousness (*conscientia*), Lord, I love thee. Thou hast struck my heart with thy Word, and I have loved Thee. But also heaven and the earth and all that therein is, lo, from every quarter they tell me I should love thee." "That is the blessed life (*beata vita*) to rejoice toward Thee, concerning Thee and because of Thee." "Give me Thyself, my God, give Thyself to me . . . All my plenty which is not my God is need."[2]

This is the heart's need of God and need to love Him, and the heart's fulness of life which that love brings. What Augustine's heart felt, his mind could analyze. "That then is love (*dilectio*, ἀγάπη) which is

[1] *Confessions*, I, 1.
[2] *Confessions*, X, 8 and 32; XIII, 9.

true; otherwise it is lust (*cupiditas*) . . . This is true love, that cleaving to truth we may live aright (*juste*); and for that reason we contemn all mortal things except the love for men whereby we wish them to live aright. Thus can we profitably be prepared even to die for our brethren, as the Lord Jesus Christ taught us by his example. . . . It is love which unites good angels and servants of God in the bond of holiness, joins us to them and them to us, and subjoins all unto God." Augustine continues: Quid est autem dilectio vel charitas . . . nisi amor boni ? Amor autem alicujus amantis est, et amore aliquid amatur. Ecce tria sunt; amans, et quod amatur, et amor. Quid est ergo amor, nisi quaedam vita duo aliqua copulans, vel copulare appetens, amantem scilicet et quod amatur ? Et hoc etiam in externis carnalibusque amoribus ita est; sed ut aliquid purius et liquidius hauriamus calcata carne ascendamus ad animum. Quid amat animus in amico nisi animum? Et illic igitur tria sunt, amans, et quod amatur, et amor.[1] True love is a loving desire of the good; love is of the person loving, and with love something is loved. Then there are three; the lover, what is loved, and love. Love is a kind of life uniting the lover and the loved. This is true in carnal loves; seeking purer draughts of life, spurning the flesh, we rise to the soul; and what does soul love in the friend save soul ?

This passage indicates the completeness of Augustine's conception. Love, *dilectio*, that which esteems and cherishes (from *deligo*), also includes love's desire

---

[1] *De Trinitate*, VIII, 10-14.

(*amor*). Love has a self-assertive, acquisitive, desir-
ous element; hence when perfected is twofold; perfect
wish for the beloved's welfare, and desire of union
with the beloved for one's own self's sake, and the
beloved's sake as well. Here is all of Plato's conception of love; and Augustine has already indicated
how he will now complete the thought with something
he did not find in Plato but in Christ. "We must
love all things with reference to God, otherwise it
is lust. Inferior creatures are to be used (*utendum*)
with reference to God (*ad Deum*); and our fellows
are to be enjoyed (*fruendum*) with reference to God,
toward God; so thyself, not in thyself ought thou to
enjoy (*frui*) thyself, but in Him who made thee; thus
also shouldst thou enjoy him whom thou lovest as
thyself. Therefore let us enjoy ourselves and our
brothers in the Lord and not dare to surrender ourselves unto ourselves, downwards as it were." [1]

Lust is an unproportioned thing; in love all motive
and desire is proportioned in the only possible universal proportionment, unto God. Thus Augustine
completes his thought of love, by relating every feeling and every person, ourselves and all whom we
love, to God; *thither* lies the standard of proportion.
Augustine has carried through an analysis of what he
felt: Thou hast made us toward Thee, and unquiet
is our heart until it rests in Thee.

The Christian conception of love was more complete than any pagan thought of love. But what was
the actual compass and range of feelings generally
approved by the Church of the fourth and fifth cen-

[1] *De Trinitate*, IX, 13.

turies? How did that compare with the range of pagan emotion? What elements of pagan feeling, what pagan limitations of feeling, passed over into Christian emotion?

The idea of Clement of Alexandria, that only with a soul purged of emotion can a man attain the logos-Christ, is connected with other phases of self-restraint and renunciation taught by later Greek philosophy; these, being part of the time's prevalent moods and ways of thinking, were introduced into Christianity. The philosophic pain arising from life's short uncertainties comes to Christian souls as a motive for keeping disengaged from life's affections and affairs. Says Gregory of Nyssa: "The moment a husband looks on the beloved face of his wife, fear of separation seizes him. One should keep disengaged from the 'Egyptian bondage' of this life's desires and cares. It is sad to care for what one cannot keep forever; and how can man on earth keep anything forever, though he love it never so passionately?"[1] This might have been written by Marcus Aurelius or a Hindoo; it represents a Hellenistic mood of the time thrusting itself into Christianity, a mood of mortality disheartened with itself. Life's transitoriness has no pain for the Christian. With the gospel's assurance in his heart, he need not shut himself against human loves. Nevertheless, such thoughts as these expressed by Gregory so make part of mortality's short vision, and are so continually borne in on man by all his life on earth, that they entered Christianity to stay for many centuries.

[1] *On Virginity*, Chaps. III, IV.

There were, however, Christians who spoke against suppression of the affections, recognizing that such a principle was pagan, while Christianity called for the use and development of all elements of human nature. It is an error of the Stoics, says Lactantius, that they would cut off all emotions — desire, joy, fear, and grief — as diseases of the human being; the Peripatetics are not so far from the truth in teaching that the affections, as a part of human nature, should not be rooted out, but moderated. Yet they too are wrong, for at times it is right to rejoice or grieve greatly. Man should not moderate the affections, but regulate their causes. He who rightly fears God is a man of right fortitude, and will not fear pain and death, which it is unworthy of man to fear. "Where there are no vices, there is no place for virtue; as there is no place for victory unless there be an adversary. There can be no good without evil in this life. Emotional desire is, as it were, a natural fruitfulness of souls (*affectus igitur, quasi ubertas est naturalis animorum*). A wild field will bring forth briars, but a cultivated field good fruit; and when God made man, He gave him emotions (*commotiones*) that he might take virtue." [1]

A greater man than Lactantius also maintained that affections and emotions were elements of Christian life on earth: "The citizens of the sacred city of God in this life's sojourning, living according to God's will, fear, desire, grieve, rejoice. And because their love is rightly directed, so are these feelings of theirs. They fear eternal punishment, desire eternal life, they groan in themselves waiting for the adoption; they

[1] Lactantius, *Divine Institutes*, V, 15–17.

fear to sin, they desire to persevere, they grieve in sins, and rejoice in good works." [1]

From the greatness of his nature Augustine recognized the emotions, above all the love of God; nevertheless, like many other Christian writers of the early centuries, he was deeply affected by pagan, and especially by Neo-platonic, thought in his conceptions of supreme blessedness in this life and hereafter. Christ had set the Kingdom of Heaven above all, and men might enter even here on earth; the life absolute, eternal, is of supreme worth for men; and on earth they may receive it. But on earth the Kingdom must be entered and eternal life attained in ways of action according with the realities of human life in its earthly conditions. Christ set forth a plan for truly perfecting the earthly life, a scheme of human progress, in which mankind must participate in modes of action suited to earth. Man shall not on earth strive to attain unearthly, and so for this life unreal, states of bliss. Neither in the synoptics nor in the gospel of John does Christ set forth as man's highest goal on earth any mystical vision of God or any mystical union of the soul with God. Here on earth communion with God comes through doing His will in faith and love and knowledge. Nor does Christ suggest that love's service shall cease in the Kingdom of Heaven.

But the Christian Fathers, steeped in the moods of the centuries which found their pagan expression in Neo-platonism, and looking forward to the final, mystic, ineffable vision of God, felt that this vision was

[1] Augustine, *Civ. Dei*, XIV, 9.

the goal of life on earth. Even here let the believer's soul, purged of its dross, unite with God. The Christian brought into this mystic union the element of love — a great reality. But otherwise this goal with Christians as with Plotinus involved the ignoring of life's realities. Christians as well as Neo-platonists were struggling in earthly life to reach beyond it, out of it, after what is for man on earth unreal. Here was an abnegation of this life's real loves and acts and knowledge. Whereas by a fulfilment of them all man does the will of God according to the gospel of Christ.[1]

[1] The underlying error lay here. The later systems of Greek philosophy were systems of renunciation. This is clearly true of later Stoicism; and Neo-platonism was a striving in the way of unreal fantasy after that which along the paths of actual human life and knowledge men had abandoned. It, too, was a renunciation — of the real. Similar ideals, which would suppress one side of human life or dream away from all of its realities, the Christian Fathers were bringing into Christianity, which was a gospel of fulfilment, attainment absolute. There could be no more comprehensive error than to direct the fulness of life, which was Christ's gospel, toward goals of apathy, of suppression of life's elements, of asceticism, or even toward goals of inactive mysticism. Yet this was done in the third, fourth, and fifth centuries. Says Augustine: "Thus two loves made these two cities: the love of self even to despising God made the earthly city; the love of God even to despising self made the heavenly" (*Civ. Dei*, XIV, 28). The love of God means not despising, but honoring self; and for Christians on earth the true love of God must show itself in doing earth's duties and living out earth's full life, and not in abandoning all for dreams, though the dreams be of Heaven.

CHAPTER VII

ABANDONMENT OF PAGAN PRINCIPLES IN A CHRISTIAN
SYSTEM OF LIFE

I. *Origins of Monasticism*

FROM the thoughts of Augustine and Lactantius regarding love and the emotions akin or contrary to it, we may turn to the practical decision upon these matters given by the lives of Christians. Was there some mode of life definitely determined on, and so strongly and widely followed as to represent Christian sentiment? The problem was, What human feelings, what loves and interests of this world, shall the Christian recognize as according with his faith, and as offering no opposition to the love of God and the attainment of eternal life? It was solved by the growth of an indeterminate asceticism within the Christian communities, which in the fourth century went forth with power, and peopled the desert with anchorites and monks.[1]

Monasticism was asceticism; it had also motives which were not ascetic. The original meaning of ἄσκησις, from the verb ἄσκειν, is exercise for the im-

---

[1] In the following pages the term "anchorite," or "hermit," is used to mean a solitary ascetic; the term "monk" to mean a cœnobite, or member of an ascetic or monastic community.

provement of the faculties exercised. More especially it signifies the practice of acts which exercise the soul in virtue or holiness, and acts, however painful, which have not this object are not ascetic.[1] Prayer, intended to move the Deity, is not ascetic, nor is sacrifice, if intended to placate Him. But another element is so universally present in asceticism that it may be regarded as essential; this is the thought that matter, or, at least, the material and animal side of human nature, is evil. Ascetic practices proceed on the idea that the desires representing "the lusts of the flesh" are evil, not merely in their excesses, but in their normal operation. And the purpose of ascetic acts and abstentions is to increase man's spiritual nature, and purify it by suppressing the senses. To the ascetic, normal comfort, not merely its abuse in luxury, is evil; so is normal diet, and not merely gluttony; not only fornication, but all sexual intercourse and every mode of life that may bring desire of it. Asceticism, then, is that course of life which suppresses the senses, purifies the soul from sensual desires, and exercises it in virtue. The ascetic act or abstention is that which has this purpose.

Christian monasticism was to be ascetic in this proper sense, in that its object was to purify and strengthen the monk's soul, and make it such that it would not fail to win eternal life. Monastic abnegation had as a further motive the love of Christ and the desire to help on His kingdom. In monasticism

---

[1] This purpose, or the cognate purpose of acquiring specific powers, was present in the austerities of Indian asceticism; it was also present in the milder practices of (late) Greek asceticism.

the ascetic principle, that the senses are evil and should be suppressed, continually joins with the motive of sacrifice for the Kingdom of Heaven's sake. Thus the system keeps itself in part accord with the life of Him who came eating and drinking and proclaiming no fasts or penances or celibacy, but announcing the Kingdom of Heaven, and bidding men live unto it in love of God and man, according to whose words there might be also eunuchs — as other martyrs — for its sake. One man must be burned, another must give up his goods, and a third renounce his heart's love — for the Kingdom of Heaven's sake, and not because marriage is lower than virginity. The motives of such sacrifice are not ascetic, but Christian.

Still another consideration: acts which may appear ascetic are a natural accompaniment of penitence. It is the instinct of the repentant soul to mourn in sackcloth and ashes. When the sinner, stung by love of the Crucified, turns to penitence, his heart cries for punishment. Or he may have fear of hell before him and seek to undergo temporal in order to avert eternal pain. In either case, penance, self-flagellation, may have motives which are not ascetic. When St. Martin came to die, he would lie only upon ashes; "and I have sinned if I leave you a different example." [1] Centuries afterward, when Cœur de Lion — no monk and no saint! — was dying, he would be beaten, hanging head downward, in penitence for his sins. What motives entered these deathbed insistences? Some, at least, that were not ascetic.

The earlier ethical ideals of Greek philosophy

[1] Sulpicius Severus, Epist. III.

included a consideration of the whole nature of
man, with subordination of the physical to the
spiritual elements. From Plato onward, there was
a growing tendency to regard the soul as supreme
and to find human welfare in the soul's freedom
and independence of circumstances. This was the
stoical ideal. But, though ascetic in tendency, stoicism was not asceticism, since it had no thought that
matter was evil, and that the soul should therefore
be purged from sense-contamination. In its own
way it reached the conclusion that the emotional
side of man should be suppressed. Neo-platonism,
however, held that matter was evil, and so presented a philosophic basis for ascetic living, which
was inculcated by its philosophers. Much in the
life of St. Anthony might have been rationally based
on teachings of Plotinus and Porphyry, whose ethics
laid such stress on the purification of the soul from
the contamination of matter and the ties of sense.[1]

So in the first three centuries of the Christian
era, ascetic thoughts were familiar to Hellenically
educated people. As Christianity spread among
them, their understanding of it was affected by conceptions derived from the later systems of philosophy. Yet it does not follow that Hellenic ideas
were among the direct causes of Christian monasti-

[1] There is at least one distinctly Hellenic note in the Athanasian
Vita S. Antonii: when many people sought Anthony out, importu-
nate to see him and imitate his discipline, Anthony, after twenty
years' solitude, came forth from his hermitage initiated in the mysteries and filled with divine spirit. His soul was pure, and undisturbed by grief or pleasure; he appeared like a man in every way
guided by reason (*Vita Antonii*, Sec. 14).

cism. The pagan Greeks were only dilettantes in ascetic practices, never virtuosos. Clement of Alexandria and Origen may themselves have been influences in the growth of Neo-platonism. At least their teachings were affected by prevalent spiritual conditions which had likewise much to do with the evolution of Plotinus's system. Again, Gnosticism was in its moods akin to much in both the Alexandrian fathers and the Alexandrian Neo-platonists. It was ascetic and distinctly dualistic. And finally throughout orthodox Christianity there was very living dualism in the strife of devils against Christ's kingdom.

Many of the men, Christian and Pagan, referred to in these pages, were not of Hellenic birth, but Copts: Origen, Plotinus, Anthony, were all Copts. But it is not safe to ascribe the insane asceticism of the Egyptian monks to the fact that many of them, like Anthony, were of this race, and so less reasonable than Greeks. Origen was the greatest intellect of the Eastern Church, and Plotinus was a supreme metaphysician. The first Christian hermits and monks in Egypt and elsewhere were influenced by the superstitions and ascetic practices of the countries in which they lived, quite as much as by influences coming through literary or scholastic channels. There was in Egypt a mass of lore upon the conflict of Set and his evil host with Horus and his host of powers seeking vengeance for Osiris slain; and the genius of Egypt had always occupied itself with imagining scenes of the future life. These notions may have affected the imagination of the Christian hermit and monk, preparing him to evolve his marvellous combats with many

devils, and the curious elaboration of his expectancy
as to the life to come. It is moreover certain that
Pachomius had been one of a band of Serapis recluses,
before becoming a Christian; and in his daily life and
ascetic practices as a Christian hermit, and then as the
head of a Christian monastery, he must have been
influenced by the habits of his former ascetic life.

But it would be an error to seek the source and power
of monasticism among the circumstances of its early
years in Egypt. It drew suggestions from its Egyptian environment; and the hermits of Egypt tended to
carry asceticism to the verge of insanity — but so did
hermits of Syria who appeared nearly at the same
time. Still greater caution is to be exercised in looking to the farther East for influences upon monasticism.
The ascetic life in both the monastic and the recluse
form had been common in India for centuries before
as well as after the time of Christ. Hindoo influences
extended north and west of India, and, in conjunction
with Persian dualism, touched Mesopotamia and the
eastern Mediterranean lands. But any Brahman or
Buddhist influence upon Christian monasticism cannot
be shown.

It is possible that far-Eastern or Hellenic influence
affected the Jewish communities of the Essenes, who
lived lives of continence in modes approaching the
monastic type. As to whether Christian monasticism
in its turn was influenced by the Essenes, or by the
more problematic Therapeutae described in the writing upon The Contemplative Life, attributed to Philo,
it may be said: the writings in which these ascetic
communities were described were known in Christian

circles, and may have furnished suggestion to Christian monks. But nothing more. Monasticism arose from within Christianity, not from without.

The circumstances of the early Christian communities were such as to develop a sense of opposition between Christianity and the pagan world. The life of the Church was many-sided conflict: to advance in spite of imperial persecution and the pagan people's hate, and to preserve the Christian faith as delivered to the saints, and keep the lives of Christians pure from corruption. Christianity was militant from the beginning. The Lord had said, " My Kingdom is not of this world." The conflict between Christ and the World was a matter of universal life; and its setting forth in the gospel of John might be misunderstood. How was the Church to realize that all positive elements of life were on the side of Christ? In the first epistle of John, the opposition between Christ and the World is absolute. Likewise in the Apocalypse all is conflict. To the seer's eye is disclosed the final storm, and then the peace of victory — a new heaven and a new earth, tears wiped away, no more death, no more mourning, no more pain, but the water of the tree of life given freely to him that is athirst; he that over-cometh shall inherit, and shall be a son of God. It is all a vision of the verity of Christian warfare, shortened in the coming of eternal peace: "I come quickly!" " Yea, come, Lord Jesus," cries the heart of the seer.

For such a mighty conflict with the world it behooved a Christian to be an athlete with his loins girded. There was no time for other matters while the conflict raged, which was so soon to be crowned with victory at the coming of the Lord. Should Christians hamper themselves with ephemeral domestic ties? The conflict was not merely with political cruelty and popular rage; it was a warfare to the death, — to the death of the soul or to the death of sin, whereof fleshly lusts are so great and foul a part. These thoughts came to communities touched by conceptions of the evil nature of matter and the cravings of the flesh. Hence, besides considerations of the incompatibility of marriage with absolute devotion to the Christian warfare, there soon came the thought that, although lawful, it was not as holy as the virgin or celibate state. This is an ascetic thought; while the remaining reasons militating against marriage spring from the desire to devote one's life entirely to other purposes.

There was no disparagement of marriage in the mind of Christ, no misprisal of the life of those whom God had joined together. But everything, as call might come, must be sacrificed for the Kingdom of Heaven, — and there are some who are eunuchs for the Kingdom of Heaven's sake; blessed are the pure in heart, for they shall see God. Such teachings received special interpretation, perhaps before the apostolic age was past. Here the mind of Paul is not the mind of Christ. The apostle sees how marriage may conflict with the demands of the Christian life; and his way of stating this — the unmarried man mindeth the things of the Lord, the married man mindeth the things of his wife — is indicative of a certain disparagement of marriage itself, a disparagement which appears in other of his utterances.[1]

[1] See 1 Cor. vii. But cf. Zöckler, *Askese*, etc., pp. 140–145.

A current of ascetic life may be traced in the early Christian communities. There are hints of the approval of celibacy for Christian teachers in *The Teaching of the Twelve Apostles ;* apparently at the date of this writing there were classes of men in the Church who abstained from marriage.[1] Soon approval of celibacy is shown in both orthodox and heretical (Gnostic and Montanist) circles ; it appears in Justin Martyr ; it is strong with Cyprian, with Clement of Alexandria — and the deed of Origen is well known. After the third century, Christian writers are well-nigh unanimous in setting the virgin or celibate state above the state of marriage.[2]

Modern scholarship has corrected the earlier exaggerated views of the corruption of the Roman Empire. Yet periods of declining strength are necessarily corrupt : in comparison with the amount of strength and virtue existing, there is a greater proportion of weakness and evil than in a period of advance, however rough. It was a phase of declining strength that men and women sought the gratification of their passions while shunning the responsibilities of marriage. The sexual intercourse of the inhabitants of the Roman Empire was disproportionately illicit. Such a condition tended to disparage marriage. Sternly the Christian Fathers condemned the corruption of the world.

---

[1] *Didaché*, VI, 2 ; XI, 11 ; and cf. I, 4.

[2] Exceptions were the monk Jovinian and the presbyter Vigilantius of the latter part of the fourth century. See Smith and Wace, *Dictionary of Christian Biography*. Basil, *Ascetica, Sermo de renunciatione saeculi*, recognizes that a married man has wider responsibilities than a monk, and that married life is harder to lead aright.

Had they been free from ascetic tendencies, they might have looked to the elevation of marriage and the fostering of family life as the true remedy of the prevailing dissoluteness. They would have deemed marriage praiseworthy and not merely permissible. But now they could not help looking on celibacy as the higher state. In Christianity all but the best incurs disparagement. With Christians, to assert that celibacy is best is to assert that marriage is not good. The Church Fathers could not close their eyes to the need of continuing the human race, nor to the plain sanction of matrimony in the Scriptures. But for these two facts, the Church of the fifth century might have condemned marriage unconditionally. As it was, the Church lauded celibacy and gradually required it of the clergy.[1]

The early Christians who lived as celibates from ascetic motives were not an organized order and apparently practised no austerities. It appears, however, from the Pseudo-Clementine Epistles, written near the beginning of the third century, that at that time

---

[1] Any one reading much patristic writing is astonished at the extent to which this struggle with fleshly lust filled the thoughts and occupied the strength of the Fathers. Anthony struggling with filthy demons is not unrepresentative of the general state of the Church. Christians had to writhe themselves free from their lusts. Grudgingly the Fathers admit that Scripture sanctions marriage, and so it is not utter sin. Says Jerome: "Laudo nuptias, sed quia mihi virgines generant!" Ep. XXII, *Ad Eustochium*, § 20, a composition which had great influence at the time. Ep. CXXX, to Demetrias, a virgin, is not quite so extreme. In the Epistle to Eustochium, Jerome also considers the non-ascetic reasons against marriage: "Nemo enim miles cum uxore pergit ad proelium" (*ib.*, § 21); and see Preliminary Discourse to Basil's *Ascetica*, Migne, *Patr. Graec.*, Vol. XXXI, col. 619.

virgins and celibates constituted recognized classes within the community. Certain precepts apply to them, and certain modes of life are recognized as fitting, especially for the men belonging to the ascetic class of wandering preachers; let these avoid women, and not lodge in the same houses with them.[1]

The functions of these preachers were gradually to be assumed by the clergy. But the celibacy which they represented could not continue among an undisciplined body of men living within the communities. Those who would keep their virgin state needed barriers between their temptations and their principles. It were best to withdraw from society; ascetics must become anchorites, "they who have withdrawn."[2] Here was clear reason why asceticism should betake itself to the desert. But the solitary life is difficult, and beyond the strength of ordinary men.[3] Solitaries would be forced to associate together for mutual aid, and then would need regulations under which to live. So anchorites tend to become cœnobites; monasticism begins.

Withdrawal from society and association in order to render existence tolerable were cognate phases of a general movement, the beginnings of which naturally are obscure. At the close of the third century an

---

[1] See "Two Letters on Virginity," *Ante-Nicene Fathers*, Vol. VIII, p. 51, etc.; also A. Harnack, "Die Pseudo-Clementinischen Briefe *de Virginitate* und die Entstehung des Mönchthums," *Sitzenberichte der Berlin Akademie*, 1891, I, 361–385. These preachers apparently were the successors to the prophets and teachers referred to in *Didaché*, XI, etc.

[2] From ἀναχωρεῖν.

[3] See, *e.g.*, Cassian, *Conl.*, XIX, 3–8.

ascetic and scholastic association existed near Alexandria under the leadership of pupils of Origen.[1] But already Anthony, the archetype of anchorites, has fled to the desert of the Thebaid.[2] Even this man, impassioned for isolation, was soon surrounded by those who yearned to emulate his example. The desert became full of solitaries, who nevertheless, as they withdrew from society, tended to draw together for helpfulness or edification.

Anthony was the marvellous devil-fighting recluse. A communal life was not to his taste, nor did its regulation lie within his genius. He was originative only as an example, and formulated no monastic rule. Such was to come from his younger contemporary Pachomius (285–345 A.D.), who dwelt in upper Egypt, and began his ascetic life as a member of a Serapis community of recluses. Afterward he became a Christian and the imitator of a mighty ascetic named Palæmon. After seven years of discipleship he departed to another place, where there came to him a vision commanding him to serve the human race and unite them to God. Disciples soon gathered to live under his direction. This was at Tabenna, on the right bank of the Nile, opposite Denderah. Pachomius ordered his growing community, and prescribed a *regula* for the life of its members. They increased in numbers, and groups of brethren went forth to found other monasteries, the members of which also lived under his direction.

[1] See Zöckler, *op. cit.*, pp. 176–178.

[2] The majority of scholars regard the *Vita Antonii* ascribed to Athanasius as genuine. See, generally, Zöckler, *op. cit.*, pp. 183–192. Anthony died in the year 356, at the alleged age of 105 years.

His *regula* was the first formulated code of monastic life. It directed that each monk should eat according to his needs, and labor according to his food and strength. It also prescribed common meals, to be taken in silence, and the manner in which monks should sleep, three in a cell; also their dress, their fastings, their prayers, their treatment of strangers, and other matter. The *regula* did not demand extraordinary austerities, nor impose burdens beyond human strength.

In the generation after Pachomius' death, when the monks of Egypt, of Palestine, Syria, Mesopotamia, and Asia Minor numbered many thousands, the great St. Basil of Cappadocia wrote *regulae* (ὅροι) in the form of questions and answers. Their extraordinary disorder and confusion made them difficult to follow as a rule of monastic life. Yet they were generally accepted in the East, and strongly influenced Western monasticism.

Thus in the East, beginning in Egypt, Christian asceticism leaves society, flees to the desert, secludes itself in hermit cells, and organizes itself in monastic life. At first it is extreme, doing acts of austerity which could but craze or brutalize; then in communities it regulates itself, restrains its insanities, betakes itself to labor, and in Christian humility bows its neck to obey. It is regulated by the Church through Basil.

The fundamental principles of labor and obedience arose from the nature and necessities of monasticism and from the spirit of Christianity. The solitary recluse must labor to supply his wants; associated monks must likewise labor, and may labor to better advantage by a division of tasks. Both recluse and monk must labor also for the wherewithal to exercise charity and hospitality, virtues which the monks of the East did not lack. No less important was labor as a discipline. This was recognized in the *regula* of Pachomius. The recluse, too, found labor a necessity, if he would retain sanity of mind and body. Only it was characteristic of the lack of practical purpose in the beginning of the movement, that hermits often set themselves absurd tasks, as they practised preposterous austerities. A man like Pachomius, finding himself at the head of a community of monks, would direct their disciplinary and other labors to usefulness, and their ascetic practices to the reasonable exercise and betterment of the soul.

The hermit must labor, though he had no one to obey. But from the first establishment of a monastic community, obedience was a necessary principle of its existence. There must be rules, and obedience to them. Christianity emanated from the example and the words of Christ. It was conformity to the one and obedience to the other, in humility of soul as a little child. The authority of the Lord was personal, and given to Him from above, not depending on human election. From above — from Christ — came the authority of the apostles, and so on downward in widening circles, ever from above. It fell in with general Christian principles that monks should obey an abbot. This also fell in with the habits of the East, where authority emanates always from a man. Obedience also sprang from the manner of monastic origins, when admiring hermits grouped themselves around one whom they looked upon as their superior in wisdom and sanctity.

The principle of obedience is assumed by the rule of Pachomius, and becomes explicit with Basil, the first regulator-general of monasticism. This mighty episcopal saint lays stress upon it. Let caution be used in permitting men to enter upon monastic life and take its vows; after that, a monk who refuses obedience commits deadly sin. A monk shall not follow his own will, but what is set by others.[1] In the West, more masterfully, monastic life was to be renunciation of the individual selfish will, and the doing of the commands of God, given through those who for the monk were God's representatives.

If the Christian churches had been kept continually in the purifying fires of persecution, ascetic devotion might have continued to find within them scope for its energy and safeguards for its life. The persecuted and the martyred did not need to crucify the flesh in the desert. Whenever persecution ceased, laxity of manners and morals invaded Christian communities. From the time of Constantine, it became convenient for the world, evil and good, to cloak itself with Christianity. The tremendous increase of monasticism, and of the celibate life even outside of monasteries, was the answering protest of the fervent Christian life. The anchorite and the monk do not represent a flight from persecution, from hardship, or from danger, but a flight from luxury and sin. Not in times of persecution, but after the

---

[1] *Reg. fusius* (A), XLI.

Church had this world's peace, their tens became thousands.[1]

[1] In the writings of the Fathers, the martyrs are called Christ's athletes; and Athanasius, if it were he who wrote the fantastic but noble *Life of Saint Anthony*, applies that term to Anthony. Anthony conceived his ascetic life in the desert as an actual warfare with devils, the enemies of his Lord. By his victories their power was weakened, and so much less evil could they work Christ's followers (see *Vita S. Antonii*, 41). Anthony fights the good Christian fight, not for his own soul alone. The story of Anthony is throughout a story of the life of a devoted man, active in love and beneficence to all who come to him: "And it was as if a physician had been given by God to Egypt. For who, in grief, met Anthony and did not return rejoicing? Who came mourning for his dead, and did not forthwith put off his sorrow? Who came in anger, and was not converted to friendship? What poor and low spirited man met him, who, hearing him and looking upon him, did not despise wealth and console himself in his poverty? What monk, having been neglectful, came to him, and became not stronger? What young man, having come to the mountain and seen Anthony, did not forthwith deny himself pleasure, and love temperance? Who, when tempted of a demon, came to him, and did not find rest? And who came troubled with doubts and did not get quietness of mind?"—*Vita S. Antonii*, 87.

Some of the thoughts inspiring the *Vita Antonii* reappear in Jerome's letter to Heliodorus (Ep. XIV), in which he exhorts this wavering monk to sever all ties and affections: Do not mind the entreaties of those dependent on you, come to the desert and fight for Christ's name. If they believe in Christ, they will encourage you; if they do not,—let the dead bury their dead. A monk cannot be perfect in his own land; not to wish to be perfect is a sin; leave all, and come to the desert. The desert loves the naked. "O desert, blooming with the flowers of Christ! O solitude, whence are brought the stones of the city of the Great King! O wilderness rejoicing close to God! What would you, brother, in the world,—you that are greater than the world? How long are the shades of roofs to oppress you? How long the dungeon of a city's smoke? Believe me, I see more of light! Do you fear poverty? Christ called the poor 'blessed.' Are you terrified at labor? No athlete without sweat is crowned. Do you think of food?

On the other hand, in the fifth century, quite opposite causes also operated to make monks. From the time of Marcus Aurelius, the Roman Empire had been weakening in numbers and in spirit; its strength could be restored only from the causes of its destruction, the barbarians. A great ruler like Diocletian could but arrest the downfall; and not for long was to be realized the promise of renewed imperial prosperity which Constantine's reign seemed to offer. It was vain for men to shut their eyes against the approaching catastrophe. Alaric sacked Rome in 410, and the Roman dream of eternal empire was broken. So Augustine began the composition of the "City of God"; it was hardly finished when he lay dying in his episcopal city of Hippo in Africa, with the Vandals battering down the walls. At no period has the civilized world felt barbarian destruction so closing in around it. *Romanus orbis ruit*, writes Jerome.[1]

The troubled condition of the world and the disastrous outlook fed monasticism. The athlete of Christ went forth from the community as from a bed of luxury. Now cowards fled for fear; and many gentle souls sought the quiet of hermitage or monastery. This also shows the elasticity and adaptability of monasticism, that it

Faith fears not hunger. Do you dread the naked ground for limbs consumed with fasts? The Lord lies with you. Does the infinite vastness of the desert fright you? In the mind walk abroad in Paradise. Does your skin roughen without baths? Who is once washed in Christ needs not to wash again. And in a word, hear the apostle answering: The sufferings of the present time are not to be compared with the glory to come which shall be revealed in us! You are too pleasure-loving, brother, if you wish to rejoice in this world and hereafter to reign with Christ."

[1] Ep. LX, *Ad Heliodorum.*

could gather numbers from so many sources and be strengthened by the accession of opposite characters.

Although Christianity was an active and militant religion, a strong influence making for the growth of monasticism lay in the impulse given by the Christian faith to the contemplative life. Among pagans also, in the first centuries of the Christian era, had come a yearning for meditation, as may be seen in the lives of many Neo-pythagoreans and Neo-platonists. There are moods of drowsiness rather than meditation, which need no incitement beyond indolence. Otherwise the growth of the contemplative life requires a definite cause. With the later schools of Greek philosophy such a cause lay in the yearning for union with the divine, and in the growing sense of inability to reach it through modes of active reasoning. Sheer contemplation of the divine, which transcended definite thought, might bring a vision of it, with ecstatic fruition. Such feelings fostered contemplation among Neo-platonists, who had but the great mystic, inconceivable, unlovable One to contemplate. But Christianity brought new thoughts of God, and a rush of loving feeling which struck the believer's heart with a new passion for the Omnipotent Lover. What greater fulness of love and life, even here in the flesh, than to dwell in this? How could the believer's thoughts leave it, any more than the lover would disperse the golden haze of thought of the beloved, which in her absence enfolds his being?

God was an exhaustless object of meditation to Hebrew psalmists. Christianity deepened the spiritual life, and filled it with love's realities. Monk and nun might live in contemplation of them. Such contemplation filled the heart as well as mind, — this sweet Christian *vita contemplativa*, this all-beloved Rachel, for whom even those active souls who have Leah for their portion must yearn in spiritual bereavement;[1] to have this, is to be like Mary, and sit at the feet of the Lord — and did not the Lord say, Mary hath chosen the better part ?

This fulness of spiritual life and love, which Christianity brought, has always been a power making for monasticism. The Christian *vita contemplativa*, with its wealth of love as well as thought, might satisfy and enrapture thousands, while but few could have held to the pagan βίος θεωρητικός which Aristotle declared the truly human life, and which Boethius beheld stamped on the garments of Philosophy. Women, as well as men, might love Christ and think of him alone; but no woman and few men could follow Aristotle's or Boethius' loveless βίος θεωρητικός. Even when the pagan contemplative life had become one of attempted visioning or ecstasy, as well as one of thought, it was so empty of real and definitely directed feeling that it could not hold its votaries. Such fantasy could not people monasteries, much less nunneries. In the Christian *vita contemplativa*, there often entered a love intense and so personally directed, toward the bridegroom Christ, that the life which held such love was no life of ascetic renunciation, but one filled with the fruition of fulfilled desire, — a life ecstatic rather than ascetic.

[1] See a beautiful passage in Gregory the Great's Ep. I, 5, *Ad Teoctistam*, and the opening of Gregory's *Dialogi*.

II. *Western Monasticism*

The monasticism of the West bears the relation to Eastern monasticism which so much that is Latin bears to what is Eastern or Hellenic, — the suggestion comes from the East and is accepted and made into something different by the West, which puts its own qualities into whatever it receives. No definite fact or single principle distinguishes Western from Eastern monasticism. Monasticism brought from the East its original moods and aims. Western monasticism, at its beginning, is not conscious of a new or different way of life, save in the modification of some details, as where Egyptian diet and dress were plainly unfit for Gaul. As in the East, so in the West, the early great founders of monasteries or monastic orders begin their ascetic lives as solitary hermits, with no such aim as the subsequent courses of their lives were to shape for them.[1] They all desire, through solitude and asceticism, to free themselves from the lusts of the flesh, and, renouncing the world, to live in contemplation of God and love of Him, and in the assurance of eternal life.[2] And as monasteries come into existence in the West, they are set far from cities, with stricter precautions against corrupting intercourse with the world than had been taken by the great regulators of Eastern monasticism.[3] Not in its beginnings did Western mo-

[1] Pachomius and Basil in the East, Martin of Tours and Benedict of Nursia in the West.

[2] This mood is so strong with Gregory the Great that it saddens his entire life after he left the monastery and became pope.

[3] Benedict's *regula* forbids intercourse with the world more stringently than Basil. Basil would have monasteries near cities,

nasticism look forward to its career of world-Christian-
ization and world-dominance.

Moreover, some features which were to characterize
Western monasticism had previously shown themselves
in the East. For example, monastic life in the West
was to be temperate, and not extravagant in its austerities. The wild asceticism and mortification of the
flesh which had distinguished the monks of Egypt
and Syria never flourished in the West.[1] But it had
been condemned in the East by Pachomius and Basil
before the West possessed communities of monks.[2]
Again, the West is active and practical. Western
monks were soon to be drawn from their cloisters to
episcopal, even papal, duties. But this had previously
happened in the East. Basil the Great, the great
monk-bishop, preceded Gregory the Great, the great
monk-pope, by two hundred and fifty years.

In fine, in Western monasticism there are not to be

so that monks could do acts of charity. He was also less stringent
in forbidding intercourse with nuns. See Basil's *Regula A*, Cap.
33; *Regula B*, 108–111; also Zöckler, *op. cit.*, p. 290; Grützmacher,
Bedeutung Benedikts, etc., pp. 42, 43.

[1] Many groups of Eastern hermits have received their names
from special ascetic practices; *e.g.*, the Omophagi, who ate no
cooked food, Cassian, IV, 22; the Grazers (βοσκοί), Sozomen, *Hist.
Ecc.*, VI, 33; or the Stylites, those who imitated St. Symeon Stylites by dwelling on tops of pillars; see *Vita Sancti Simeonis*,
Migne, *Patr. Lat.*, Vol. 73, col. 326; Delehaye, "Les Stylites, Saint
Symeon et ses imitateurs," *Revue des questions historiques*, Vol. 57
(1895), pp. 52–103. These people, to be sure, are hermits, rather
than monks; yet they constitute groups, and no group of hermits
or monks was ever in the West called after any special form of
asceticism practised by them, for the reason that extreme and
remarkable forms of asceticism were not practised in the West.

[2] See Basil, *Regula A*, 18–20; *B*, 128–133.

found novel creations, and new purposes consciously conceived. What passed from East to West was altered by circumstances, and modified by the Western character and the exigencies of the advance of Christian civilization among barbarous peoples. Unconsciously Western monasticism became filled with new energies and inspired with new aims.

Some early distinguishing traits of Western monasticism can be pointed out. In the fourth and fifth centuries, the Romanized West [1] retained something of the order and intellectual definiteness which marked that most original creation of the Latin genius, the Roman law. The West was more capable than the East of formulating rules of conduct and of ordering them in practical schemes of living. It was stronger than the East in the power of self-control and self-discipline; and it still preserved more of the youthful energies of life. Accordingly, Western monasticism soon evolved a regular order, a regular discipline, and a power of obedience and command, which Eastern monasticism did not possess. Hence an ordered and regular corporate life was attained, the members of which were trained in like effective modes of discipline. Monks and abbots became as privates and officers of an army; they could carry out commands and execute enterprises in obedience to authority. And that authority tended toward a unity at the apex, — Rome. Practically viewed, Eastern monasticism remained contemplative, pointless, inefficient; while in the West monasticism became a mighty and mightily directed

[1] That is to say, North Africa, Gaul, Italy, and Spain.

power, often directed anew by the intelligence and energies and devotion within itself.

In the moral life also, Western monasticism orders and systematizes its rules. Humility, obedience, chastity, and other Christian virtues had been inculcated and practised in the East. But in the West, moral precepts take form as a regular and possible code of daily living for every monk, and a code constituting a systematic education in the Christian life. Moreover, Western monasticism becomes more completely Christian than its Eastern prototype, which contained much Hellenism, and sometimes was regarded as a philosophy, or as a way of life based on knowledge and wisdom. Western monasticism tends to omit the Hellenism, while it codifies the Christian principles of Eastern monasticism, and completes them with more absolute conceptions of Christian faith and love, such as came to Augustine and to those he influenced.

Ascetic tendencies began early in Latin Christianity. A wide interest in the celibate or virgin life, led in retirement, arose in Rome near the time of Athanasius' sojourn as an exile there, about the year 340. There was much material for monasticism whenever the movement should seek the solitude of the waste places. These modes of ascetic living were encouraged by the three great Latin Fathers, Jerome, Ambrose, and Augustine, with whom, two hundred years afterward, Gregory the Great is ranged as the fourth great Father of the Latin Church, and arch-laborer in the establishment of monasticism.

Of these great leaders of Latin Christianity in the fourth century, Ambrose directed a cloister of monks near Milan; Jerome wrote enthusiastic and extravagant letters to his admirers, urging the virgin life, which he himself led, whether in Rome among adoring women, or in his cell in Palestine, where he also counselled and directed. The youngest of this triad, Augustine, from the time of his conversion earnestly advocated virginity. Late in life he wrote a "libellum" as a *regula* for a convent of north-African nuns.[1] The qualities which were to distinguish Western monasticism speak in this writing. It does not discuss; it is not enlightening or educational; it lays down rules for the nuns to follow in their daily life, orders them to hear the "libellum" read once a week, and—let them give thanks to God when, on hearing it, they find they have carried out its precepts. Augustine's "libellum" was not a comprehensive monastic *regula*; but its directions were clear. Inchoate as it was, it presented a mode of daily life and governance which any nun or monk could understand, remember, and follow. The Roman capacity for definite legislative precept is here.

Before Augustine wrote his libellum, men who had experience in monastic and anchorite life began to write. Rufinus, friend and enemy of Jerome, translated freely the *Regulae* of Basil, condensing the matter, but introducing no order into that chaos.[2] In other Western writings the practical and legislative genius of the West may be observed ordering monasticism and preparing it to be a way of life fit to accomplish tasks other than Eastern monks had dreamed of.

[1] Ep. 211, written 423 A.D.
[2] Printed in Vol. I of Lucas Holstenius, *Codex Regularum*, pp. 67-108, and made up of 203 Questiones et Responsiones.

First are to be noticed the writings of Cassian, the Western compiler and arranger of the data of monasticism; and then the Western regulae, the legislative documents proper, which direct and order the life of the monk.

Cassian wrote two works upon monasticism. The earlier of these, written between the years 419 and 426, was entitled *De institutis Cœnobiorum et de octo principalium vitiorum remediis libri XII.*[1] It presented a picture of Egyptian monasticism. His later work, the *Conlationes,* composed between 426 and 428, purports to give the discourses of Egyptian abbots, edifying to those who should seek to perfect themselves in monastic virtues. The names of the abbots are given; and the *Conlationes* probably reflect their utterances.[2] Cassian was not a legislator, but a com-

[1] For the life of Cassian, perhaps a native of Gaul (cir. 360-cir. 432), see prolegomena to the translation of his works by E. C. S. Gibson, in *Nicene Fathers,* Vol. XI, 2d series. Cassian, *Inst.,* V, 4, says that Anthony said that a monk should not go to one man to learn all the virtues, but go to many, seeking to learn from each the virtue in which he excels. St. Basil the Great travelled through Egypt, Palestine, Cœle-Syria, and Mesopotamia to see saintly anchorites and monks. Thus many finished their education in asceticism. Compare also the trip of Jerome and Paula, described by Jerome in Ep. 108, *Ad Eustochium.*

[2] For example, he reports the discourse of Abbot Moses of the desert of Scete upon the scope and purpose of monastic life. Says Moses, in Aristotelean-Ciceronian way: " Omnes artes ac disciplinae scopon quendam, id est destinationem, et telos, hoc est finem propriam habent." The Kingdom of Heaven is the monk's final goal; but we may distinguish between that and the means which form a subsidiary end: "Finis quidem nostrae professionis ut diximus regnum dei seu regnum caelorum est, destinatio vero, id est scopos, puritas cordis, sine qua ad illum finem impossibile est quempiam pervenire " (*Conl.,* I, 2-4).

piler of information. He does not give positive directions for the daily life of monks, but a systematic presentation of monastic customs. He may be expected, also, to set forth the ethical principles of monasticism in such a way that they can readily be made into a mode of life.

In the preface to the *Institutes* he says that he will not speak of the miracles wrought among the monks, but will set forth the "institutions and rules of their monasteries, and especially the origins, causes, and remedies, according to their traditions, of the principal vices, which they say are eight." He believes that nothing wiser can be found for the West than the customs and rules of the ancient monasteries of Egypt or Palestine, except that, owing to the difference of climate or habits, certain details may, for Gaulish monks, need to be balanced by borrowings from the other parts of the East. Whereupon, he tells in the first book what he has observed regarding the dress of monks in Egypt. In the second and third books he describes the "modus canonicus" of prayers and psalms by night and by day. The fourth book explains more generally the institutes of the renunciants, to wit, the monks, those who renounce this world; their probation before admission; why they may not bring anything into the monastery; why they must lay aside their clothes and receive others from the abbot; and other rules for their daily life and conduct. The author gives many examples of the proficiency of the Egyptian monks in virtues of obedience and humility, and he quotes an abbot's discourse to a candidate, in order to show how true and spiritual must be the monk's renunciation.[1]

The author passes, at the beginning of the fifth book, to a discussion of the eight principal vices of monastic life which are the following: "*primum gastrimargiae* (gluttony), *quae interpretatur gulae concupiscentia, secundum fornicationis, tertium filargyriae, quod intelligitur avaritia, vel ut proprius exprimatur, amor pecuniae, quartum irae, quintum tristitiae, sextum acediae, quod est anxietas sive taedium cordis, septimum cenodoxiae, quod sonat vana seu inanis gloria, octavum superbiae.*"[2]

This series is given by two Greeks, Evagrius Ponticus (d. cir. 401)[3] and St. Nilus Abbas (d. cir. 430).[4] They describe these eight vices and speak of their ill effects upon the monk; they also mention means by which he may overcome them. But Evagrius is too inexplicit to afford practical help in daily life; and Nilus is discursive and rhetorical in his comments on these vices and their remedies. He is also touched by the Eastern Hellenic apathy or absence of desire; ἀπαθεία, he says, is the strong defence of the monk against tristitia (λύπη) and other vices.[5]

It is uncertain whether Cassian was acquainted

---

[1] On the three kinds of call (*vocatio*) to be a monk, and the three renunciations, see *Conl.*, III, 4–6; and compare Basil, "De renunciatione," *Reg. fusius* (A), 8.

[2] Cassian, *Inst.*, V, 1.

[3] Πρὸς 'Ανατόλιον περὶ τῶν ὀκτὼ λογισμῶν (De octo vitiosis Cogitationibus), Gallandus, *Biblioteca Veterum Patrum*, VII, p. 575.

[4] Περὶ τῶν ὀκτὼ πνευμάτων τῆς πονηρίας (De octo spiritibus malitiae), Migne, *Patr. Graec.*, 79, col. 1146. The Greek names are: γαστριμαργία, πορνεία, φιλαργυρία, ὀργή, λύπη, ἀκηδία, κενοδοξία, ὑπερφανία.

[5] Nilus, *ib.*, Cap. XII.

with these writings of Evagrius and Nilus: his treatment sometimes closely parallels theirs;[1] at any rate all drew from the same general sources. But the Latin writer is more explicit and systematic, and more practically helpful in setting forth the remedies and showing how the monk may direct his efforts toward perfecting himself in the virtues which are the destroyers of these faults.[2] His exposition of the eight vices and their remedies constitutes a coherent scheme for perfecting the monk in the virtues of the Christian life. The vices are treated as if they were spiritual diseases; rules are given for their diagnosis; the remedies are stated with directions as to using; and a regimen of virtuous thought and conduct is set for the convalescent soul.[3]

Moreover, Cassian's exposition represents a scheme of life in which the ethical principles are Christian, not pagan, stoical-eclectic for example. They are not self-reliant principles, but religious; prayer and the grace of God enable the monk to fulfil them. And the seal of Christianity is set upon this monastic scheme of life by holding pride to be the worst of sins:[4] for so it is from the Christian standpoint, being

[1] *E.g.*, compare Evagrius, *ib.*, Cap. VII, on ἀκηδία with Cassian, *Inst.*, X, 1–3.

[2] All three writers regard these various vices sometimes as vices or evil thoughts or dispositions, and sometimes as evil spirits, — *spiritus*, πνεῦμα, δαίμων; *e.g.*, πορνείας δαίμων, ἀκηδίας δαίμων, Evagrius; and notice Nilus' title, and the title of Cassian to Books V to XII of the *Inst.*, " de *spiritu* gastrimargiae," etc.

[3] See, *e.g.*, Cassian's treatment of *tristitia* and *acedia* in Books IX and X of *Inst.*, also, especially, XII, 29–33, on the symptoms and remedies of spiritual pride.

[4] *Inst.*, XII., 1 et seq.

a thing self-reliant and God-defiant, with none of the spirit of the little child. Pride might be a pagan virtue; in Christianity it could only be the worst of vices. Rooting it out means the expulsion of the pagan spirit from Christian ethics. In Benedict's still more constructive exposition the chief Christian virtue is humility, pride's opposite.

The greatness and efficiency of the regula of Benedict of Nursia[1] did not lie in its inventive originality, but in its wise revision and constructive use of monastic principles and experience. A tabulation of the special resemblances and divergences between Benedict's regulations and those of his predecessors would not give an adequate idea of his regula. He was acquainted with the writings of Jerome and Augustine; but appears to have made chief use of Basil and Cassian.[2] It is doubtful whether he knew of the regula of his contemporary, Cæsarius of Arles. Using his materials with discrimination, he added to them from his own spiritual life and from his experience as director of monks.

The regula of Benedict gained universal dominion among the monks of the West, superseding other authorities. Compared with the regulae of Basil, it was as a clear and ordered code is to a mass of questions and answers. No one could find a definite and explicit rule of conduct in Basil; Benedict's regula was just such a rule. Again, the works of Cassian, though systematic, contained no regula. Yet the necessary principle of monasticism was obedience;

---

[1] 480–543 A.D. Foundation of Monte Cassino, 529 (cir.).
[2] He read the regulae of Basil in Rufinus' Latin version.

so it needed a definite law authoritatively prescribed. The rule of Cæsarius of Arles was such; but it was too short, and left much unprovided for.[1] The rule of Columban lacked definite directions for the details of daily living, and was excessive in its ascetic demands. Benedict's rule was wise and temperate, definite and explicit in its regulations for the guidance of the monk through each hour of the night and day.

Where the regula of Benedict differed from any of these writings, it differed by containing more of the distinguishing qualities of the Latin West. It embodied and expressed these in so far as they were passing into monasticism. The Roman qualities which made the Roman law practical, definite, orderly, and comprehensible, appear in Benedict's regula, and distinguish it from the regulæ of Basil. The authoritativeness of Rome distinguished Benedict's regula from the *Institutes* and *Conlationes* of Cassian; it was law and not discussion. Its sufficiency of detail and clear definiteness made it practical and Roman, while distinguishing it from the regulæ of Augustine, Cæsarius, and Columban. And Benedict's regula was sufficiently strict, sufficiently stern, and adapted to the character and needs of Western monasticism. Few writings can be compared with it for effective combination of religious precept and practical direction. *Discretione praecipua, sermone luculenta,* is Gregory's comment on it.[2]

Potent influences made for its dominance; it was

---

[1] It is not over two folio pages in length. See Holstenius, *Codex Regularum*, I, pp. 145–147; Migne, *Patr. Lat.*, 67, col. 1098.

[2] *Dialog.*, II, Chap. 36.

authoritatively recommended by Gregory the Great.
Wheresoever his activity reached, there reached his
influence in favor of monasticism and the regula of
Benedict.[1] His successors also zealously favored it.
Gregory and his successors, however, did not happen
accidentally to advocate Benedict's rule instead of
some other, but because it was the best. The fame of
Benedict's piety and of the miracles ascribed to him
may at first have promoted the acceptance of his
regula, which in turn increased the marvels of the
great saint's legend.

In order to make clear some of the qualities of the
Benedicti regula monachorum, its ethical precepts may
be noticed, and then the character of its more specific
regulations. The former are contained mainly in the
prologue and in the fourth to the seventh chapters,
and thus are grouped together in the first part of the
regula. In spirit and letter these precepts are religious and Christian, with no trace of stoico-pagan feeling or principles. They are simple and frequently
Biblical in phrase. Considered individually, they are
direct, pertinent to daily life, and widely applicable;
collectively, they constitute a complete scheme of religious ethics and a consistent mode of holy living.[2]

[1] Thus the regula of Benedict reached England with Augustine
of Canterbury. See, generally, Grützmacher, *Bedeutung*, etc.,
pp. 51–71, who, however, underestimates the effect of the distinguishing qualities of the regula itself. An important circumstance
was that the monks of Monte Cassino, after the destruction of their
monastery by the Lombards in 580, went to Rome, and were given
a cloister near the Lateran by Pope Pelagius, Gregory's predecessor.
Gregory became pope in 592.

[2] Gregory says that Benedict's regula was a reflection of his life.

"Hear, O son, the precepts of the master and incline the ear of thy heart;[1] freely accept and fulfil the admonitions of the good father, that through the labor of obedience (*oboedientiae laborem*) thou mayest return to Him from whom thou hast departed through the desire of disobedience." Thus the prologue opens with words of exhortation addressed to those who would renounce their own wills and take up the arms of obedience to fight under the Lord Christ, and in all their strivings turn to him with instant prayer. The prologue sustains throughout the opening note of exhortation, and speaks in tones adapted to impress an humble, obedient and devoted mood upon the hearer: Let not our evil acts distress Him who thought us worthy to be called sons; that the angered father may not disinherit his sons, nor the angry lord give over to everlasting punishment those wicked servants who will not follow him to glory.[2] Let us arise from sleep, as the Scriptures bid us, — and keep our tongues from evil. Lord, who shall dwell in thy tabernacle? Brothers, hear the Lord answering: He who goes without spot and works justice; who, speaks truth in his heart, and whose tongue speaks no guile; who does no evil to his neighbor; those who, fearing the Lord, are not elated over their due observances, but, knowing they can do nothing good in themselves, say with the prophet: Not unto us, O Lord, not unto us, but unto Thy name give glory.

The Lord says in the gospel, Whoso heareth My

[1] Cf. Psalm xliv. 11 and Jerome, Ep. 22, 1.

[2] God is looked to both as *master* and as *father* through these opening paragraphs.

words and doeth them, I will liken him unto a wise man who built his house upon a rock. Behold, for the correction of sins, the day of this life is accorded unto us, as the kind Lord says, I desire not the death of a sinner, but that he should be converted and live. Therefore, let our hearts and bodies be prepared to carry on the warfare of obedience ; and what to our nature is impossible, we must ask of the grace of God.

The fourth chapter is a statement of the rules of the Christian life (*instrumenta artis spiritualis*) — *in primis* to love the Lord God with all thy heart and thy neighbor as thyself. Then, not to kill or steal or commit adultery, and what we would not have done to us not to do to others ; to deny ourselves and follow Christ ; to chasten the body and love fasting ; to refresh the poor, clothe the naked, comfort the sorrowing ; to keep oneself a stranger to temporal affairs (*saeculi actibus se facere alienum*) ; to set nothing before the love of Christ ; to hold no anger, nor falseness ; not to return evil for evil, to suffer injury with patience ; to love enemies ; to bless those who revile ; not to be proud or drunken, or gluttonous, or sleepy or sluggish, or a grumbler or backbiter ; to hope in God ; to attribute the good in us to God, knowing that our acts are always evil ; to fear the day of judgment, tremble at Hell (*gehennam*), ardently desire eternal life, with the expectation of death daily with us ; to know that God sees us everywhere ; to bring to Christ the evil thoughts coming to our hearts and disclose them to our spiritual superior ; to keep our mouths from evil or foolish speech, and not love much speaking, or utter words causing laughter; to hear the holy readings (*lectiones sanctas*) willingly; to be diligent in prayer; daily with tears to confess our sins in prayer to God; not to do the desires of the flesh; to hate our own will; to obey the words of the abbot, though he do otherwise himself; to wish to be holy sooner than to be called so; to fulfil the commands of God in daily acts, love chastity, hate no one, have no envy, love not strife, avoid conceit, venerate the elders, love the juniors, pray for enemies in the love of Christ, agree with thine adversary, and never despair of the mercy of God.

If all these *instrumenta artis spiritualis* are sedulously fulfilled by us day and night, that reward shall be ours from the Lord, as He has promised; what eye hath not seen, nor ear hath heard, which God hath prepared for those who love Him.

The fifth chapter is devoted to the mighty virtue of obedience, — *oboedientia sine mora* — so befitting those who deem nothing dearer to them than Christ. For the sake of the sacred service which they have professed, or from fear of hell or for the glory of life eternal, as soon as anything is commanded by a superior (*a majore*), as if it was divinely ordered, let him make no delay in doing it. Those upon whom presses the love of attaining eternal life, who do not follow their own decision or obey their own desires, but walk according to the judgment and bidding of another, living in monasteries (*in coenobiis*), desire an abbot to be over them. Surely these imitate Him who said, I came not to do My own will, but the will of Him who sent me. Such obedience will be acceptable to God and sweet to men, if what is ordered is performed *non trepide, non tepide, non tarde, aut cum murmorio.* The obedience which is yielded to superiors (*majoribus*) is offered to God; for He Himself said: Whoso heareth you, heareth Me; and, God loveth a cheerful giver. But if the disciple obeys with a bad will, and with murmuring, he will not be accepted of God nor will grace come to him from his act; and he will incur the penalty of those who murmur, unless he make amends.

The prologue of Benedict's regula exhorts the hearers, affects their mood, and impels them toward ready acceptance of all that follows: the fourth chapter contains the sum of the precepts constituting the piety of a monk; while the fifth and sixth speak more specifically of obedience and silence. The seventh chapter is in itself an ethical system in which one virtue, that is, one fundamental principle of monastic piety, is analytically expanded, to show that its fulfilment includes and requires a complete Christian life. This chapter "on the twelve stairs of humility" is the great example of how the precepts of monastic and Christian living, having been gathered and systematized by others, are by Benedict's regula made anew into an organic unity fitted to constitute the life of a Christian monk. This chapter pictures a type of character.

The divine Scripture calls to us, brothers, saying: Every one that exalteth himself shall be abased, and he that humbleth himself shall be exalted. Thus it shows us that every exaltation is a kind of pride. Therefore, brothers, if we wish to touch the summit of complete humility and reach that heavenly exaltation to which we ascend through the humility of the present life, we must by our ascending acts erect those stairs which appeared in Jacob's dream, on which the angels were shown to him descending and ascending. By this we should understand descent through exaltation and ascent through humility. The upright stairway is our life on earth, which a heart humbled by the Lord raises to heaven. The sides of this stairway we call our body and soul; in them the divine summons (*evocatio*) sets the stairs of humility or discipline to be ascended.

The first stair of humility is, if, setting the fear of God continually before our eyes, we never forget His commands, always remembering that those who despise Him go to Hell because of their sins, and that eternal life is prepared for those who fear Him: and we must guard ourselves every hour from sins and faults of thought, tongue, eye, hand, foot, will, and cut off the desires of the flesh, knowing that we and our deeds are always beheld by Him and told Him by the angels.

The second stair of humility is, if any one, loving not his own will, delights not in fulfilling his desires, but imitates in his deeds that saying of the Lord, I came not to do my own will, but His who sent me.

The third stair is, that each for the love of God, should subject himself in all obedience to his superior (*majori*), imitating the Lord, of whom the Apostle says, He made Himself obedient to the Father unto death.

The fourth stair is, if in hard and vexatious matters,

and even when suffering undeserved injuries, we obey readily, and weary not, nor turn aside: He who perseveres to the end shall be saved.[1]

The fifth stair is, if we conceal no evil thought or privily committed sin when humbly confessing to the abbot.

The sixth stair is, if the monk is content under every deprivation and indignity and whatever is imposed upon him, and deems himself as but a bad workman.

The seventh stair is, if the monk not only call himself least and vilest of all, but believe it in his heart.

The eighth stair is, if the monk does nothing save what the regula of the monastery or the example of the elders bids him.

The ninth stair is, if the monk keeps his tongue from speaking, and preserves silence until questioned. The tenth is, if he be not prone to laughter; the eleventh is, when the monk speaks, that he speak gently and humbly with gravity, in few words and rationally.

The twelfth stair is, if the monk not only in his heart, but in his demeanor, show humility always — in God's work, in the oratory, in the monastery, in the garden, in the road, in the field, or wherever he may be, and always stand or walk with head inclined and with looks fixed upon the ground. At all times

---

[1] Here and elsewhere, when I have tried to translate the substance of Benedict's paragraphs, I have omitted for the sake of brevity a number of Scripture quotations, which are admirably chosen.

he should judge himself guilty of his sins, saying in his heart with the publican in the gospel, Lord, I a sinner am unworthy to lift my eyes to the heavens.

The monk who rises by all these stairs of humility will quickly reach that perfect love of God which sends away fear, whereby all those things which formerly he kept to, not without trembling, he will begin to guard without any labor, naturally from habit, not now from fear of Hell, but from love of Christ and delight in the virtues.[1]

The precepts of Benedict's rule are strikingly positive, prescribing rather than forbidding. The great abbot knew that vices are best eradicated by cultivation of the opposite positive virtues. So his great

---

[1] With Benedict's chapter on humility compare Cassian, *Inst.*, IV, 32-43, especially Chap. 33, which contains a like arrangement of the humilities. These chapters of Cassian purport to contain the discourse of an Egyptian abbot to a young monk. The summary at the end of Chap. 43 is interesting in form: "Audi ergo paucis ordinem, per quem scandere ad perfectionem summam sine ullo labore ac difficultate praevaleas. Principium nostrae salutis ac sapientiae secundum scripturas timor domini est. De timore domini nascitur compunctio salutaris. De conpunctione cordis procedit abrenuntiatio, id est nuditas et contemptus omnium facultatum. De nuditate humilitas procreatur. De humilitate generatur mortificatio voluntatum. Mortificatione voluntatum exstirpantur atque marcescunt universa vitia. Expulsione vitiorum virtutes fruticant atque succrescunt. Pullulatione virtutum puritas cordis adquiritur. Puritate cordis apostolicae caritatis perfectio possidetur." The form of this summary recalls to mind Gotama's Chain of Causation; see Taylor, *Ancient Ideals*, I, p. 87. Doubtless, the symbolical number twelve — *twelve* stairs of humility — contributed to the observance of the seventh chapter of Benedict's regula, just as the fact that Chap. 4 contained *seventy-two* "instrumenta artis spiritualis" impressed that chapter on mediaeval minds, who were so fond of certain significant numbers.

seventh chapter says little of that chief of vices, pride;
but shows how to develop to the full that chief Christian virtue, humility, which will leave no place for
pride. The monk's soul shall be filled with virtue,
and not merely void of vice. His life shall be positive
and not negative.[1]

Having thus set the principles of the monk's righteousness so as to form a way of living, the monastic
lawgiver has yet an important task. The monk's
heart is inclined to listen; he has received his lessons
in the principles of his righteousness, — he is humble
and obedient. But the days and hours of his life
need definite regulation; for his rule of life is humility and obedience, and he must have detailed orders,
in the carrying out of which he may know that he
is always obeying. Hereby will each monk, and, in
greater measure, the order collectively, gain the habit
and form of disciplined and efficient obedience.

The remaining and by far the larger part of Benedict's rule is taken up with definite directions for each
hour of the day and night. And as Benedict's constructive righteousness appears in his statement of
general principles, so equal practical wisdom and moderation, combined with requisite disciplinary strictness,
are shown throughout the more detailed regulations for
the government of the monastery and the lives of the
monks. Those general principles had for their aim
the attainment to the love of God and life eternal
through the cultivation of the Christian virtues; the

[1] The spirit of Benedict's rule is in accord with the Augustinian
conception of sin as deficiency, — the absence of righteousness and
love of God.

detailed regulations have likewise the purpose of perfecting the monk in these virtues, that they may work their perfect work.[1]

The rule provides for the choice of an abbot, and points out what qualities he should possess and how he should rule.[2] That the choice might fall on one of the younger monks, and that they also might speak in the counsel of the brothers,[3] was likely to make for progress. On the other hand, the principle of subordination, for the most part of younger to older monks, was recognized in orders of precedence established among them.[4] Moreover, the abbot is to be obeyed as the representative of the Lord; and between him and the monks were ranged the *praepositus* and the deacons, to aid his administration of the monastery.

The mode of receiving candidates, and their discipline until the time of taking the threefold vow of *stabilitas, conversio morum,* and *oboedientia,* is carefully regulated.[5] And the regula has definite and detailed provision for all matters which make up the substance of monastic life. For example, it regulates the psalms and prayers and readings for the hours of the day and night, and for the different times and seasons; also the punishments for lighter and more serious faults in monks, extending to expulsion from the order; the care of the sick, the cooking, and other necessary work for the monastery; the meals and the measure and character of the monks' food and drink, their hours of daily labor, their garments, their manner of

---

[1] Cf. Chap. 73.   [2] Chaps. 2 and 64.   [3] Chap. 3.
[4] Chap. 63.   [5] Chap. 58.

sleeping, and their conduct when away from the monastery; also the reception of strangers, and the relations of the monks toward outsiders. Monks might not own property; [1] but this restriction did not apply to the monastery.

Through these practical regulations run deep chords of Christian piety; all acts are to be done in the spirit of the principles of the regula, that is, in the spirit of humility and Christian love, and the following of Christ. "Let the Cellararius (steward) of the monastery be chosen from the congregation, wise, sober, temperate, not puffed up, nor turbulent nor insolent nor wasteful, but fearing God, — who shall be a father to all the congregation. Let him not afflict the brothers; if a brother asks what is unreasonable, he should not spurn the request, but, explaining with humility, he may deny what is ill-asked." [2] Such a man shall the Cellararius be; and likewise the *portarius* (doorkeeper), *senex sapiens qui sciat accipere responsum et reddere.*[3] Regarding the treatment of strangers applying at the monastery: "Let all strangers be received as Christ, because he himself shall say, 'I was a stranger, and ye took me in.'"[4]

Notwithstanding its directness as a moral code and its detailed regulation of monastic life, the regula of Benedict was such that further aims than it expressed could be introduced among the companies of monks who lived according to its commands. The regula said nothing of the pursuit of learning, or of the missionary and civilizing activity of monks. It did prescribe manual labor; and also made provision for

[1] Chap. 33.   [2] Chap. 31.   [3] Chap. 66.   [4] Chap. 53.

the study of Scripture and the writings of the Fathers.[1] *Otiositas inimica est animae, et ideo certis temporibus occupari debent fratres in labore manum, certis iterum horis in lectione divina:*[2] and therefore it fixes the hours of manual labor and of *divina lectio* for the different seasons of the year. All labor was not the same; the heavier labors of the field were not required of the weak;[3] and if there were *artifices* among the monks, they might humbly ply their arts, and the product should be sold at a low price for the monastery.[4] There was nothing in the regula which should forbid monks, under the abbot's approval, turning from the labor of the plough to the labor of the pen, after Cassiodorus and others had shown the Benedictines this way of serving God.

The regula of Benedict drew stricter bands of closure than the regulae of Basil. The Benedictine monastery should include all necessaries for the monks, "that there may be no need of their wandering abroad, which does not profit their souls."[5] Moreover, when strangers were received within the walls, no monk, unless directed, could associate or speak with them;[6] nor could a monk receive letters from parents or others in the world, without the abbot's permission.[7] And his vows of obedience to the regula, once finally made, were irrevocable. This all helped to perfect discipline. Seclusion from the world was for the monk's salvation, which, however, demanded also that the monk should do the will of Christ. And the closure provisions of Benedict's regula held greater

[1] See Chap. 73. [2] Chap. 48. [3] Chap. 48. [4] Chap. 57.
[5] Chap. 66. [6] Chap. 53. [7] Chap. 54.

possibilities for monastic action upon the world than Basil's laxer rules. Impelled by exigencies which were opportunities, the genius of the West was to enter into Benedict's monastic rule, and find it to be a goodly mode of life, in which he who would could serve God mightily in missionary labors among barbarians, as well as in prayer and contemplation, or by copying manuscripts in the cloister.

III. *The Monastic Character*

Monasticism and dogma, these are two great legacies bequeathed by the transition centuries to the Middle Ages: dogma the interpretation of Christianity in doctrinal formulation, monasticism the interpretation of Christianity in a way of life, the chief practical mode of Christianity set by the transition centuries and accepted by the Middle Ages as the perfect Christian life. Dogma was expressed in terms of Greek philosophy; but pagan elements have been eliminated from monasticism. It is the contrast of contrasts with all that is antique. Although not a complete interpretation of Christianity, still it is Christian. And one reason why the man of the Middle Ages in his religious thought and feeling is less pagan than the Græco-Roman Christians of the third, fourth, or fifth centuries lies in the fact that the Middle Ages received Christianity through monasticism and looked to that as the ideal Christian life.

The monastic life, as it assumed definite form under the regula of Benedict, might hold divergent motives.

Its strength and inspiration was the love of God and the desire of an eternal life wherein the chief element of bliss should be the love of God more nearly realized in ecstasy and vision.   On earth, the love of God must be fostered, and the conditions of attainment of eternal life must be fulfilled, in the spirit and according to the precepts of Christ as interpreted in the transition centuries.   Western monasticism takes its form from the interpretation of Christianity by the Latin Fathers and the Western monastic regulators, who unconsciously modify and add to the interpretations of the East.   Its constant endeavor is to eliminate the emotions and desires which oppose entire consecration to the love of God and the attainment of eternal life; and to cultivate the human qualities which serve these final ends, and the relationships with fellow-men which fulfil the love of God in love of man according to the words of Christ.

Chief among the emotions and desires — to wit, the lusts — to be eliminated was passionate love between the sexes.   Hence one most holy form of human love was excommunicated from the perfect Christian life. The reasons for this rejection include well nigh all the causes of monasticism heretofore discussed.   All sexual desire was condemned, every mode of life involving it was excluded, and whatever might occasion it was forbidden.   Mainly to this end was the monk's diet regulated, his fasts prescribed, and his intercourse with the world restricted.

Sexual desire was evil.   Moreover, marriage and the claims of family were an impediment to a life led in devotion to the love of God.   Consequently monasti-

cism barred or sternly held in check the love springing from ties of blood, the father's love, the mother's,
the son's, the daughter's, the brother's, the sister's.
There was no sensual lust in these; yet any one of
them might distract the soul. Gluttony was also evil
in itself and conducive to still more evil lust. It
should be checked by sparing diet and set fasts. Anger was likewise evil. There could be no place in the
monk's heart for this passion having ill as its desire.
Nor might the monk be covetous, a base and selfish
feeling, involving lust for the vainglories of this life,
manifestly distracting from devotion to God's glory,—
indeed, a passion fastening the monk to earth. Top-
ping all other sins was pride, the swelling vanity of
self-reliance and self-love, an obstacle to any right
attitude of the Christian soul. These vices might be
suppressed and yet the soul be barren if it were rest-
less and despondent over the lost vanities of life and
the tardy coming of the love of God. This was failure
in devotion, emptiness, when the soul should be filled
with love of God.

The soul pure from fleshy lusts, nor distracted by
affections leading aside from God; the soul which
knows not anger, and does not desire the glittering
vanities of life, which is not puffed up in conceit, and
yet has all devotion's energy,—this soul is a fit recep-
tacle for the holy spirit and the grace of God. Energetic, yet not trusting in itself, devoted, yet unto
nothing save what comes from God and leads to Him,
hopeful and proud in Him alone, this soul is strong in
faith, obedience, and humility. The spirits of these
virtues unite in love of their great end and aim and

source and sanction, — God. The soul has nothing in and through itself, but all from God and in Him. He is its life, its joy, its love, its contemplation, as it waits expectant on His grace to do His will. And God so great, so infinite, so near, so guarding and caretaking, so closely loving, who suffered for every man and every woman — to such a God such a soul clings in the passion of devotion, begotten by God's love. It will dwell ever in the thought of Him, a happy pilgrim moving along the sweet, quiet, yearning ways of the Christian *vita contemplativa*.

Yet this soul dwells also in the flesh, among fellow-sojourners. It is human, and its great relationship to God must be in part reflected and fulfilled in consistent relationships toward men. As the Christian spirit lived through its desert hermit life and regained its sanity and wholeness, this became clear to monasticism. The relationship of the soul to God was supreme; relationships toward men must never ignore their final end, the fulfilment of the relationship to God. To order and adjust them to this end was the problem; its solution was the cloister, where the lives of all reflect the love of God in human relationships. The monk shall love his brethren unto God, exercising obedience and humility, in the energy of love and patience. This is the key to monastic organization and its rules. The love of God, the attainment of eternal life in Him, is the monk's end and aim; he cannot love his brethren or himself save in love ordered toward this end; he must love himself, and them as himself, unto this end. Therefore it is his brother's spiritual welfare, as his own, that his love serves; it cannot cherish evil in the brother or himself, or aught distracting from the common end. In love and humility toward God and man, the abbot must direct, and the monk obey: in love and humility monks must go through their days, perform their acts of labor for the good of all and the glory of God, act toward each other not in idle foolishness of intercourse, but so that all may advance toward God and eternal life. To these ends were monastic regulations, so that each act of the monk's life should be an act of obedience and humility, done in love of God and man. Even in prayers and spiritual devotions, the monk shall observe set times and seasons, lest he be proud or puffed up at his progress.

The ideal monastic character was that which corresponded to these principles. And in hundreds of instances a personality with such a character did result; a personality when directing faultless in humility and obedience to God, faultless in humility and obedience when obeying; knowing neither pride nor vanity, nor covetousness nor lust, nor slothful depression; grave and silent with bent head, yet with an inner peace, even an inner passionate joy; meditative, mystic, an other-world personality; one that dwells in spiritual facts, for whom this world has passed away and the lusts thereof; one that is centred in God and in eternal life, and yet capable of intense activities; a man who will not swerve from orders received, as he swerves not from his great aim, the love of God and life eternal. Such a character was narrow in that it lacked the qualities developed by those normal human activities which monastic life excluded; and it might be set and rigid and uncreative in its obedience. But in its spiritual wealth and power lay compensation for its misprisal of the life that circles unto God through loves which are partly of this earth. Only by suppression and exclusion of what seemed opposing and in reality was too difficult to fulfil, could men of the transition and mediæval centuries formulate and carry out an ideal of the perfect Christian life. It was not for them, as it is not for other ages, to fulfil all of Christ.

Evidently the contrast between the monk and the antique pagan man is well-nigh absolute. If we should take the foregoing outline of the monastic character sentence by sentence, and prefix a negative to each, we should find that the antique man was thereby not untruly, if but partially, described.[1]

The monastic character manifested different phases in monks and nuns of diverse temperaments living under various conditions. A consummate expression of it, toward the end of the Middle Ages, is the *De Imitatione Christi* of Thomas à Kempis. But we may rather turn to certain great men of the transition centuries. Their characters and the range of their faculties will indicate the scope of manhood and human quality existing among Latin Christians, and will also illustrate monastic prototypes. Jerome, Ambrose, Augustine, Benedict, and Gregory the Great

[1] This is true, although the monastic ideal had something in common, not only with certain problematic Jewish modes of life (*ante*, p. 141), but also with Neo-platonism, which was mainly Greek. Yet any elements which Neo-platonism may be deemed to have in common with monasticism will be found to be those characteristics which indicate departure from the antique.

were mighty factors in mediæval life and thought, and their lives bore close relation to monasticism, though not all were passed in monasteries.

Of these five, Jerome was the least. He was a gifted not a great man. His was a sensitive, irascible, almost hysterical temperament, but with fine touches of sympathy and understanding. He had an especially sympathetic understanding of women; there was much of the woman in this great director of widows and virgins. He was an admirable scholar, a violent controversialist, and a great letter-writer.[1] He was possessed with a fiery enthusiasm for Christianity and celibate life, which perhaps was even over-expressed in his letters; for Jerome always felt dramatically and imaginatively. At all events, he led an ascetic and effusively celibate life in Rome and afterwards in his retreat at Bethlehem. His enthusiasm for Christian scholarship proved itself real in his mighty labors upon Biblical translations.

Jerome's temper, appreciations, and affections clamored ceaselessly at the barriers of his austerely conceived life. This heart, shut against fleshly lures, has much confessorial tenderness for women; and this mind which deems that a Ciceronian is not a Christian, continually hungers for the fair classic literature. Although a Greek scholar, it was his own Latin that made part of him; and his preferences appear in his letters. These contain more quotations from Virgil than from all other pagan writers together; less frequently he quotes from Horace, and has scattered lines from other classics, Naevius, Persius, Terence, Lucan.

[1] *Post*, p. 211.

The saint suppressed feelings connected with sense; but his nature quivers. No stoic, he knows that he feels intensely, and he finds it well to feel. He felt the passion of devotion, which inflames his exhortations for virginity. He felt another love — for saintly Paula and her daughter Eustochium, a love fervent if not impassioned; but certainly not that of lover for mistress; "Salute Paula and Eustochium, mine in Christ, whether the world will or no,"[1] he writes, about to sail for the Holy Land, disgusted with Rome and his disappointed ambitions there, and the scandals touching him and these ladies. They followed him thither, and established convents at Bethlehem, near their teacher's dwelling. The loving friendship of the three gains inspiration from their Christian fervor. Christianity has increased their capacity for feeling, though the passions of mortal love are barred.

A different person from Jerome was the great Bishop of Milan, an entirely masculine and authoritative personality. Jerome was gifted; Ambrose was great. In him the power of Roman command abides; he is a Roman Christian, a jurist, a statesman, a consul-bishop. The range, the greatness, of his personality consists in the intelligence which understands and directs, and in fortitude and power and goodness. Like a Roman and a Stoic, he inculcates Christianity and Christian conduct, and is unfaltering in defence of Christian principles against the orthodox Theodosius, as he is tireless in upholding Christian dogmas against Arians.

[1] Ep. 45, *Ad Asellam*; and see his eulogy on Paula, Ep. 108, *Ad Eustochium.*

Ambrose is not irascible, nor does he appear sensitive or emotional. In harmony with his juristic and dogmatic mind, the sentiments of his heart flow evenly and strongly, not made to eddy by quick quivering sympathies, which, if the Roman temper feels, it will ignore. Ambrose's emotion flows steadily toward that goal which moves it, God — the Trinity, Father, Son, and Holy Spirit. His admonitions are stern, true, unangered; his appeals are not impassioned by his feelings toward the person he addresses. Yet his human feelings are not suppressed; they gather greatness in the current which they do not disturb, but which carries them onward toward God. Such is the quality of the feeling which rolls so calmly in his hymns, springing from the power of his thought of God, and sobered by the compelling sobriety of that thought, — reverential, awe-struck, correct, mightily loving:

> *Deus creator omnium,*
> *Polique rector, vestiens*
> *Diem decoro lumine,*
> *Noctem soporis gratia.*

This is the reverence of the Christian Roman mind; the heart turns to God in the *Veni, redemptor gentium.* Dogmatically one hymn is as correct as the other. They may seem unemotional and too correct in statement. But the power of their reverent adoration moved Augustine to tears.

A supremely great man may contain in his nature what has been attained in those prior periods of human development which constitute the past for him. Such a man does not feel and include the past as it was, but

as it still is — transformed in the present. He draws
this into himself, forms it anew and reëxpresses it for
the inspiration of the future. Homer expresses the
ideal of the past heroic age as that ideal still lived in
the life of his own time. Virgil sums up in himself
and in his work the great Roman past as it lived in
the power of the Augustan era. Dante is preëminently
the scholastic poet, who apparently sums up an actual
past, which ends in him. Nevertheless, Dante is of
his present; and in him, as in all great men, there is
dawn as well as twilight.

Augustine was not a poet; yet as the supreme man
of his time he summed up the past as it still lived,
remoulded it, added to it from himself, and gave it a
new unity and form wherein it was to live on. It was
a fact of paramount importance for the Middle Ages
that Augustine lived to purge and unify and complete
his era's understanding and appropriation of the first
four Christian centuries. He embodied in himself and
expressed in his writings a large and veritable Christianity. He eliminated pagan ethics and substituted
Christian love of God, with the principles which it
involves. On the other hand, his personality held
antecedents which were not specifically Christian.
His intellect was greatly Roman. The Roman law
was inborn in him; its spirit appears in his writings,
occupied with God and man, with sin and grace. He
prizes government and is impassioned for order. The
Roman order, the *pax Romana*, the concord of citizens,
is re-set in the kingdom of God: *Pax civitatis, ordi-
nata imperandi atque obediendi concordia civium. Pax
coelestis civitatis, ordinatissima et concordissima societas*

fruendi Deo et invicem in Deo.   Pax omnium rerum,
tranquillitas ordinis.   Ordo est parium dispariumque
rerum sua cuique loca tribuens dispositio.[1]   For earthly
peace and order there must be the concord of citizens
in commanding and obeying; and for this life's true
ordering and pacifying unto life eternal, there must
be an authority on earth to transmit peace and grace
from God.   The Roman in Augustine completes the
labors of prior Roman-minded Christians, and makes
the Church absolute in authority to bind and loose.

Augustine had also the training of rhetoric and the
enlightenment of the philosophies, especially Neo-
platonism.   He combines Greek metaphysical conceptions and late philosophic moods with his own intense
Christian love of God and ardent practice of the other
Christian virtues.   Yet he remains a man of the Latin
West.   This appears in his abiding Roman qualities,
and in the character of the topics interesting him; for
example, the problem of grace and free will, the nature
of the soul and its relationship to God, rather than
the metaphysical dogmas of the Eastern Church,
which he simply accepts.   He had a genius for psychology, in which branch of mental science his predecessors were Latins rather than Greeks.[2]

The greatness and completeness of Augustine's
Christian nature consisted in the greatness of his love
of God and the completeness which his mind carried
out the convictions of this love to their conclusions.
In this, with power unequalled since Paul, he was
appropriating Christ, feeling and thinking back to

---

[1] *Civ. Dei*, XIX, 13, and cf. *ib.*, 10–12.

[2] *E.g.*, Tertullian and Arnobius.

Christ's teachings and the teachings of the Old Testament. He veritably feels in the words of psalmist or prophet or evangelist, or in the words of Paul.[1] Yet in his Biblical phrases, and much more in his own expressions of Christian feeling and all that Christianity is to him, he is interpreting and reëxpressing Christianity. And inasmuch as his intellectual and emotional appropriation of Christianity was more comprehensive than that of any man for centuries after him, his understanding and expression of it laid the lines and set the tone of mediæval theology and piety. It is he, for example, that strikes the mediæval keynote of Christ's sublimity in his humility, and the note of reverence for humility;[2] *omne bonum in humilitate perficitur*, would have been a good text for Benedict's twelfth chapter. *Robur in infirmitate perficitur ; illa aedificans caritas a fundamento, quod est Christus Jesus :*[3] what keynotes these of mediæval piety. Augustine represents the sum of emotion and the capacity for love which had been gathering in Christian souls and drawing toward Christ and the love of God. Conceiving and feeling the love of God which was in Christ Jesus, he reëxpressed it in terms which were to voice the Christian feelings of the mediæval soul.

The great heart, the great mind; the mind led by the heart's inspiration, the heart guided by the mind — this is Augustine. Both mind and heart contribute

---

[1] Augustine's recurring note is the *mihi adhaerere Deo bonum est*, which is from Ps. lxxiii. 28. For how he sets his principles and feelings in words of psalmist and prophets, see, *e.g.*, *Civ. Dei*, X, 5, 6, 18, 25, 32.

[2] Cf. *Conf.*, VII, 24–27 ; Harnack, *Dogmengeschichte*, III, 118–121.

[3] *Conf.*, VII, 26.

to the intensity and harmony of life included in a single aim — God: *mihi adhaerere Deo bonum est.* Augustine's works are never the product solely of the mind; the whole man speaks in them, the entire human consciousness recognizing that the truths of love are as valid as the truths of reason. His thoughts are not mere thoughts, but expressions of the whole soul, and therefore always involving desire and aversion; his supreme conception, God, is also his supreme desire. The life of the soul is not mere knowing or contemplation, but includes a striving according to desire or aversion; for the soul has always these, *cupido, amor, ira,* or *timor.*

Augustine is primarily sure of his own thoughts and feelings. In accord with them he constructs his conception of God, and loves Him: so his theology rests on his psychology. God and the soul are the objects of his love and his desire to know: *Deum et animam scire cupio. Nihilne plus? Nihil omnino.*[1] Therefore he abjures the blithe world around him, and creates a new world of God and the soul of man.

Augustine's personality includes qualities which singly were possessed by other men. He may not have been the Roman imperator that Ambrose was, but he had an equally authoritative character; the flock-guiding Christian bishop speaks in his sermons. There also exists in Augustine the juristic nature of Tertullian. That great African's flame of reason is matched by the fervent arguments of Augustine's more balanced, but equally impassioned mind. And the woman-nature which was in Jerome exists more

[1] *Solil.,* I, 7.

greatly in him; for his is the woman-nature turned toward God, poured out at His feet, bathing them with its flood; the repentant woman-nature, grateful, devoted, surrendered, and abased, utterly filled with love of Him; and the woman-nature which is not narrowed by love's devotion, but is broadened through it to include tender consideration of whatever needs love's sympathy.

In matters of sheer intellect Augustine rises creative above his contemporaries. He anticipates Descartes' *cogito ergo sum,*[1] and almost Kant's thought of the subjectivity of time.[2] He has also a grand conception of spiritual progress, — of the people of God, advancing from age to age.[3] And he discountenances the worship of martyrs, who yet may be honored.[4] Still, he had some of the limitations of his time. His Platonism was mainly Neo-platonism; and this means much; it led him to speak of Porphyry as *nobilissimus philosophus paganorum.*[5] He believed in miracles, and gives a list of many known to him or occurring in his time.[6] But he argues excellently, showing them to be less wonderful than creation and man and the world and God.[7] He thinks that demons have bodies superior to those of men.[8] He could not have doubted the existence of demons without lifting himself out of the fifth century, when their existence was assumed,

---

[1] *Civ. Dei*, XI, 26.

[2] *Civ. Dei*, XI, 6; *Conf.*, XI, 36.   Cf. Flottes, *Études sur St. Augustin*, pp. 188–197.

[3] *Civ. Dei*, X, 14.   [4] *Civ. Dei*, VIII, 27.

[5] *Civ. Dei*, XXII, 3.   [6] *Civ. Dei*, XXII, 8.   [7] *Ib.*, X, 12.

[8] *Civ. Dei*, VIII, 15.   He does not doubt ancient heathen prodigies, which he regards as the work of devils (*Civ. Dei*, X, 16 and 21).

just as we now assume their non-existence. Likewise he assumes the existence of angels, and reasons on their creation,[1] and on their knowledge of God.[2] He had also the universal habit of allegorical interpretation,[3] with fancies for the symbolism of numbers.[4]

Augustine's final, most fatal, limitation was also of his time, as well as of the centuries which followed him. This was the prurient misconception of the normal and lawful relations between the sexes. The love of man for woman which holds passion could be but lust for Augustine; it could not be holy, it held the creature down. He knew not the love which draws man and wife toward God. His words speak only of concupiscence. As his thoughts are wavering toward utter devotion to Christ, it is not the yearning for the companionship of a wife that distracts him. He is hindered by the passions of the flesh; it is the habit of these that he cannot lay aside, that he longs for most sinfully, that in the end he will cut off utterly. His thoughts correspond to the verse which met his eyes as he suddenly opened the gospel in the crisis of his conversion, — not in rioting and drunkenness, not in chambering and wantonness, not in strife and envying; but put ye on the Lord Jesus Christ, and make not provision for the flesh *in concupiscentiis*.[5]

---

[1] *E.g.*, *Civ. Dei*, XI, 9 and 32.   [2] *Ib.*, XI, 29.

[3] See, *e.g.*, *Civ. Dei*, XI, 8 and 34; XIII, 21; *Contra Faustum*, XXII; Sermo XXIV, on Gospel of John. In Sermo XVII, Sec. 8, etc., on Gospel of John, Augustine interprets Christ's words, "Take up thy bed and walk," to mean "Love your neighbor."

[4] *E.g.*, *Civ. Dei*, XI, 30.

[5] *Conf.*, VIII, 29. See *ib.*, VI, 25; VIII, 12, 13, 17. Compare *Civ. Dei*, XIV, 16 et seq.

But how could Augustine have high thoughts of
love and marriage ?   Could he lift himself out of his
time, and forestall the development of future ages ?
He would have been obliged to create such conceptions.
Christ recognized the holiness of marriage, yet hardly
in fifteen centuries did marriage reach its full sanctification in the spirit of His teachings.   The causes
which brought about monasticism prevented the recognition of the absolute holiness of marriage within the
Christian communities.   Life in those communities
was environed by pagan conceptions of love and marriage, in which there was little to present an ideal
according with Christianity's continual exaction of the
best.   So marriage fell below the demands of Christian
idealism ;   it was not raised to their level, but was
definitely numbered with those things which might be
tolerated but could not be admired.   Absolute holiness
lay only in virginity.   This was the monastic outcome.
And strange were to be the far effects.   For, in the
course of centuries, love's inspiration was to assert its
own nobility, but not always within the bonds of
matrimony.   Through the Middle Ages the thought
of love as inspiration grew indeed, but whether there
was marriage or adultery between the lovers was not
the first consideration.[1]

Benedict of Nursia was holy from his youth; from
his childhood carrying an old man's heart, *ab ipso suae
pueritiae tempore cor gerens senile*,[2] a phrase revealing
monastic ideals of holiness.   The character of Bene-

[1] The Arthurian cycle of poetry and the *Roman de la Rose* bear
witness to this.
[2] Gregorius Magnus, *Dialogi*, II, prologue.

dict is reflected in his regula; as Gregory says, *Cujus si quis velit subtilius mores vitamque cognoscere, potest in eadem institutione regulae omnes magisterii illius actus invenire : quia sanctus vir nullo modo potuit aliter docere quam vixit.*[1] The regula not only reflects the character of Benedict generally, but contains touches revealing distinctly the soul of him who set it. Thus the reference to the rule as this *minimam regulam inchoationis,*[2] tells the utter humility of Benedict and the ideality of his endeavor for a life of holiness. His regula is but a slight beginning; for what more could he, poor workman, set ? it is also but a beginning, as the saintly soul sees all his acts small and poor in the light of the perfection for which he yearns. Likewise the characterization of the proper abbot mirrors Benedict, his lovingness and his sufficient strictness when needed : *oderit vitia, diligat fratres . . . studeat plus amari quam timeri.*[3]

Gregory's words, quoted above, disclose the aspects of Benedict which impressed Gregory's generation, and the centuries following: " He who would gain minuter knowledge of Benedict's life, may, in the institution of the regula, find all the acts of that *master;*[4] for the *holy man* could in no wise teach other than as he lived." These are the two aspects of the same Benedict, the master, the abbot, the wise and temperate

---

[1] Gregorius Magnus, *Dialogi*, II, 36.

[2] *Reg. Benedicti*, Cap. 73, — one of the chapters possibly not written by Benedict, yet reflecting his spirit.

[3] *Reg.*, Cap. 64.

[4] I have thus translated *illius magisterii*. *Magisterium* properly means office, not magistrate. But here I think the sense is arrived at by translating " master."

lawgiver, and the holy man, whose holiness wrought miracles. Herein he was the prototype of mediæval saints, whose characters combined a like miracle-working sanctity with the wisdom, firmness, and force which make the possessor a director of those about him and sometimes of the wider destinies of men. The holiness of Benedict's life was reflected in tales of miraculous deeds, many of which tales carry human life and holiness and poetic beauty;[1] and, as for the other aspects of his career, his regula gave the fundamental form to the monasticism of the West.

As Benedict is both saint and monastic lawgiver, so even more strikingly the writings of Gregory the Great exhibit two aspects of the man, which make him also one of the great prototypes of the mediæval monk-rulers of the Church. A strange but frequent combination of traits and faculties: the same man is well nigh a mystic, one to whom spiritual communion with God is blessedness, one to whom the career which disturbs the peace of this communion comes as a banishment; on the other hand, a man of marvellous practical sagacity and capacity for the management of affairs and the direction of men, a man of dauntless will and untiring energy, a man of power and authority, strong in exhortation, terrible in reproof,[2] whose commands are not to be withstood, and whose love is commensurate in fervor. Gregory is moreover a prototype of the mediæval union of humility and authority. He outlines such a character in his Book of Pastoral Rule: the bishop shall be humble, but

[1] See, e.g., Gregorius, Dialogi, II, 6 and 7.
[2] See, e.g., Ep. V, 15, Ad Johannem Episcopum.

authoritative in suppressing sins; he must lord it, not over the brethren, but over their vices.[1]

Gregory's Pastoral Rule is an authoritative work of episcopal — inchoate papal — precept. Its purpose was to supply the bishop with rules for his conduct, just as Benedict's *regula monachorum* sets the rules for monks. Both writings are regulae authoritatively prescribed. They are thus typical of the later transition centuries and the Middle Ages; the former yearned for such regulae as these to obey, and created them; the latter accepted the same, modifying them according to the further development and needs of mankind.

As pope and head of Western Christendom, Gregory assumed a title expressive of his humility, and prophetic of the nature of the papacy's future dominion: *servus servorum Dei.*[2] It was as a servant of servants that the pope was to command the world, in obedience to God and in exaction of obedience to authority given and enjoined by God.

Gregory is a man of the late transition centuries, a man far more mediæval than Augustine. Augustine had summed up Christian doctrine and feeling for the West; Gregory accepts the work of Augustine, but reëxpresses Augustinian feelings and conclusions in conformity to his own character, which is more definitely touched by the spirit and the new ignorance of the Middle Ages. His mind is occupied with topics which were to occupy coming centuries; he is filled with allegorism; he discusses the affairs and details

---

[1] See, *e.g.*, *Pastoralis Regulae Liber*, II, 7; also cf. *ib.*, I, 10 and 11.

[2] Thus he begins Ep. I, 1.

of the life to come; and the doctrine of a purgatorial
fire, which purges lesser sins after the sinner's death
but before the Last Judgment, has come to him.[1] His
great practical insight and ability does not prevent his
ready credence of miracles preposterous or otherwise;
they occupy the greater part of his *Dialogi de Vita et
miraculis Patrum Italicorum.* He has, likewise, a full
mediæval reverential fear of relics, which can work
miracles or death.[2] And he is mediæval in that he is
a sombre character, upon whom weighs the responsibility of his pontificate, and over whom already
impends the mediæval *Dies Irae.* He bids his corre-
spondents be mindful of that Day: *In interitu ergo rerum omnium pensare debemus nil fuisse quod amavimus.
Appropinquantem itaque aeterni judicis diem sollicita
mente conspicite, et terrorem ipsius poenitendo praevenite.
Delictorum omnium maculas fletibus lavate. Iram quae
aeterna imminet temporali lamento compescite.*[3] These
are dark words; the joyful world is no more. Contemplation of God is blessedness in the present life, which
otherwise is danger and distress; in such contemplation there is fear of Hell and love of God, a love which
also does not cease to shed tears of penitence.

[1] *Dialogi*, IV, 39; see this fourth book of the *Dialogi, passim.*

[2] See Lib. IV, Ep. 30, *Ad Constantiam Augustam;* also VII, Ep.
26; VIII, Ep. 35.

[3] "In the face of the destruction of all things, we ought to hold
what we have loved as nothing. Gaze upon the Day of the Eternal
Judge with a solicitous mind, and forestall its terror by repentance.
Wash out with tears the stains of every sin. With present lament
quiet the wrath hanging over us from eternity" (Lib. III, Ep. 29,
to the clergy of Milan).

CHAPTER VIII

CHRISTIAN PROSE

I. *Christianization of Style*

CHRISTIAN literature from the second to the fifth century does not follow the lines of literary degeneracy which mark the course of pagan literature during the same period. For Christians had new matter, and new power to set it forth. There had come to them the gospel, which they had received according to their capacities and characters. This was new matter which Christian writers were to set forth as they understood it. With the gospel, new elements of life had entered the natures of these men, renewing their powers, enlarging their personalities, giving them new points of view. A new message, a new faith, a new love, impelled them to exhort and instruct each other. Sometimes persecuted, usually despised and hated, they had constant need to justify before the world their faith and way of life.

Thus, novel circumstances, a new message of exhaustless import, a new manhood in those to whom the message had come, combined to create a new literature. Its fulness and pertinency of contents contrast strikingly with the emptiness and irrelevancy of contemporary pagan writings. From the second century, moreover, a steadily increasing proportion of the intellect of the Empire is to be found among the Christians, until at the end of the fourth century there are Greek and Latin Christians who are great writers, while there is no pagan to compare with them. In this century the Christian triumph checked the decline of art; and the same period produced a body of writings of great power, constituting a revival of literature in a time of literary emptiness. In both cases the inspiration was the Christian faith and the Christian situation.

The first Christian writings [1] constituted a group unlike anything in classical Greek and Latin literature. Their theme was the Christian faith and the spiritual and temporal needs of Christians; they presented a view and way of life contrasting with all that was Greek and Roman. Another fundamental contrast was presented by their emotional contents. Through the classical periods of Greek and Roman literature a deepening of emotional capacity may be traced and a quickening of sympathy, which culminate in Virgil's great human heart with its pity for all mortal life. This was a growth of feeling touching fellow-men. Pagan literature has nothing like the fear and love of God, and the accompanying sense of sinfulness, felt and uttered by the prophets and psalmists of the Old Testament. In the New Testament these feelings are Christianized; they are perfected in

---

[1] The New Testament, the Epistle of Barnabas, the *Shepherd of Hermas*, the *Didaché of the Twelve Apostles*; then the writings of the Apostolic Fathers, Ignatius, Polycarp, Clement of Rome. The language is Greek.

that love which casteth out fear, and are given new power through the heart's devotion to Christ. "For the love of Christ constraineth us; . . . and he died for all, that they which live should no longer live unto themselves, but unto him who for their sakes died and rose again."[1] The love which in and through Christ we bear to God is poured out on earth in love of man, as Christ exemplified and commanded. This is the love to which Paul gives lyric utterance.[2] The New Testament voices in great notes the emotions of the Christian soul, which were to reëcho in Christian writings from Augustine through the Middle Ages.

Finally, the New Testament writers were by nature more Hebraic than Hellenic; their Hellenic education was meagre. Absorbed in the contents of their writings, they had no care for style or vanity of authorship. As a result, the writings are void of self-consciousness, and, from a classical standpoint, are formless. Here again they offer a total contrast to Greek and Roman literature, which had striven always for excellence of form. But the first three gospels betray no thought save for the subject-matter; the Fourth Gospel feels the infinite import of its contents, yet is not stylistically self-conscious. In the epistles, Paul writes as he would speak, without artifice or rhetoric. He often thinks of himself, but never of his style. He has not the faintest literary self-consciousness. Unless a man in writing Greek observed the rules of rhetoric, his writing, viewed from the standpoint of classical tradition, would be formless and barbarous. This applies to the first Christian writings. The Gospels, the

---

[1] 2 Cor. v. 14. [2] 1 Cor. xiii.

Epistles, the Apocalypse, are as un-Hellenic as anything could be and be written in Greek.[1]

Formlessness and absence of the rhetorician's art do not characterize Christian literature so markedly after the middle of the second century. Educated men were joining the circles of believers; and education meant primarily the study of rhetoric. These men did not lay aside their education. Moreover, the necessity of writing in a style that would appeal to the educated pagan world was tacitly recognized in practice, however vehemently Christians disavowed the tricks of rhetoric.[2] From the fourth century onward, the Church writers frequently insist that all matters pertaining to the faith and to the edification of the faithful should be set forth in simple style without rhetoric or grammatical fastidiousness. It was nevertheless asserted that, as against heretics and other falsifiers of truth, the champion of the faith should not be unskilled in the use of his weapons, but avail himself of all resources at his command.[3]

[1] Cf. generally, Norden, *Antike Kunstprosa*, pp. 479-512.

[2] The manner and form of the rhetorician's productions were part of the time. Christians might, without conscious imitation, cast their thoughts in like forms. For example, there has been found a likeness (Hatch, *op. cit.*, p. 90) between the Life of Apollonius and the Clementine *Recognitions*, a production probably of the third century, in which the pseudo-Roman Clement tells of his accompanying the Apostle Peter on his journeyings, and of Peter's teachings, and especially of the mighty contests, waged in public, between Peter and the arch-deceiver Simon Magus, whom the Apostle pursues from city to city.

[3] See Augustine, *De doctrina christiana*, IV, 2, 3. This passage, and others insisting upon a simple open style (*e.g.*, Basil, Ep. 339; Migne, *Patr. Gr.*, 32, col. 1084; Jerome, Ep. 21, 42, *Ad Damasum*;

A language, when required to express the thought and feeling of a new religion, will suffer change. In the works of Christian prose writers from the close of the second century onward, the written Latin language passed through changes from which it emerged Christianized.[1] Many popular words were admitted to literary use, and new words were formed after the analogy of the usages of popular speech; again, new words were formed or old ones altered in their meaning in order to translate Greek (Christian) words, and phrases were constructed in imitation of Greek idioms; Semitic words and idioms were introduced; and finally, the balanced periods of classical composition were replaced by a style and order of words suggesting the formative stages of the Romance tongues.

A permanent separation from the classical Latin language was thus brought about, and a Christian diction was evolved which could express Christian thoughts and give voice to Christian feeling, — the passion of Augustine's *Confessions* could not have been put into the balanced periods of Cicero. A new diction and a new style had risen, Augustine himself being a potent influence. Still further declassicizing, barbarizing, Christianizing of Latin will be needed before Latin will voice the feeling of the *De Imitatione*, or of the well-nigh singing lyric passages in the early Latin lives of St. Francis.[2]

ib., Ep. 49, 4; Augustine, on Psalm xxxvi, v. 26; Sulpicius Severus, *Vita Martini*, praef.; Gregory the Great, preface to *Moralia*), are collected in Norden, *Antike Kunstprosa*, pp. 529–535.

[1] Cf. Ozanam, *La civilisation au Ve siècle*, II, pp. 134–167.

[2] Cf. T. Celano, *Vita Prima*, Cap. X, ed. Amoni (Rome, 1880); *Legenda Trium Sociorum*, ed. Amoni (Rome, 1880); *Legenda*

The changes in Latin style and diction between Cicero and Augustine were not entirely due to Christian writers. Apuleius and Petronius had broken with the classical tradition, as preserved by Quintilian. So had at least one pagan poem, the *Pervigilium Veneris*. The language was loosening from its classic balance and stately self-control; it was becoming flexible in a way pointing to the later Christian changes. These innovations within the field of pagan literature were due to the writers who had something living to express. It is the well-bred emptiness of a Symmachus that at the very end is found preserving the old form.[1]

In the conflict between the classical style and the innovations, not all Christian writers were on the same side. The division is marked in the two earliest Latin Christian authors: Minucius Felix skilfully maintains classical form; Tertullian forcefully develops a Christian style. The former introduces no novel idiom; the latter was the first creator of a Christian Latin diction. He translated Greek words into new-coined Latin words, and made over Greek phrases into strange Latin equivalents.[2] Even more largely and more fruitfully he drew from the spoken Latin of the people, the *Sermo Plebeius*. The language of literature, fashioned under Greek influence, was artificial, and had but cramped powers of

Antiquissima Speculum Perfectionis, V, 81, and VIII, 95, 96, ed. Sabatier (1898).

[1] On Symmachus, see Teuffel-Schwabe, *Gesch. des Röm. Lit.*, § 425.

[2] Cf. Norden, *Antike Kunstprosa*, 593–598, 606–615.

growth. By its side had always existed the spoken
Latin, different in many forms and words. The latter represented the vernacular, un-Hellenized genius
of the Latin tongue; it was living, adaptable, capable of growth.[1] In Tertullian's writings, apparently
for the first time, appear a mass of words either
drawn from this spoken language or formed after its
analogies.[2]

[1] Cf. P. Monceaux, "Le Latin Vulgaire," *Revue des deux mondes*,
July 15, 1891.

[2] The following words (taken mostly from F. T. Cooper, *Word
Formation in the Roman Sermo Plebeius*, 1895) are examples of the
words thus introduced by Tertullian and other Christian writers: —

TERTULLIAN

ablatio	novatio	visibilitas	nunciator
abominatio	(*law Latin*)	(*same in ad-*	oblator
adimpletio	praemonitio	*jectives in*	operator
benefactio	prostitutio	-bilis)	peccator
blasphematio	reprobatio	impassibilis	persecutor
compassio	resurrectio	irreligiositas	protector
concarnatio	retributio	corporalitas	recreator
concatenatio	revelatio	nuditas	salvator
contribulatio	sanctificatio	profanitas	sanctificator
contristatio	tribulatio	sensualitas	transgressor
detectio	vivicatio	spiritalitas	vivificator
dilectio	vivifico	temporalitas	justificare
discretio	episcopatus	trinitas	acceptabilis
eradicatio	expiatus	animator	virginari
exaltatio	creatura	annuntiator	angelificare
fornicatio	concupiscentia	confessor	castificare
humiliatio	delinquentia	damnator	glorificare
jejunatio	improvidentia	dubitor	mortificare
(*or* ievinatio)	praescientia	expiator	nullificare
illuminatio	corruptibilitas	illuminator	revivificare
incorruptio	incorruptibilitas	miserator	sanctificare
mortificatio	invisibilitas	negator	jejunare

Classified according to their nature and significance, the words entering the written Latin with Christianity were: words relating to Christian worship (*e.g. baptizare,* from the Greek); those relating to the customs or government of the churches (*episcopatus,* from the Greek; *excommunicatio*); abstract nouns, in which the classical Latin was poor (*ingratitudo,* classical Latin would be *ingrata mens*); words signifying qualities, feelings, or opinions, which originated, or at least reached definite consciousness or a new importance through Christianity and the sentiments which it inspired, — for example, *carnalis,*[1] *sensualitas,* repre-

Apparently first used by the following are: —

ARNOBIUS	LACTANTIUS	AUGUSTINE	
abnegatio	mirabilitas	convictio	resplendentia
passibilitas	levitudo	(*from* convinco)	somnolentia
possibilitas		delapsio	monstrositas
	AMBROSIUS	excommunicatio	beatifico, -cator
HIERONYMUS	dissuetudo	imperfectio	exstirpator
excommunicatio	meditator	mansuefactio	justificator
impeccantia		perfruitio	luminator
impoenitentia	COMMODIANUS	ploratio	deificare
vilificare	hymnificare(?)		

A number of words from the Greek; *e.g.:* —

TERTULLIAN	ITALA
prophetare	agonizare
zelare	anathematizare
Christianizare	baptizare
eleemosyna	catechizare
	judaizare
AUGUSTINE	prophetizare
anathemare	sabbatizare

[1] Used by Tertullian, Minucius Felix, and *Acta SS. Perpetuae et Felicitatis.*

sented ideas novel to the pagan world, *i.e.* they represented disapprovals which were new; likewise *peccator* — paganism had not the Hebraic and Christian conception of sin; *compassio* (Greek συμπάθεια) was a quality incarnate with Christ — quite different from Virgil's saddened pity for all life; *dilectio* was a sort of love different from *amor; creatura* stood for a Christian (and Hebraic) conception not existing in the pagan world, whose gods were not creators; *resurrectio, revelatio, sanctificatio*, were thoughts first definite with Christianity; *spiritalitas* — there had been nothing in the pagan world corresponding to this quality of the Christian soul; *salvator* — nor had there been a Saviour before Christ; with reference to Him, the conception of temporal preservation changed to that of eternal salvation and was spiritualized; a Christian word was needed to express this. A mass of words came into Latin with the growth of monasticism. Some of these were taken from the Greek,[1] and some were newly coined Latin equivalents. A number of them had originally passed over into the Christian Greek vocabulary from Stoicism and Neo-platonism.

Classical writers were on the verge of using many of these words, and used words from the same roots. But in Christianity the novel forms, as well as many words previously in classical use, gained new and spiritual significance. The whole matter represents a Christianizing and spiritualizing of the Latin language, and may be compared with the Christian transformation of the Teutonic tongues.

[1] See, *e.g.*, Cassian's list of monastic vices, *ante*, p. 162.

II. *The First Four Centuries of Christian Prose*

A brief reference may be made to the different classes of prose Christian literature — Greek and Latin — which had come into existence by the fifth century, in order to observe what continuance of classic form and style there is with the authors, what abandonment of classic form, and what development of Christian style and diction, and capacity of voicing Christian thought and feeling.

Christianity quickly took root in many cities, and the widely separated churches felt themselves members one of another. Epistles began to circulate at once. The earliest Christian documents are the epistles of Paul, the formlessness of which from a Hellenic point of view has been noticed. Their author has little thought of rhetoric in his eager rush of argument and loving exhortation.[1] Their style, reflecting the author's intense personality, is individual in the highest degree, but with Hebraic rather than Hellenic affinities. The Epistle to the Hebrews and the Epistle of Barnabas are more Hellenic. Also quite simply Hellenic is the epistle written by Clement of Rome as the spokesman of the Roman Church (cir. 92 A.D.), and addressed to the church at Corinth. On the other hand, the epistles of Ignatius of Antioch are as indi-

---

[1] Paul's own judgment is expressed in 2 Cor. xi. 6, ἰδιώτης τῷ λόγῳ, ἀλλ' οὐ τῇ γνώσει. Cf. 1 Cor. ii. 1 et. seq. Yet he may have had some training in Greek rhetoric; antithesis seems natural to him, *e.g.*, Rom. ii. 6, etc.; 1 Cor. i. 18; 1 Cor. iv. 10, etc.; 2 Cor. vi. 9. See Norden, *Die antike Kunstprosa*, pp. 492–510, and compare the different view of E. L. Hicks, *St. Paul and Hellenism*.

vidual in style as the epistles of Paul, whom one almost feels in reading them. Like Paul, Ignatius makes occasional use of antithesis,[1] which by itself indicates little; for, although antithesis was carefully developed in Greek rhetoric, it is also a natural form of fiery utterance. Ignatius is no more a rhetorician than Paul, nor under the influence of Greek literary style. Like the apostle, the apostolic Father makes his own Greek, mangling his periods as the spirit moves him.

Thus, from a literary point of view, there is little that is Hellenic in these Greek Christian epistles of the apostolic and post-apostolic time. Ordinarily the language adopted by a writer modifies the expression of his thought. But in these epistles the Greek language does not affect the thought as much as the thought and feeling distort the Greek diction. The language has been compelled to express thought and feeling alien to its genius. Such violent Christianizing of the Greek tongue might not endure among Christians of Hellenic birth or education. These early Greek epistles had no more literary influence than the Greek gospels upon the subsequent development of Greek Christian literature.[2]

When Rome became the mistress of the East and West, many Roman acquaintances found themselves

---

[1] *E.g.*, in the passages: " Three mysteries to be cried aloud which were wrought in the silence of God." — Ign., Eph. xix. " I am God's wheat, and I am ground by the teeth of wild beasts that I may be found pure bread." — Ign., Rom. iv.

[2] Cf. Overbeck, " Ueber die Anfänge der patristischen Literatur," *Historische Zeitschrift*, Neue Folge, XII (1882). This is also true of the *Shepherd of Hermas*.

scattered through the subject provinces. As facilities of transmission abounded, they naturally wrote to each other. Letter-writing became more common than it ever had been with the Greeks. The fact that the Greek race was spread through the East caused no such separation of friends as resulted from the constant exodus of Roman officials or exiles to the provinces. A great part of Cicero's Correspondence was occasioned by the situation thus created, and the example of that greatest of letter-writers made letters an important part of Latin literature.[1] The Romans were better letter-writers than the Greeks; and from the time when Latin Christendom, turning from the language which had brought Christianity to Rome, speaks its own tongue, the most interesting letters are Latin and not Greek.

The earliest collection of Latin letters is the correspondence of Cyprian,[2] the cultured and authoritative bishop of Carthage, who was martyred in the persecution of Valerian (257–258). The might and order of the organized Church speak in them, and the writer's zeal. They show a masterful grasp of the situation. Their style betrays the saint's former profession of a rhetorician.[3] It has little affinity with that of Tertullian, whom he calls his master and from whom he draws

---

[1] The poetic epistle, though it may have had its obscure Greek forerunner, was a Latin creation; it became a favorite with the poets of Latin Christendom.

[2] Not all these are by Cyprian; some are written to him.

[3] Many a Christian saint of the third and fourth centuries had been a professor of rhetoric, though we do not read of their having been professors of other matters, — a fact showing the primacy of rhetoric in the schools.

much of his substance. Nor does Cyprian approve of
the style of the Old Latin Bible. He is a purist in
diction, avoiding so far as possible Latinized Greek
words and words not sanctioned by classic use. His
Latin is smooth and round, containing much rhythm,
rhyme, and alliteration, and tending toward a har-
monious parallelism of structure between the clauses
of the same sentences. Although Cyprian never fails
to use the skill which his profession brought him, his
letters have the fire of the real situation, as when
from banishment he writes to the brothers in the
mines, exhorting and congratulating them: "They
have put fetters on your feet and bound those blessed
limbs and temples of God with vile chains, as if the
spirit could be bound with the body! To men devoted
to God, and testifying to their faith, such fetters are
ornaments; nor are Christian feet bound unto infamy,
but glorified unto a crown. O blessedly bound feet,
which God shall release! O blessedly bound feet,
which are guided in the way of salvation to Paradise!
O feet, bound in the present time that shall be always
free before the Lord! O feet, delaying in fetters for
a little, but soon to run the glorious course to Christ!
. . . Not with pillows and couches is the body cherished in the mines, but with the comforts of Christ.
Wearied it lies on the ground; but it is not pain to
lie down with Christ."[1]

From the third century the volume of Christian
correspondence increases; and letters form a goodly
part of the writings of the Greek and Latin Church

---

[1] Ep. 76. Cf. Ep. 15, 24, 25. Cyprian's letters contain vivid
pictures of the times, *e.g.*, Ep. 1.

Fathers. They do not fall within any one literary category, but reflect the activities of the leaders of the Christian world. They include polemic writings and doctrinal treatises, and all manner of epistles called forth by the situation of the Church at large, or of some particular community, or of the writer or recipient. They compare with the letters of pagans of the same period as Christian literature in general compares with the last centuries of pagan literature; the one has novel substance, the substance of the other is exhausted. Christian letters discuss matters vitally affecting Christian communities, or disclose the actual situation of affairs; pagan letters are apt to be empty and formal, like the letters of Symmachus, for example, telling little about anything.

The careers and characters of the Latin Fathers of the fourth and fifth centuries are disclosed in their correspondence. For example, the scope of Augustine's activities appears as, in his letters from Hippo, he writes polemics, answers questions, informs, instructs, and admonishes. Some two hundred and fifty of them still exist, covering the years from 387 to 429. They are of several classes, official letters, sometimes written in the name of a synod, letters upon topics of Christian exegesis and theology, letters of pastoral exhortation, personal letters of an intimate and confidential character, which are least numerous of all.

But the best Christian letter-writer was Jerome, whose letters from Palestine were a power making for monasticism, and a power in all matters of Christian learning. His letters, like Cicero's, are real letters, reflecting his personality and his mood as affected by the immediate situation and his feelings toward his correspondent. A true letter is personal to both writer and receiver; the writer writes not only as he alone would write, but as he would write only to this particular person on this particular occasion. Jerome's sympathetic and irascible temperament, so quickly sensitive to another's personality, keeps his letters real, while his vivacity and power of picturing people and situations keep them interesting. In no other class of writing does he so finely show himself the literary virtuoso that he is. The resources of rhetoric are all drawn upon in them, nor are they void of the vanity of authorship. Jerome edited the collection in his lifetime.

In those writings of Jerome that may be called literary, — his letters, his lives of saints, his *De Viris Illustribus*, his translation and continuation of Eusebius' chronicle, — he is in language and style a great mediator between classical antiquity and the times which came after him. His language is flexible, it is freed from the Ciceronian period, it can voice Christian feeling; but it still is pure, and preserves the classical speech as fully as is compatible with the expression of feeling and sentiments that were unknown in the times of Cicero and Virgil. In all these works Jerome is the brilliant man of letters, one who has made classic culture his own so far as that culture might pass into the transformed nature of a Christian of the fourth century. But there was another Jerome, and another side to his work as an author. He was a great Christian scholar, whose powers were consecrated to gaining the most fundamental knowledge of the Scriptures and to the most exact rendering in Latin of their meaning. This Jerome cares more for substance than for form; he does not hesitate to use or even invent words at which classic writers would have gasped, if only they truly render the thought. In translating Scripture he uses words from the common speech most of which were already used in older Latin versions of the Bible; [1] nor does he stumble before necessary Greek or Hebrew words; and in his learned Commentaries on the books of the prophets and the Gospels, or in his translation of Origen's abstruse Homilies, he forms the needed words along the free lines of development of the common spoken Latin. [2] So this painstaking learned Jerome is a potent factor in the declassicizing — the barbarizing if you choose — of Latin.

Besides letters, the Christian situation soon evoked apologetic writings. The earliest extant Apology is in Greek, that of Justin Martyr, [3] a Latin-descended native of Samaria. His ἀπολογία is addressed to the Emperor Antoninus Pius. It sets forth the Christian demand for justice from the government; the injustice of condemnation for a name; refutes the charge of atheism; shows the folly of idol worship; lays stress on the righteous, law-abiding lives of Christians, passed under God's eye in expectation of no earthly kingdom, and in obedience to the civil authorities. Then it argues for the resurrection, refers to

[1] Cf. Rönsch, *Itala und Vulgata* (1875), Einleitung.

[2] Cf. Goelzer, *La Latinité de St. Jerome*, Introduction. Jerome introduced about three hundred and fifty words into Latin.

[3] Born about 114, martyred at Rome, 166.

the Sibyl and to Plato for foreshadowings of Christian doctrine, and points out analogies to the history of Christ in pagan mythology; and then sets forth the Hebrew prophecies of Christ's birth, life, crucifixion, resurrection, and final glory. It gives an account of Christian worship and customs, to show their innocent character, and concludes with a warning to the Emperor that he shall not escape the final judgment of God.

An ἀπολογία is an argumentative explanatory defence. Early Christian apologies might be addressed to the Greeks or Gentiles (πρὸς Ἕλληνας, adversus gentes, ad nationes) or to some distinguished person, or might be directed against a named opponent, as Origen's Contra Celsum (κατὰ Κέλσου). They might be controversially directed against paganism or Judaism,[1] or against both.[2] Unlike previous pagan defences (e.g., Plato's Apology of Socrates), the Christian apology was a defence of Christianity rather than a personal plea for the writer.[3] The form and contents differed according to the situation and the nature of what was to be refuted. Thus Origen, Contra Celsum, quotes in separate excerpts the entire work[4] of his antagonist, and answers all in turn.

Latin apologists wrote with originality and ready

[1] Justin's Dialogue with Trypho.

[2] Jewish arguments were advanced by the pagan Celsus and refuted by Origen.

[3] After Christianity became the State religion, a personal defence or attack might be called an Apology. Jerome and Rufinus wrote " Apologies " against each other.

[4] Celsus called his work λόγος ἀληθής. Cf. Keim, Celsus' Wahres Wort.

grasp of at least the Christian side of the situation. Their writings were not modelled on the work of Origen or Justin. The earliest, apparently, is the much-admired *Octavius* of Minucius Felix. This is in form a Ciceronian dialogue, and argues for Christianity from a general theistic stoical standpoint. Specifically Christian themes are hardly touched. Style and language are classical; there is no approach to a Christian style or vocabulary.

No more than the Greek-writing Justin does the Latin-writing Minucius break with classic culture, but only with polytheism. Tertullian, however, stands for the Christian revolt against everything classical or pagan. He denounces pagan literature and philosophy as well as pagan superstition and the tyrannical suppression of Christianity by the pagan government. As a writer he is extraordinarily individual and original. His mind is filled with Christian thoughts, and his masterful endeavors to express them in a language not yet fitted to Christianity made him the great originator of a Christian Latin diction. But passionately as he was a Christian and greatly as he was himself, his style and literary habits were affected by his study of Roman law and the art of rhetoric. He is as much a rhetor as Apuleius, knowing every latest trick of word-twisting. His writings abound in marvellous antitheses, in rhythms and in rhymes. A virtuoso in the advocate's art, he was a creator of Christian arguments, some sophistical, but all impassioned and full of power. His works were a store for later apologists.

Tertullian had declared that no misfortune could

come to men, but the cry arose — *Christianos ad leonem*. This was true, for the pagans ascribed public misfortunes to the anger of the gods at Christian impiety. The charge was not to slumber till the Empire's overthrow was laid at Christian doors. Cyprian writes to refute it on the occasion of a pestilence.[1] A refutation of like charges is the leading motive of the lengthy *Adversus Nationes* of the African Arnobius, written shortly after the last and most thorough of all the persecutions, that under Diocletian. Conversely, writing after the persecutions had ceased, Lactantius,[2] in his historical writing, *De Mortibus persecutorum*, directs his polemic narrative to show the evil ends of the persecuting emperors. His great work was the *Divinae Institutiones*, written when the Christian cause was nearing its imperial triumph under the rising star of Constantine. There was then no urgent need to free Christianity from blame for the ills of an Empire which, for the time, appeared to be renewing its strength; but there was need to set forth systematically the elements of Christian truth, and Lactantius calls his work the *Divinae Institutiones*, using the title of elementary legal treatises. Its general purpose was to show that pagan worship and philosophy did not accord with reason and truth, while Christianity was both true and reasonable. Accordingly, in philosophic manner and with elegant

---

[1] *Ad Demetrianum*, Migne, *Patr. Lat.*, Vol. IV.

[2] Lactantius, as well as his teacher, Arnobius, was a professor of rhetoric before his conversion to Christianity. His style is classical, and expresses little Christian feeling. Nor does his work represent a deep understanding of Christianity.

diction, Lactantius begins by enlarging upon themes already sketched by Minucius Felix. He then sets forth in detail the entire volume of pagan foolishness and the invalidity of pagan philosophy; he expounds the Christian faith, shows its superiority in reason, and the warrants of its truth afforded by the miracles of Christ and the predictions of the prophets. He discourses upon justice, and finally upon the purpose of the world's creation and the course of the *saecula* until the conflict with the Antichrist; whereupon follow Christ's thousand years of reign, and then the final conflict with the unchained devil and his hosts; the wicked are overthrown and cast into Hell, and the righteous rise from their graves to enjoy forever the *vita beata.*

If the *Divinae Institutiones* was written when happier times might be expected, a hundred years had not passed when Alaric sacked Rome, and the world tottered. Pagans, who still constituted a large part of the Empire, laid the catastrophe to Christianity. There was no wide reaction toward paganism — of which there was enough in Christianity. But there was cause for the greatest of Christian intellects since Origen, to construct a work more positive and systematic than the *Contra Celsum;* a work which, with more profundity of thought than could be claimed for Lactantius' *Divinae Institutiones,* should set forth the aim and course and final goal of God's Commonwealth. Augustine's *Civitas Dei* undertook to expound the polity of Him who made the world and man. Under His providence waxed the Empire of the earth, the *civitas terrena,* with its own aims leading away from God. Within the guidance of His love, endured and grew the other city, the heavenly, the *civitas dei*. Two opposite desires — *amores* — made these two commonwealths, and carry them along divergent paths to different ends, the one toward the false good of this life, the other toward the true good of life eternal: *Fecerunt itaque civitates duas amores duo ; terrenam scilicet amor sui usque ad contemptum dei, coelestam vero amor Dei usque ad contemptum sui.*[1] The fortunes of the earthly commonwealth appear through the history of States, until finally all elements of earthly greatness converge in the imperial destiny of Rome. The course of the other commonwealth is traced through the Old Testament; which is shown to be in harmony with what its events and teachings prefigure and prophesy, Christ and the universal Church.

Even the earthly commonwealth, represented in Rome, had not gained its power through the heathen gods, but by its energies, under God's providence. Augustine's work refuted pagan assertions that Rome had stood by the power of her gods: it set forth all the calamities which had come before Christianity; it showed the evil folly of pagan worship, the futility and falsity of pagan philosophy. With all-embracing arguments of universal scope the *Civitas Dei* should utterly invalidate paganism and its claims, and show Christianity's absolute and universal truth.

Like Lactantius, like Arnobius and Cyprian, Augustine had been a professor of rhetoric, and his training often appears in the use of antithesis and word-play

---

[1] *Civ. Dei*, XIV, 28.

in the *Civitas Dei*. It was a work of mighty plan;[1] but its author gave his genius free course in this his final message, and allowed himself to introduce whatever served his general purpose, though it might infringe upon the continuity of some leading theme. The work was too universal to be commonly understood in its entirety, though it was to be a many-chambered store, from which future men were to draw according to their power. Imitation of it as a whole was never attempted.

The *Civitas Dei* attempted to harmonize the validity of Christianity with the verdict of universal history, and to direct the argument *adversum paganos*. The third book took up the story of Rome, to show that her greatness was not due to the aid of her gods, but that it came to her under the providence of the one true God. Augustine's disciple, Orosius, at the master's suggestion, undertook to expand similar historical themes in a history of the world, *adversum paganos*. "Thou hast commanded me that as against the vain rhetoric of those who, aliens to God's Commonwealth, coming from country cross-roads and villages are called pagans, because they know earthly things, who seek not unto the future and ignore the past, yet cry down the present time as filled with evil, just because Christ is believed and God is worshipped; — thou hast commanded that I should gather from histories and annals whatever mighty ills and miseries and terrors there have been from wars and pestilence, from famine, earthquake, and floods, from volcanic eruptions, from lightning or from hail, and also from

---

[1] Augustine tells its scheme in *Retractations*, II, 43.

monstrous crimes in the past centuries; and that I
should arrange and set forth the matter briefly in a
book." [1]

Orosius finds that there were four great kingdoms
corresponding in the *ineffabili ordinatione* (sc. Dei) to
the four quarters of the earth; first the Babylonian
in the East; then the Macedonian in the North; the
African in the South; and, finally, the Roman in the
West.[2] Of these, the two intervening kingdoms of
Africa and Macedonia act as the tutors and curators of
the heritage of empire, which is Rome's from Babylon.
Rome was not ready to assume this empire when the
Babylonian power fell. For Sardanapalus was the
last successor of Ninus, the founder of the Babylonian
empire; and the Medes overthrew Sardanapalus the
same year that Procas, the grandfather of Rhea Silvia,
began to reign over the Latins. All these matters
were so disposed in the mysteries and fathomless
judgment of God, and did not take place through
accident or human power.[3] Following upon these
statements, Orosius sets forth certain further ineffable
chronological coincidences and parallels.

[1] Orosius, *Hist.*, prologue. Beyond the Old and New Testaments
and the Jewish Apocrypha, Orosius uses Latin sources exclusively,
and chiefly those near to his own time. He knows nothing of the
Greek histories of Herodotus or Thucydides. He draws from the
following writers: Livy, Eusebius (Jerome's trans.), Justin (who
drew exclusively from Trogus Pompeius), Eutropius; far less frequently, Cæsar, Suetonius, Virgil, Hirtius, Cicero, Sallust, Florus,
Rufinus, Augustine.

[2] The oldest part of *Sibyllina Oracula*, III, 159–162, has eight
kingdoms: 1, Egypt; 2, Persians; 3, Medes; 4, Ethiopians; 5, As-
syria-Babylonia; 6, Macedonia; 7, Egyptian; 8, Rome.

[3] *Hist.*, II, 2.

The notion of four great monarchies set the plan according to which the Middle Ages divided ancient history; and to mediæval men, chronological correspondences, which never existed in fact, were to be evidences of God's providential guidance of history, as they were to Orosius. It has been said that Orosius finds for history a new principle of organic unity in the thought that all events occur within the purpose and control of God's providence.[1] He discerns most interesting evidence of this in the providential bringing of all nations beneath one rule and into one great peace, under Augustus, in order that when Christ was born the gospel might readily spread among mankind.[2]

The chief argument of Orosius' presentation of history, as against the opponents of Christianity, lay in the long pre-Christian tale of slaughter, pestilence, and calamity. His story is confined to war, seen in its carnage, and to other ill-fortunes of mankind. He had no eye for human progress, for the growth of institutions or culture, nor had he any conception of such development. His main apologetic contention is that the world in his time was less infelicitous than in the periods covered by his histories.[3] His work was the Christian argumentative summary of history, a true

---

[1] Ebert. For the earliest Christian reference to Providence, Ebert cites from Minucius Felix's *Octavius*, Chap. 25, sec. 12: Et tamen ante eos (sc. Romanos) *Deo dispensante* diu regna tenerunt Assyrii, Medii, Persae, Graeci, etiam et Aegyptii. The Stoics had developed an idea of Providence. See Zeller, *Philosophie der Griechen*, III¹, pp. 157 et seq. (3d ed., 1880).

[2] *Hist.*, VI, 1 and 22, and VII, 1.

[3] *Ib.*, V, 1, 2, and 24.

work of the transition period, and one that gave the form for mediæval conceptions of ancient history.

Other Christians had written history before Orosius; as, for instance, Lactantius, also with apologetic aims, *adversum paganos*. The Greek church historian, Eusebius, had composed a history, to show the dignity and antiquity of the Jewish race and the Mosaic teaching, as compared with heathen culture. Jerome translated this, and continued it to his own time. Such writings were narrative arguments for Christianity and its sacred prefigurement in Judaism. With somewhat similar purpose, Jerome wrote his *De Viris Illustribus*, or short accounts of illustrious Christians, in order to show the pagans that the Church was not unlettered, but had its philosophers and scholars. The strain of narrative glorification of the Christian Church is taken up by Jerome's friend and enemy, Rufinus, the diligent translator of Greek Christian writings. His *Historia ecclesiastica* was an abbreviated rendering of Eusebius' Church History; while a more original compilation was his *Vitae Patrum* or *Historia eremita*, which he wrote to commemorate the wonders of ascetic piety seen by him in Egypt.

Sulpicius Severus is another historian of the early part of the fifth century. His classic elegance of language contrasts strangely with the transitional and mediæval character of the substance of his work. His *Chronica*, or *Historia sacra*, a chronological history of Christians and of the Jews regarded as their forerunners, does not appear to have been popular; but his *Vita Sancti Martini* was to be one of the most widely read books in the Middle Ages. Its style was easy,

and its abundance of miracle fell in with mediæval
taste.   It is a typical example of the *Legenda* or *Vita
Sancti*, the number of which becomes legion from the
fourth century onward.[1]

Not unallied with apologetic literature were the
writings directed against heretics, or intended to con-
firm Catholics in their orthodoxy as against heretical
arguments.   Even in the time of the apostles, there
was call for argumentative protests against imperfect
acceptations of Christianity, as appears from Paul's
epistles.   Thereafter came tracts *contra Judaeos* which
served as arguments to show that Judaism had been
superseded by Christianity.   These took the form of
dialogues.[2]   The anti-heretical treatises proper begin
with those against the Gnostics of the second century,
who were quite as much latter-day pagans as Christians.   Hereunder came the anti-gnostic writings of
Irenaeus, bishop of Lyons, and the *Contra Marcionem*
of Tertullian.   This kind of early Christian literature
may be regarded as closing with Augustine's anti-
Manichæan treatises.

Besides writings directed against those whom all
the Church might deem without the Christian pale,
there were dogmatic controversies within the large
and loose circle of men who made claim to orthodoxy.
This mass of theological writing, which was hardly
literature, represented Christian controversies; yet
much of the thought and terminology came from
Greek philosophy, in the terms of which and in the
Greek tongue the dogmas of orthodox Christianity

[1] Cf. Ebert, *op. cit.*, I, 331 et seq., 612 et seq.
[2] Justin's *Dialogue with Trypho* is an example.

were at last formulated by the Eastern Church, and therefrom translated rudely to the Latin of the West.

There was a kind of actually spoken Christian literature, the growth of which was due to the inspiration of Christian teaching and Christian needs. This was the sermon, the Homily, that spoken combination of instruction and exhortation. The Christian themes were more real and living than the productions of pagan rhetoric; but rhetoric gave the form in which Christian orators spoke. The great Greek preachers, Basil, Gregory Nazianzen, Chrysostom, were trained rhetoricians, who employed all the resources of rhetoric in their florid sermons, which, however, contained much matter and were adapted to the situation and the needs of the congregation.[1] The sermons of the great Latin preachers, Ambrose and Augustine, were less florid and more direct and practical.[2] Yet they contain like rhetorical devices, or rather bear witness to a like rhetorical education of their authors. For example, antithesis with a rhyming ending to the contrasted parallels is a characteristic of Cyprian's sermons and of Augustine's. The great Western preachers did not spare pathetic appeals to the emotions of their hearers in a style and language departing from the antique.

The writings already noticed were by well-known men of dignified position in the Church. There remains to be mentioned another sort of prose literature

[1] As, for example, Chrysostom's sermons to the people of Antioch on the destruction of the emperor's images.

[2] The practical moralizing of sermons of Pope Leo I in the middle of the fifth century is noticeable.

of dubious origin, but destined to extraordinary popularity and influence. This was anonymous or pseudonymous. It received the forms in which it survived at an early though indeterminate period, and its puerile character rendered later remodelling unnecessary to adapt it to the romantic credulity of the Middle Ages. Its main source lay in the legends which had grown up around the canonical accounts of the ministry of Jesus and his apostles, and its chief extant examples are the apocryphal Gospels and the apocryphal Acts of the different apostles.[1] These were originally written in Greek. Some of the Greek texts still exist, while in other instances only Latin or Syriac or Arabic translations remain; or again both the Greek version and the translation in one or more of these other tongues are extant. Much of this apocryphal literature received its earliest form among Gnostics or Ebionites; and the narratives were shaped in accordance with the teachings of these heretical or imperfectly Christianized circles. Yet the substance probably was drawn from legends or traditions which were spreading through Christian communities. Later orthodox revisions of these Gospels and Acts omitted the markedly heretical features which made the narratives conflict with Catholic doctrine.

When events have occurred which stir the feelings

---

[1] The titles of the latter in Greek were: —

πράξεις	= acta
περίοδοι	= itinera
θαύματα	= miracula, virtutes
μαρτύριον, τελείωσις	= Passio, consummatio

See Lipsius, *Die Apokryphen Apostelgeschichten*, Einleitung.

and impress the mind, the first accounts relate to facts most vitally affecting those concerned. Whatever lies beyond the central story may be actually forgotten, leaving a fair field for the imaginations of succeeding generations. The four canonical Gospels were properly a εὐαγγέλιον, a good tidings, the announcement and account of the salvation offered to man through Christ. It was left to the affectionate and creative curiosity of the next decades and centuries to supplement the facts of the Gospel story with matter satisfactory to the imagination. Thus the apocryphal Acts fill out the details of the careers of the apostles, regarding whom the Church preserved the scantiest information; and the apocryphal Gospels represent the expansion of tradition, or rather the growth of legend, concerning the portions of Christ's life in regard to which the Four Gospels are silent.[1] There was also need to construct a story of Mary's parentage, childhood, and decease, comporting with the divine dignity of the Blessed Virgin.

The Christian apocrypha tells the story of Joachim and Anna, the parents of the Virgin, a story suggested by narratives of hardly hoped for children, late-born to Sarah in the Old Testament and to Elizabeth in the New, monkish ascetic fancy adding some curious features. It also tells of Mary's girl-

[1] Such a writing as the Gospel of Peter does not come in this general category. That contained topics covered by the Four Gospels, and, with knowledge of their narrative, changed the same to accord with Docetic doctrines. It was written with the purpose not to supplement, but to modify, the canonical accounts; and the extant fragment preserves the distinctly Docetic characteristics of the writing.

hood passed as a virgin in the Temple, until she is given into the guardianship of Joseph. And it narrates her final glorification.[1] In the religious art and literature of the Middle Ages the romantic story of Joachim and Anna is as well known as the Gospel story of the life of Christ, which it regularly accompanies.[2] And from the Middle Ages on through the Renaissance, few subjects in religious art vie in frequency and beauty with the Assumption of the Virgin.

The same Gospels that tell the parentage and girlhood of Mary give details of the Saviour's birth and childhood alike miraculous and foolish, quite on a level with early mediæval miracle-story. Mary's virginity before and after Jesus' birth is established by such naïve circumstantial narrative as would address itself to the common, uneducated mind.[3] Corresponding to like puerile taste, the journey to Egypt is filled with silly miracle,[4] and even more meaningless and void of goodness are the miracles of the child-Saviour. He possesses magic powers, with which he amuses himself, or takes malicious vengeance on his playmates. Where he is, there is no safety for other children; "Teach him," say their parents to Joseph,

[1] See *Protevangelium* of James, *Gospel of Pseudo-Matthew, Gospel of Nativity of Mary, Story of Joseph the Carpenter, Book of John concerning the falling asleep of Mary, The Passing of Mary*.

[2] See the whole story greatly painted by Giotto in the Church of the Arena at Padua.

[3] See *Protevangelium*, 19, 20; *Gospel of Pseudo-Matthew*, 13. J. Strzygowski, *Byzantinische Denkmäler*, Bd. I (1891), refers to representations in art of the proving of Mary's virginity according to the *Protevangelium*.

[4] See *Gospel of Pseudo-Matthew*.

"to bless and not to curse, for he is killing our children." [1]

Not all of this apocrypha touching Jesus confines itself to the periods of his birth and childhood. The story of his trial, crucifixion, and ascension was told in the canonical Gospels; the apocrypha expands even these authoritatively narrated subjects. [2] But where was Jesus' spirit while his body lay in the tomb? The late canonical writing of Jude says that he descended to Hades. This suggestion or tradition was soon mightily elaborated, and the legend comes down to us in the second part of the *Acts of Pilate*, otherwise called the *Gospel of Nicodemus*. [3] This is a narrative of considerable power and dignity; perhaps no other story regarding Christ more forcibly impressed the Middle Ages.

The apocryphal Acts of the various apostles have literary and intellectual traits of the apocryphal Gospels. They offered greater opportunity for the growth of romantic episode. [4] The normal starting-point of

---

[1] *Gospel of Thomas*, 4. See also *Gospel of Pseudo-Matthew*, 26–29. This part of the apocryphal narrative may have been fostered by certain of the Gnostic doctrines of the completed divine nature of Christ from his birth.

[2] See, *e.g.*, the *Acts of Pilate*, first part.

[3] With *Gospel of Nicodemus*, etc., compare *Sib. Orac.*, VIII, 310–313, which mentions the descent into Hades "heralding hope to all the holy ones" there. Ephraim Syrus (died 373 A.D.) describes this descent and the conflict with death and Satan in the *Nisibene Hymns*, XXXV et seq. See *Library of Nicene Fathers*, 2d series, Vol. XIII.

[4] For instance, in the *Acts of Thomas*, the Lord sells Thomas as a slave and handicraftsman to an Indian merchant, the agent of an Indian king, and the merchant takes the apostle to India, to the royal court. This is romantic.

their narratives was the variously told story of the separation of the apostles after Pentecost, in order that each might proceed to the country which the casting of lots had declared to be the field of his missionary labors.[1] Sometimes the apostles set out at the command of the Lord Jesus; and it is often through his miraculous intervention that they reach their haven. The Lord not only guides or transports them there, but continues with them an ever present aid in many forms; he appears as pilot, as a little child, or in the form of an apostle.

These various apocryphal Acts appear to have originated in heretical settings together of tradition, and to have been revised in Catholic circles, as was the case with the apocryphal Gospels. They contain many beautiful legends;[2] yet on the whole, they constitute a popular and puerile literature wherein the magical and the romantic unite. The miracle is the unfailing occurrence; only the natural and rational is absent. It is a mountebank propagation of the faith that these Acts set forth.[3]

Further, the Christian apocryphal Gospels and Acts show traits of puerility, if not of literary decadence, similar to much in the Greek love-romances and the romance of Alexander.[4] They answered to a popular and crude literary taste. They have no perception of fitness. Vitally related sequence is lacking; things

[1] See, *e.g.*, beginning of *Acts of Thomas.*

[2] Above all, the *Domine quo vadis* of the *Acts of Peter and Paul.*

[3] See, for example, the *Acts of Andrew and Matthew in the City of Man-eaters.*

[4] *Ante*, Chap. III.

happen, and, of course, miraculously. Yet the reader may be certain that the Lord Jesus will bring about the conversion of many people through his apostle, as well as that apostle's glorious martyrdom, just as the reader of the Greek romance may be sure that Fortune will bring hero and heroine to wedded bliss at last. Likewise, there is scant delineation of character in this Christian apocrypha; all the apostles suffer meekly, though miraculously destroying, for the example's sake, many of their tormentors; all Jews and heathen rage, until their conversion; the purity of the Virgin Mary is the formal priggishness of a nun; Joseph is uninteresting; the child-Saviour shows no character beyond malice, vengefulness, and premature powers of disputation.

In many forms these apocryphal writings reappear in the Middle Ages. Their incidents are frequently reproduced, or an entire writing is translated, and is altered or added to according to the racehood, the environment, and the individual taste of the translator or adaptor. In its literary and intellectual inferiority, the Christian apocrypha bore the same relation to the New Testament that the Jewish apocrypha bore to the Hebrew Canon of the Old Testament. The Jewish apocrypha was popular in the Middle Ages, and as authoritative as the books of the Hebrew Canon. Likewise, much from the Christian apocrypha was accepted by Church and people, and fills as large a place in popular literature as the canonical narratives.[1]

[1] " On ne s'est pas borné à faire entrer le prétendu évangile de Nicodème dans la plupart des histoires de la passion et de la résurrection de Jésus-Christ; il a pénétré dans la littérature profane.

III. *Mediævalizing of Latin Prose*

The death of Augustine closes the great constructive period of Latin Christian prose, which thereafter is rapidly mediævalized. The diction falls away from what had been idiomatic and correct; it abandons the classic order of words and loses at the same time all feeling for the case endings of nouns and the conjugation of verbs, for which it substitutes prepositions and auxiliaries; many novel words are taken from the common speech.[1] The substance also becomes somewhat debased and barbarized. It frequently consists in a recasting of what the fourth or fifth century had produced, with the addition of whatever appealed to an insatiable credulity.[2] As for literary form, as signifying the unity and artistic ordering rather than the diction of a composition, this does more than decline; judged by any antique standard, it ceases to exist. One cause was the unintelligent recasting of matter taken from the writings of a more intellectual period,

Le récit de la délivrance de Joseph d'Arimathie par le Seigneur a été le point de départ des fictions relatives au 'saint-graal,' et la scène qui nous représente la délibération des princes de l'enfer paraît avoir servi de modèle au conseil des diables par lequel s'ouvre le *Merlin* de Robert de Boron." Gaston Paris, *Trois versions rimées*, etc., Introduction, p. ii.

[1] The *Historia Francorum* of Gregory of Tours (538–594) is an illustration of all of this. Cf. Monceaux, "Le Latin Vulgaire," *Revue des deux mondes*, Tom. 106 (1891). "Mieux vaut être le premier des chroniqueurs romans que le dernier des cicéroniens," *ib.* His Latin is becoming French.

[2] Thus Gregory the Great makes over much doctrinal material from Augustine, while his *Dialogi de vita et miraculis Patrum Italicorum* are filled with monkish miracle.

a recasting which was always attended by an infusion of barbaric and extraneous elements. A vigorous barbaric mind may express fittingly simple subjects of its own devising; but less simple subjects taken by semi-barbaric or partly barbarized writers from works of men their superiors in intellect and culture, will not be adequately treated, and the structure of the composition will be bad. The writer cannot present what he does not understand; and, not perceiving the proper nature and the scope of the subject, he is apt to wander from it. The misappreciation and mishandling of borrowed subjects are one cause of the formlessness of mediæval literature; the effect may appear in the chaotic representation of misappreciated topics from pagan literature, as well as in the distorted treatment of matter taken from the Christian prose writers of the fourth and fifth centuries.

Moreover, the boundless reach of Christian thought, the limitlessness of Christian emotion, and the unfathomable mysteries of the Faith could not be adjusted to those literary forms which suited the clear finitude of classic themes. All attempts thus to adjust Christian topics failed, whether in prose[1] or metre. At the very first, Christian prose writing had only such excellence of form as comes with the sincere and ardent expression of a deeply felt subject; no conscious attention was paid to style or structure. Afterward, when Christians used the resources of pagan literary education, the Christian spirit still had its own con-

---

[1] Whenever a Christian wrote in classic form, his work was apt to be more pagan than Christian, in tone and feeling, if not in thought. *E.g.*, the *Octavius* of Minucius Felix or the *De Officiis Ministrorum* of Ambrose.

tempt for form.[1] All of this prevented mediæval literature from deriving any sense of form from the classics ; and, however else a classic pagan work might be valued in the Middle Ages, the beauty of its form was not thought of. It may also be said, with reference to the mediæval lack of form, that mediæval writers were not anxious to have a subject clear-cut and limited ; but preferred one which was universal or which wandered far and wide — a preference marking the difference between the romantic and the classical.

Through the Middle Ages, however, there were always men who tried to imitate the diction of classic writers, although they did not think to imitate them in the form and structure of their works. This was especially the case in the Carolingian period, when conscious imitation of the Roman past prevailed. Eginhard in his *Vita Caroli* imitates the classical style. Traces of the same tendency appear with his contemporaries, Paulus Diaconus and Servatus Lupus, and afterward with Lambert von Hersfeld.[2]

Such life as there was in mediæval Latin literature was not in this imitation of classic style, but in the disintegration, the barbarization, of Latin diction, to wit, in the tendencies of the written Latin to follow, though at an ever increasing distance, the lines of evolution of the Romance languages from the vulgar

[1] As in the oft-cited words of Gregory the Great, — " quia indignum vehementer existimo, ut verba coelestis oraculi restringam sub regulis Donati," Epistola opening the *Moralium libri;* Migne, *Patr. Lat.*, 75, col. 516.

[2] Cf. Norden, *Antike Kunstprosa*, pp. 748–753, and pp. 680 et seq.

Latin — an evolution unretarded by the classical literary tradition. These vulgar Romance tongues and the barbaric Teutonic languages, which attained their growth under the auspices of the Christian religion, were to develop the capacity of expressing Christian thoughts and voicing Christian feeling. A like though narrower capacity was reached by mediæval Latin prose from which all vestiges of classical style were gone.[1] But a deeper volume of Christian feeling rolled through the Latin hymns, which of all mediæval Latin compositions departed farthest from every classic prototype and advanced farthest in the creation of an original style and form of verse. These currents of life in mediæval Latin were finally extinguished through the attempt of the humanists — Petrarch first and above all — to reawaken and restore classical Latin.

[1] *E.g.* the *De Imitatione Christi.*

CHAPTER IX

CHRISTIAN POETRY

I. *Classic Metre and Christian Emotion*

In order to appreciate the formal and substantial changes through which poetry passed in its course from paganism to Christianity, and from the antique to the mediæval, a clear idea is needed of some general characteristics of Greek verse. The due appreciation and proportionment of life's elements was a principle of Greek life and art and literature. It forbade excess. It was also in happy unison with the Hellene's clear mental vision, his love of definiteness, and his aversion to whatever was unlimited or vague. All of which is exemplified in Greek poetry. Its contents are clear and proportioned, unfailing in artistic unity. Its structure consists of metre, to wit, ordered measure, the ordering of what has definite quantitative proportion.

The contents and form of Greek poetry were closely united. Pindar, creating an epinician ode, composed metre, music, and words. The simpler lyric metres — sapphics, alcaics, iambics — were more fixed; and yet they had been created in correspondence with the nature of verses which express the writer's circumstances and his hates and loves. This was personal poetry, quite different in form and contents from the partly impersonal sententiousness of the elegy, and from the epic, where the heroes, not the poet, speak and act. Both epic and elegy were uttered in moderate musical modes, which in the course of time were levelled into recitative. Such poetry could not be sung, sung fully, like Sappho's love poems or Alcæus' proud personal lyrics. With Sappho and Alcæus words and music were cast together so as to make one song. The music was syllabic, so to speak; one syllable, one note. Nor did the ethos of the music differ from the ethos of the words. The words, however passionate, avoided the monstrous and unmeasured; the music avoided vagueness and excess. Its nature, like theirs, lay in measure and proportion.

The Greeks were eager for the full round of life. Their intellects ordered and proportioned their desires. Many emotions entered their lives and are uttered in their poetry. Beyond reason's dictates they recognized no principle of exclusion. Greek life within its finitude was rounded and complete, both actually and in the idealizations of poetry and sculpture. Emotion contains within itself no leaven of proportionment. It may be strong or weak, violent or gentle; but it remains an impulse to satisfy itself. One emotion may quell another; but, apart from such a conflict and from the exhaustion or satisfaction of an emotion, it is the intellect that imposes restraint and proportion. When these qualities are shown in emotional action, they are imposed by the intellect at the time, or else have been so constantly impressed upon the emotions as to have become spontaneous emo-

tional habit. Because of the intellectual character of
the Greek race the emotion in their poetry is clear
and distinct, definite in its cause, its nature, and its
object, and measured and proportioned. All emotions
are limited; none is excluded.

Thus in the *Iliad* and *Odyssey* no feeling natural
to an early age is barred or even disapproved. A
hero may feel anger, hate, revenge, grief, or fear; he
may feel affection, love, or sexual passion; he may
entertain desires or repulsions of any kind. It is
the same with the women within their lesser range.
Only let no hero do what is shameful or infatuate.
Such action is forbidden by wisdom and by honor
(αἰδώς), which together insure success, respect, and
fame. Honor or reverence, called by Pindar " the
child of forethought," is an ethical sentiment springing from broad intellectual approvals; honor and
wisdom impose measure upon emotions and the acts
they prompt. Measure is never absent from the
characters and conduct of Homer's heroes. They are
passionate, but not unrestrained; and their emotions
are not limitless. One may feel the power of wrath
of wise Odysseus, when at last, bow in hand, he
springs upon the platform, his heart filled with a
rage that was not out of proportion to its cause, a rage
which, once sated, shall fall to calm, the suitors slain.
It is a mighty passion, which the man's strong intellect has held restrained; it is a beautiful passion, and
has its cadences like the bowstring which sang so
sweetly to his ear. Neither are the passions unrestrained of him who was the most deeply passionate
of the heroes. Athene caught him by his yellow

hair, and he thrust back his sword into its sheath.
He also yielded up Briseis. Achilles' deepest passions were his love for Patroclus, his grief for him
slain, and his rage against the slayer. Even this
grief and wrath find their cadences and final calm.
Once the hero feared lest, passion mastering restraint,
he should do a shameful act — so he warns Priam.[1]
The passions of the epics were fitted to the mighty
but finite hexameter. They were like the waves of
ocean, which never lose their measure of rise and fall,
never lose their metre, be it of calm or storm.
Achilles' anger and the torrent of his grief and wrath,
rising, falling, and again rising, resistless but not unrestrained, ever roll within the harmonies of the metre.

The elegiac metre likewise accords with the measured grief which is its burden. Its couplets are composed of a hexameter and a pentameter, that is to
say, a hexameter in which the unemphatic second
half of the third foot is omitted, as well as the first
syllable of the sixth foot, which would have been a
spondee. The result is a solemn slowing of the movement in the middle of the line, and an increase of
stress upon the final syllable by the omission of the
long syllable before it. The pause in the middle of
the pentameter and the stress at its close make it the
emphatic line of the elegiac couplet. The hexameter
is the preparation, the anacrusis, as it were; while
the weight of sententiousness, when the couplet is
gnomic, and the stress of the feeling, when the couplet
is proper elegy, fall on the pentameter, and sometimes with marked emphasis upon the last syllable of

[1] *Il.*, XXIV, 560.

each hemistich. This regular recurrence of emphasis
in an elegiac couplet renders its sententiousness definite and its expression of feeling strikingly measured.
Some examples may be taken. The following couplet
of Theognis summarizes much Greek ethics : —

> Μηδὲν ἄγαν σπεύδειν · πάντων μέσ᾽ ἄριστα · καὶ οὕτως,
> Κύρν᾽, ἕξεις ἀρετήν, ἥντε λαβεῖν χαλεπόν.[1]

These lines express the universal Greek warning,
μηδὲν ἄγαν, "nothing excessively"; also the converse
positive ideal of the "mean," and the relation of these
principles to the achievement of excellence which is
difficult to gain. The stress in the pentameter falls
on the final syllables τήν and πόν, which are the strong
syllables of emphatic words.

Simonides' epitaph on the Spartan dead at Ther-
mopylæ illustrates the preparatory anacrusis function
of the hexameter line, and the weightiness of the
pentameter : —

> ᾿Ω ξεῖν᾽, ἀγγέλλειν Λακεδαιμονίοις, ὅτι τῇδε
> κείμεθα, τοῖς κείνων ῥήμασι πειθόμενοι.[2]

And, finally, the beautiful epitaph on the Eretrian
exiles, ascribed to Plato, exemplifies the measure, the
control, the exquisite rhythm of pathos, which the
elegiac metre might contain.[3]

---

[1] Bergk, *Anthol. Lyrica*, Theognis, 335: "Not too much eager-
ness; best of all is the mean; thus, Kurnos, shalt thou have excellence, which is so hard to catch."

[2] "Stranger, tell the Lacedæmonians that here
We lie, to their laws obedient."

[3] Οἵδε ποτ᾽ Αἰγαίοιο βαρύβρομον οἶδμα λιπόντες
᾿Εκβατάνων πεδίῳ κείμεθ᾽ ἐνὶ μεσάτῳ.
χαῖρε κλυτή ποτε πατρὶς ᾿Ερέτρια, χαίρετ᾽ ᾿Αθῆναι,
γείτονες Εὐβοίης, χαῖρε θάλασσα φίλη.
— BERGK, *Anthol. Lyrica*, Plato, 9.

Little need be said of the iambic trimeters and trochaic tetrameters, so well adapted to narrative which was not of epic size and dignity; adapted also to personal attack and satire. These metres were not suited to pure song, and in a lyric time could hardly hold their own. Yet Archilochus expresses himself as a true Greek in them and bids his soul consider the rhythmic beat of destiny: "Soul, soul! stricken with overwhelming troubles, bear up! and cast back the opposing evil, breast to foe! and neither, conquering, foolishly exult, nor, conquered, wail and cry. But in joys delight, and in evils grieve — not overmuch; so learn what rhythm holds men."[1]

The verses of Sappho give voice to the Greek passion for beauty, beauty the vision; they are poems of the passion with which beauty fires the senses. The intensity of these molten verses has never been surpassed. Yet the emotion is utterly Greek in its expression — limpid, definite, complete, perfect in form, free from vagueness and mysticism. It is controlled and modulated in the exquisite metre through which it is vocalized; nothing unmeasurable is suggested. Reading the two odes which are entire, one is struck with the definiteness of statement as to the cause and nature of the emotion, and the finiteness of the emotion itself.

[1] θυμέ, θύμ' ἀμηχάνοισι κήδεσιν κυκώμενε,
ἀντέχευ, δυσμενῶν δ' ἀλέξευ προσβαλὼν ἐναντίον
στέρνον, ἐν δοκοῖσιν ἐχθρῶν πλησίον κατασταθείς
ἀσφαλέως· καὶ μήτε νικῶν ἀμφάδην ἀγάλλεο,
μήτε νικηθεὶς ἐν οἴκῳ καταπεσὼν ὀδύρεο·
ἀλλὰ χαρτοῖσίν τε χαῖρε καὶ κακοῖσιν ἀσχάλα
μὴ λίην· γίγνωσκε δ' οἷος ῥυσμὸς ἀνθρώπους ἔχει.
— ARCHILOCHUS, *Fr.* 66.

Pindar is a final example of the unison of words, metres, and music in Greek poetry. Emotion is not the most palpable element in his stately strophes, those supremely Greek strophes, themselves such examples of measure and proportion, of which they also sing. Whatever emotions are expressed in his epinician odes are framed in a consideration of all life's factors and are modulated by reason. Pindar is not as naïve as Homer in the admission of emotional desires. Yet he excludes only the unseemly. Likewise the dramatists. Theirs also is a complete consideration of life's factors, including the emotions which come to mortals. Æschylus and Sophocles are deeply concerned with the conflict between human will and overhanging destiny. They contribute to its ethical adjustment by dramatizing the ruin entailed by unrestrained impulse and lawless act. He who does not modulate his acts finds himself wrapped within fate's dread measures.

The metres of the dramas correspond to their substance. The iambic trimeter, well suited to narrative verse, is strengthened and dignified with frequent spondees, while the too rapid anapæst is avoided, though Euripides often uses the still quicker tribrach. The varied strophes of the choral odes suit the substance as closely as with Pindar. Æschylus' weighty thoughts roll in periods unrivalled in sweep and melody. With Sophocles words, metre, music, produce the perfect dramatic whole. Disintegration begins with Euripides. His choral odes tend to fall away from perfect pertinency to the drama. With such discrepancy of contents there can be no perfect form.

His dramas have novel excellences, yet fail in unity and proportion. The emotional contents are more unrestrained. Passion runs riot, though the results still are dire.

The unison of form and substance ceases in the Alexandrian period of literature. Hexameter is used in dialogue and narrative unsuited to the dignity of that metre;[1] or it is used to set forth science or philosophy.[2] The latter was an affectation with the Alexandrians; for an adequate prose was ready to their hand. They had not the reason of Xenophanes or Parmenides for using hexameter — that prose hardly existed. As for the metres of lyric song, the Alexandrians have lost command of them.

Lack of instinctive feeling for the right metre may have been related to the falling away of metrical quantity from the spoken language. Quantity had probably passed from Greek speech before the Christian era; and from whatever time quantity ceased to be the basis of speech, poetry composed in metre necessarily became academic. Its rhythm no longer corresponded with the living language; and the more complicated the metre, the more palpable would be the artificiality of the poem. The tendency was to use the simpler metres, which also passed over into Latin literature. That literature was to be academic rather than spontaneous in its development, the work of men educated in Greek poetry, rhetoric, and philosophy. Greek metres, in somewhat blunted modes, constituted the structure of Latin poetry, and Greek qualities en-

---

[1] *E.g.*, Theocritus, *Idyl*, XV.

[2] *E.g.*, in the Φαινόμενα of Aratos.

tered Latin literature.   Latin feeling was not Greek
feeling.   Yet the expression of emotion in poetry
is necessarily in some accord with the structure of
the verse; and emotional expression in Latin poetry
was affected by the use of Greek metres.   Their early
development had been in unison with the evolution of
the thought and feeling of Greek poetry; they would
always carry with them something of the quality of
its ancient thoughts and sentiments, which might also
survive in the words of the Greek poems or in borrowed Latin phrase.

It may be doubted whether Homer's spirit dwelt in
Ennius' stiff hexameters.   It might be more at ease
in the epic poem in which classical Latin poetry culminated. A lover woos by self-surrender. Virgil wooed
and won the epic hexameter. With what mastery he
made that his own is beautifully and subtly shown in
the Virgilian expression of emotion.   The pagan heart
had matured in the centuries between Homer and Virgil; it had gained in tenderness; sentiments had re-
fined, emotions had deepened.   The older poet com-
passed the emotional range of his age.   Virgil's pure
nature and supremely sympathetic genius held the
noblest feeling of his time.   His contemplative, saddened temperament endued all human situations with
the pathos of mortality, the pathos of heroic endeavor
frustrated or saddened in its success by the hardship
of the toil.   Through all his modes of feeling, through
his great heart's grief over the helplessness of life, his
expression is controlled, beautiful, always in harmony
with the music of his hexameters.   The lover of Virgil may take as illustration any pathetic passage and

may find therein some phase of pathos hardly to be found in a Greek poet. Moreover, Virgilian pathos usually differs from prior modes of emotional expression in that the pathos of the individual situation is deepened by its suggestiveness of the woe of the whole world, whereof it is part. Yet the mode of expression always embodies the Greek qualities of control, modulation, clarity, and beauty. Inasmuch, however, as Virgilian pathos has broader range than pathos in Sappho or Homer, it is not quite so definite and finite in its expression.[1]

Thus Virgil is Greek, and something more. The intense passion of other Latin poets also presents qualities of the metres used and of the sentiments expressed in the Greek poems written in them. Lucretius' contempt and pity seem never to break the roll of his hexameters. Catullus' expression of emotion has the Greek qualities of definiteness, adequacy, point, and necessary limitation. The Greek control is pronounced in Horace, with whom the emotional element is at times hardly strong enough to make his verses poetry. There is genuine feeling whenever he touches upon themes of mortality; but the classic modulation of expression never fails.

The time of a new religion was at hand, and novel thoughts, changed views of life, and modes of emotion heretofore unfelt were soon to seek appropriate poetic forms. Such forms did not exist in the opening centuries of the Christian era. The old metres were no longer in accord with actual speech. The Christian

[1] Cf. Taylor, *Ancient Ideals*, II, pp. 32–40, and examples of pathos from Homer and Virgil there cited.

soul could not express itself in artificial verse. It needed poetic forms which should draw their life from living speech as the classic metres had drawn theirs.

There were other reasons why the old metres were not suited to Christian poetry. The spirit of Christianity was not the spirit of paganism. Christian emotion differed from the emotions of pagan life or pagan literature, and, if it was to become articulate in poetry, it must evolve its own forms of verse. Control, moderation, and inclusiveness were characteristic of the emotions as expressed in classic Greek and Latin poetry. Christian emotion was to be characterized by qualities the opposite of these. Control, moderation, inclusiveness, were absent. Instead, there were both excess and exclusion. The classic μηδὲν ἄγαν was abandoned; the Christian heart could not hold too much love of God. There was no bound to the passion with which the soul should cast itself down before Him. Then there was exclusion. For as Christianity was interpreted in the fourth century and through the Middle Ages it excluded one side of human emotion. True, in the love of God there might be a larger inclusiveness than in the pagan range of feeling; it might hold the proportionment of all mortal affections, as Augustine saw. But the application of such thoughts was defeated by the causes which were making monasticism the ideal of Christian life.

Again, emotion as expressed in classic literature was clear, definite, and finite. Christian emotion was to know neither clarity nor measure. Its supreme

object, God, was infinite; and the emotion directed
toward Him might be vague and mystic, so unlimited
was it. God was infinite and man's soul eternal;
what finitude could enter the love between them?
Classic metres expressed measured feelings. Hexameters had given voice to many emotions beautifully,
with unfailing modulation of calm or storm. They
had never revealed the infinite heart of God, or told
the yearning of the soul responding; nor were they
ever to be the instrument of these supreme disclosures
in Christian times. Such unmeasured feelings could
not be held within the controlled harmonies of the
hexameter nor within sapphic or alcaic or Pindaric
strophes. These antique forms of poetry definitely
expressed their contents, although sometimes suggesting further unspoken feeling, which is so noticeable
with Virgil. But characteristic Christian poetry, like
the Latin mediæval hymn, was not to express its meaning as definitely or contain its significance. Mediæval
hymns are childlike, having often a narrow clearness in
their literal sense; and they may be childlike, too, in
their expressed symbolism. Their significance reaches
far beyond their utterance; they suggest, they echo, and
they listen; around them rolls the voice of God, the
infinitude of His love and wrath, heaven's chorus and
hell's agonies; *dies iræ, dies illa* — that line says little,
but mountains of wrath press on it, from which the
soul shall not escape.

Christian emotion quivers differently from any
movement of the spirit in classic measures. The new
quiver, the new shudder, the utter terror, and the utter
love appear in mediæval rhymed accentual poetry : —

Desidero te millies,
Mi Jesu ; quando venies ?
Me laetum quando facies,
Ut vultu tuo saties ?

Quo dolore
Quo moerore
Deprimuntur miseri,
Qui abyssis
Pro commissis
Submergentur inferi.

Recordare, Jesu pie,
Quod sum causa tuae viae ;
Ne me perdas illa die.

*　　*　　*　　*

Lacrymosa dies illa
Quâ resurget ex favillâ,
Judicandus homo reus ;
Huic ergo parce, Deus !
Pie Jesu, Domine,
Dona eis requiem.

Let any one feel the emotion of these verses and then turn to some piece of classic poetry, a passage from Homer or Virgil, an elegiac couplet or a strophe from Sappho or Pindar or Catullus, and he will realize the difference, and the impossibility of setting the emotion of a mediæval hymn in a classic metre.[1]

II. *Greek Christian Poetry*

Christian poetry would naturally be drawn from the narratives of the Old and New Testaments, and the

---

[1] The *Veni sancte spiritus* (Clement, *Carmina e Poetis Christianis*, p. 404) is an example of how much there is outside the lines, yet carried or suggested by the hymn.

continually increasing volume of Christian story, or would consist of the sentiments and emotions which were deepening from generation to generation in Christian souls. Holy Scripture could not be moulded anew to suit the needs of creative poetry in the way that the Greek and Roman poets recast the tales of pagan mythology. The canonical narratives remained indubitable facts authoritatively stated. Although they were interpreted both allegorically and literally, no one changed them. Original narrative Christian poetry was not written until the heroism of martyrs furnished material which the imaginative Christian memory might cherish reverently and hand on through that universalizing process which raises fact to poetry. The poetic intention still would be to tell the truth, but the poet was not hampered in his truth-telling by sacred narrative.[1]

Somewhat analogous conditions affected and perhaps retarded the composition of Christian lyric poetry. The fundamental, as it were, theistic, emotional attitude of the Christian soul was already authoritatively

---

[1] The first Christian narrative poems, which were creations and not paraphrases, were in Latin, the ballads of Prudentius upon the heroic careers of martyrs, composing his *Peristephanon*. To these we might add two hymns from his *Cathemerinon;* IX, *Hymnus omnis horae*, and XII, *Hymnus Epiphaniae*, which are lyrical narrative poems with Biblical subjects. It was after his time that Avitus wrote a veritable poem on the Fall of Man. This is the piece of Biblical narrative that has been most successfully treated in narrative poetry; the brief Biblical account is suited to dramatic and narrative expansion. The subject-matter of the Old and New Testament narratives has lent itself more frequently to great art than to great poetry; for the sacred story came down authoritatively told, but not authoritatively illustrated.

voiced, and with fervor and universality. The first
Christians were Jews, and the Christian communities
took from the synagogue the custom of singing God's
praises, as well as the songs in which to sing them.
For three centuries the Psalms constituted the main
body of Christian devotional song. It was a paschal
psalm that Christ and his disciples sang on the night
of his betrayal.[1] The apostle Paul bids his hearers
be filled with the Spirit, speaking one to another in
psalms and hymns and spiritual songs (ψαλμοῖς καὶ ὕμνοις
καὶ ᾠδαῖς πνευματικαῖς), singing and making melody
(ᾄδοντες καὶ ψάλλοντες) in your heart to the Lord.[2]
Here the "psalms" mean psalms of David or psalms
derived from them;[3] the "hymns" are songs of praise;
the "spiritual songs" (cantica spiritualia in the Latin
version) are more specifically songs directly inspired
by the Spirit. But the exhortation "be filled with
the Spirit," and speak or sing, applies to all these
utterances, and indicates that, just as the brother
might be moved to sing an Old Testament psalm, so
in the singing he might be moved to vary from it, or
voice his feelings in new-formed utterances, probably
consisting mainly of combinations of Biblical phrases.

Canonical examples of these Christian hymns are
Mary's Magnificat, and Zachariah's song of praise,[4]
both of which consist largely of Old Testament
phrases. The angel's song, Glory to God in the highest and on earth peace, good will to men,[5] was enlarged

---

[1] Mat. xxvi. 30; Mk. xiv. 26. See Thayer's *New Testament Lexicon*; Edersheim, *Life of Christ*, Bk. V, Chap. 12.

[2] Eph. v. 19, 20; Col. iii. 16.   [3] Cf. 1 Cor. xiv. 15, 26.

[4] Luke i. 46, etc., and 67, etc.   [5] Luke ii. 14.

into the matin hymn, the ὕμνος ἀγγελικός of the Greek liturgy, of which the Latin *doxologia magna* is the equivalent. These compositions are not metrical, and their structure preserves the parallelism of Hebrew poetry.

Thus the earliest poetical expressions of Christian emotion in the Greek tongue were Hebraistic in form. Likewise their contents were more Hebraic than Greek. The Hebrew devotion to God was the prototype of the Christian's love. It had always been unmeasured, absolute, quite different from anything in classic Greek or Latin literature. Now a like devotional feeling was to seek expression in strange languages whose chief poetic forms were dead or academic. Yet, although academic and otherwise unsuited to express Christian feeling, metre was the only form of verse familiar to educated Greek and Latin Christians, and metrical Christian poetry was written in both these tongues. We may trace its failure and early disappearance in Greek. In Latin it had some temporary success.

In the first place there was a partly pre-Christian Græco-Jewish hybrid. The earliest portions of the extant pseudo-Sibylline Oracles were composed at Alexandria by Hellenized Jews in the second century before Christ. Judaic Christians added some hundreds of lines toward the close of the first century A.D.; and in the course of the second and third centuries, Christians or Judaic Christians brought the collection to its present bulk. Much space would be needed to analyze the contents of this series of pseudo-prophetic pictures of the world's history from the creation to the

Last Times. They are lurid with hatred of the heathen nations, of Rome above all. From the time of Justin Martyr many Christian Fathers accepted them, and so the ancient Sibyl entered the company of those who prophesied of Christ. Through the Middle Ages the Sibyl remained a great name in poetry and art.

These Sibylline Oracles show some Hellenistic literary skill. The metre is hexameter, and many lines contain queer twisted survivals of Homeric phrase, which impart a grotesque epic flavor to the whole. Jewish fanaticism and Christian feeling break through occasionally; but on the whole, hexameter metre and epic reminiscence dominate the form and influence the matter of the verses, curiously affecting the emotional contents. Even in the oldest Jewish[1] or Judaic-Christian[2] portions, there is slight trace of Hebraic parallelism of statement, but much Homeric adjective and epithet.

Christian feeling struggles to expression in those portions of the sixth and eighth books which are not earlier than the third century; but the expression is still affected by epic phrase and by the hexameter. The famous acrostic begins at line 217 of Book VIII: ΙΗΣΟΥΣ ΧΡΕΙΣΤΟΣ ΘΕΟΥ ΥΙΟΣ ΣΩΤΗΡ ΣΤΑΥΡΟΣ. It closes with a glorification of the Cross; and then comes a reference to Moses conquering Amalek by faith, stretching out his arms;[3] in which act Moses is symbolical of Christ. Lines 256–259 delineate Christ's in-

---

[1] *Sib. Orac.*, III, 97–294; *ib.*, 489–817 (second century B.C.)

[2] Bk. IV, cir. 80 A.D.

[3] VIII, 251.

carnation as his first coming to judgment, and with a
realization of its great condescension;

> Οὐδὲ γὰρ ἐν δόξῃ, ἀλλ' ὡς βροτὸς εἰς κρίσιν ἥξει,
> Οἰκτρὸς, ἄτιμος, ἄμορφος, ἵν' οἰκτροῖς ἐλπίδα δώσει . . .

There follows a short review of Christ's works until
he gives himself for the world a 'pure virgin,' παρθένον
ἀγνήν.[1]

In a subsequent part of the same book is told the
annunciation, the incarnation, and then the birth of
Christ, — a child from "virgin parents a great marvel
to mortals," μέγα θαῦμα βροτοῖσιν;[2] and if this phrase
does not transport us from Bethlehem to Troy, we are
at least carried part way to Ida by the lines which
follow: —

> Τικτόμενον δὲ βρέφος ποτεδέξατο γηθοσύνη χθών ·
> Οὐράνιος δ' ἐγέλασσε θρόνος, καὶ ἀγάλλετο κόσμος.[3]

Such passages relate to Christian matters, yet contain little Christian feeling,[4] which, however, breaks
through the hexameter in the sixth book, when the
blessed Cross is apostrophized in words prefiguring

[1] VIII, 291.

[2] VIII, 473; cf. Od., XI, 287. The more frequent Homeric phrase
is θαῦμα ἰδέσθαι; e.g., Il. XVIII, 83, 377, — but the βροτοῖσιν is so very
classic in its suggestion.

[3] The words are not those of the description of Zeus and Hera
on Ida, in Il., XIV, 347, etc.; but compare Il., XIX, 362. These passages, like others in the Sibylline Oracles, suggest passages in Homer,
but do not reproduce them.

[4] The incompatibility of hexameter with Hebraic feeling appears
in the translation by the younger Apollinarius (390 A.D.) of the
sixty-sixth psalm into Greek hexameters. The result is something
too Homeric for a psalm and too Hebraic to be really Greek, as
Bouvy says, Poètes et Mélodes, pp. 43–51.

that veneration of power in humility which encircles
thoughts of the Cross in later literature and art: —

Ὦ ξύλον ὦ μακαριστόν, ἐφ᾽ ᾧ θεὸς ἐξετανύσθη, . . .

"O most blessed wood on which God was stretched;
earth shall not hold thee, but thou shalt see the heavenly house when the face of God shall gleam burning
anew."

The later portions of the Sibylline books contain
metrical irregularities indicating that quantity as the
principle of verse formation was beginning to find a
rival in a fresher principle more in accord with the
actualities of speech, to wit, accent. Frequently in
these verses a short syllable appears lengthened because of the accent, or a long syllable shortened, when
the accent falls on another syllable of the word.[1]

The struggle for supremacy between metre and
accent appears in two early Christian compositions,
which express true Christian feeling. The first of
these is a poem found at the end of the *Paedagogus* of
Clement of Alexandria, who died between 211 and
218 A.D. If not written by him, it is not much later
than his time. The lines are short and simple; but
metricians differ as to whether the metre is iambic
or anapæstic. It seems to be constructed largely of
anapæstic words rather than anapæstic feet; that is
to say, it contains many words of three syllables,
accented on the final syllable, which is also long in
quantity. At all events, accent is asserting itself as
a vital force. The verses are addressed to Christ, and
are filled with images showing the many ways in

[1] See Bouvy, *op. cit.*, pp. 127–132.

which Christ was then thought and felt by the Christian soul.

> "Bridle of untamed colts,
> Wing of straight-flying birds,
> Sure helm of helpless ones,
> Shepherd of the King's sheep,
>> Thine own simple
>> Children lead
>> Holily to praise
>> Guilelessly to sing
>> With sinless mouths
> The children's leader, Christ.
>
> King of the holy ones,
> All conquering word
> Of the highest Father,
> Prefect of wisdom,
> Support of burdens,
> Rejoicing eternally,
> Of the mortal race
> Saviour Jesus.
>
> Shepherd, husbandman,
> Helm, bridle,
> Heavenly wing
> Of the hallowed flock,
> Fisher of men
> Who are saved,
> Catching with the bait of sweet life
> The holy fishes
> From the hostile wave
> Of the sea of evil.
>
> Lead, shepherd
> Of the speaking sheep,
> Lead, holy one,
> King of unharmed boys.

Footprints of Christ,
Heavenly way,
Word everlasting,
Time unbounded,
Eternal light,
Font of mercy,
Doer of good,
Holy life,
God of those who sing praises,
Christ Jesus,
Heavenly milk
Of the sweet breasts
Of the bride of grace.

* * * *

Let us sing together,
Let us sing simply
The mighty child,
(We) the choir of peace,
The Christ-begotten,
The sober folk,
Let us sing a psalm
To the God of peace.[1]

If we disregard the lyric passages of the New Testament, this hymn is perhaps the earliest outpour in verse of the Christian soul that has come down to us.

The second of these compositions is the work of Methodius (martyred in 311, probably at Tyre). In his didactic and partly allegorical work, the *Symposium of the Ten Virgins*, modelled — afar off — on Plato's *Symposium*, each virgin talks lengthily in praise of virginity. Their views and sentiments, however, are at the end fused into feeling in a genuine

[1] The translation is literal, line for line, but does not attempt to reproduce the metre.

lyric, the hymn of praise to Christ the bridegroom, which is sung by one of the virgins, while the others respond in chorus with recurring refrain. The metre is iambic, but with so many violations of quantity as to indicate that the poet — a learned man — realized the existence of accent as a principle of verse. In form the hymn appears related to the classic Parthenia, as of Pindar and Alcman, some fragments of which remain. But instead of Greek maidens singing a glad farewell to maidenhood, here Christian virgins utter the soul's ecstasy on its mystic espousals unto everlasting virginity. "I am pure for thee, and bearing lighted torches, O bridegroom, I go to meet thee" — this is the choral refrain; and the verses hymn the joy of the virgin soul as it hears the call of the heavenly bridegroom and hastens to meet him clothed in white, gladly fleeing the marriage bed and the mournful joys of mortals, yearning for the shelter of the bridegroom's life-giving arms and for the sight of his beauty. The closing strophes draw the Old Testament types of virgin chastity into this song of praise.

A comparison of these poems with the correct metrical compositions of Gregory Nazianzen and Synesius goes far to show that the simple and sincere tone of the earlier compositions is not unrelated to their violation of metre and recognition of the force of accent. The poems of Synesius and Gregory, on the other hand, illustrate the final failure of metrical Christian poetry in Greek. Synesius, the younger of the two, never dropped his Neo-platonism.[1] He composed a number of hymns metrically correct; but his

[1] *Ante*, p. 78.

confused sentiments did not allow him to express distinctly Christian feeling. It was quite different with the fervent Gregory Nazianzen, whose pulpit oratory held Christian hearts enthralled. His was a poetic, emotional nature; his rhetorical powers were great; and he composed many metrical hymns quite Christian in their sentiments. But they never touched the people, as his sermons moved them; nor were they ever taken into the liturgy. They afford an example of compositions according with the literary taste of the latter part of the fourth century, a taste so trained in classical poetry and metre that it could not readily conceive of poetry based on other principles. Such academic taste was scarcely conscious that metre no longer bore any real relation to the sound of living speech, and that metrical poems in consequence could no longer possess the breath of life.

There was, however, a living speech and utterance based upon that which makes a polysyllabic word a unity and gives to spoken language rhythm and emphasis. This was the word-accent. Although colloquial language was not cast in the balanced periods of orators, and oratorical utterance outsoared common speech, accent was as dominant in one as in the other. However, as metre was the only principle of verse-structure recognized in the Greek world, all unmetrical compositions were regarded as prose. The Old Testament, as used by the Eastern Church, was a translation from the Hebrew; and the New Testament was written in a Semitically influenced Greek which expressed thought simply and directly, regardless of rhetorical conventions. Both Testaments were unsuited for translation in any classic metre. The churches were accustomed to give utterance to their faith and feeling in scriptural phrases. There always had been singing. The simplest singing is melodious, and tends to bring into a rhythmic order whatever words are sung. It was natural and easy to bring Greek words to an accentually rhythmic order, that is, an order having a regular recurrence of accented syllables. Since the men who directed this choral worship had little conception of poetry based on accentual rhythm, they were not conscious that they were bringing into existence a new form of poetry. But such was the fact.

There existed, moreover, rhythmic precedents which influenced the progress of liturgical chant. From the time of the Sophist Gorgias, all Greek prose that had style, and embodied rhetorical principles as understood by antiquity, was rhythmical; that is to say, within its periods the succession of strong sounds was ordered so as to yield a rhythm pleasing to the ear, and suited to the elevated and semi-musical manner in which dignified compositions were read or recited.[1] Such prose was not regarded as poetry, and did not in classical times develop definite parallelisms of accentual and strophic forms. So long as quantity survived in speech, the rhythm of prose would in part depend on it; but as quantity ceased to exist, the prose rhythm became more exclusively dependent upon accent, which had always made part of it. Rhythmic prose continued in vogue among rhetoricians and orators into the Christian period. It is marked in the

[1] See Norden, *Die antike Kunstprosa*, p. 41 et seq.

sermons of the Greek preachers, Chrysostom, Basil, and Gregory Nazianzen. Such rhythms needed only to be more definitely ordered into parallel cadences and strophes to present forms of accentual verse.

Thus Greek accentual verse probably sprang from rhythmic prose.[1] And so in all likelihood did rhyme. The word rhyme has no connection with the word rhythm, nor is rhyme necessary to accentual verse. Nevertheless, rhyme was usually present. On the other hand, in classical Greek metrical poetry, rhymes, if not accidental, were never an essential element of metrical verse structure. But apparently it was otherwise in Greek rhythmic prose, where frequently rhymes occur deepening and defining the accentual rhythm; they are marked in the emotional climaxes of oratorical speech, and are clearly intended to add emphasis. As Greek accentual verse took the suggestion of its rhythmic structure from rhythmic prose, it probably took rhyme from the same source.

Besides his metrical hymns already alluded to, Gregory Nazianzen composed two hymns, the rhythm of which was dependent on accent. They were not fully successful, for accentual verse was in a rudimentary stage.[2] Its forms, perfected in line and

---

[1] Cf. Norden, *op. cit.*, p. 843, etc.; Krumbacher, *Geschichte der byzantinischen Literatur*, § 291, pp. 702–705 (2d ed.). For another view, that Latin and Greek Christian accentual poetry was deeply influenced by Semitic — *i.e.* Syrian — forms, see W. Meyer, " Anfang, etc., lat. und griech. rhythmischen Dichtung," *Abhand. Bayr. Akad. Philos.-Philol. Classe*, Bd. XVII (1886), p. 369 et seq.; Hubert Grimme, *Strophenbau in den Gedichten Ephraems des Syrers* (1893), p. 77 et seq.

[2] These two hymns were Gregory's *Evening Hymn* and his *Hymn upon Virginity*. See, for metrical criticism and text, W. Meyer,

strophe, were yet to be created.   The history of
Greek accentual hymns during the fifth century is
obscure;   but at its close they attain the climax of
their glory in the work of Romanos.   Before his time
the accentual hymn had been reaching that stage where
a great poet might bring it to its perfection, just as
choral poetry had by the time of Pindar progressed to
the point where he received and perfected it.   There
is a parallel between the culmination of the choral
lyric in Pindar and the Greek hymn in Romanos; as
Pindar composed together words, metre, and music,
Romanos composed music, words, and the accentual
strophic forms, though sometimes he made repeated
use of the same tunes and strophic forms, which was
not Pindar's way.

The structure of Romanos' hymns rested upon accent and the number of syllables.   Each hymn opens
with a procemion of from one to three strophes.   Then
follows the body of the hymn, written in a different
verse, the first strophe of which was called the *hirmos*.
Every line in the hirmos differs from the others in
rhythm and the number of syllables.   The succeeding strophes, called *troparia*, correspond with the hirmos line by line in accent and number of syllables.
Thus these hymns fulfilled the requirements of songs
to be sung to a tune, which extended through one
strophe and was repeated in the next.   Every strophe
closes in the same words, making a refrain throughout

op. cit., pp. 313 and 400 ; Bouvy, op. cit., p. 133 ; Christ, Anthol. Gr.
Car. Chr., p. 29.   In the manuscripts of Gregory's writings these
hymns are placed among his prose works, a fact of interest in connection with the origin of accentual and rhyming Greek Christian
verse.

the hymn. Rhyme is present, but the verse does not depend on it as essentially as upon accent and number of syllables. Acrostics also are frequent.

The hymns of Romanos are not short, nor are they simple either in verse-structure or contents; but they are magnificent. They are lyrical and dramatic narratives, long for lyrics, though short for narrative poems, like Pindar's fourth Pythian ode or the seventy-eighth Psalm. They carry much feeling, and they pray or exhort. They exhibit tendencies toward the expression of theological dogma, wherein they reflect the Eastern Church. Also, in their stateliness and form and in their occasional lack of diversity, they exhibit the qualities which may be seen in ecclesiastical Byzantine art. A Byzantine poet, amid the pomp of the present, and with the ecclesiastical and dogmatic development of the past inbred in him, could hardly reproduce the evangelical simplicity of the Gospels. Romanos' hymns were farther removed from this than the hymns of the Western Church. In his hymn to the nativity the baby Christ is ὑπερούσιος (supra-essential), and is felt to be so throughout the hymn. In its refrain he is παιδίον νέον, ὁ πρὸ αἰώνων θεός, the "new-born child, God before all ages." Likewise the *Hymn of the Virgin at the Cross* is a stately dialogue between the Virgin and her divine Son, in which he shows her the necessity of his crucifixion. It has none of the convulsed sorrow of the *Stabat Mater*. On the other hand, there is deep emotion in the hymn upon Judas the Betrayer, with its refrain of Ἵλεως, ἵλεως, ἵλεως, γενοῦ ἡμῖν! The poet's dramatic power is marked, some of his hymns moving dramatically to a climax.

Romanos was the greatest of Greek hymn writers. Yet he was not the author of perhaps the most celebrated hymn of the Greek Church, the ᾿Ακάθιστος of Sergios, so called because it was sung with the congregation standing. This magnificent and prolonged chant of adoration to the Virgin, uttered by all creatures, appears to have been written in 625. After this time, though the liturgic poetry of the Greek Church made some formal progress, the period of poetic decline soon set in.

III. *Early Latin Christian Poetry*

Latin Christian poetry differed in many ways from the Christian poetry of the Hellenic East. In the West, metre was abandoned more slowly,[1] and accentual verse came through a different process. The Greek accentual verse was not reached through substitution of accent for quantity in the old metrical forms of poetry, but had its antecedents in Greek rhythmic prose. In Latin Church poetry, quantity gradually gave way to accent, while some of the metrical forms of verse were retained. Accentual verse, so derived, tended for some centuries to keep to strophes composed of lines of the same rhythm and

[1] The long maintenance of metre in Christian Latin poetry was not unconnected with the circumstance that Latin, as written, was becoming a learned language, in diminishing correspondence with the common speech of daily life; poetry written in it would not be so strongly drawn from metre to accentual rhythm by the actualities of speech. In daily life men used the vulgar Latin, which was turning into Provençal, French, Spanish, and Italian.

number of syllables; there was no such tendency in Greek accentual verse, derived from the freer and more diversified periods of rhythmic prose.

Besides preserving the general forms of certain of the old verses, mediæval Latin poetry developed new forms of verse, characterized by novel and effective rhymes. The origin of these rhymes is not clear. We know merely that assonance turning to rhyme gradually became a marked feature of Latin verse during the period from the fifth to the ninth centuries, while the cognate change from quantity to accent was in progress.

In contents, also, and in form as affected by the contents, Latin Christian poetry differed from the Greek.[1] Beginning with Hilary and Ambrose, there

---

[1] With the exception of some Latin adaptations of early Greek hymns (e.g., the *Gloria in excelsis*), the Greek accentual hymns do not appear to have exerted direct influence upon the development of Latin Christian poetry. It was otherwise with regard to the music and the manner of singing the antiphonal psalms and anthems. Antiphonal psalmody originated in the church of Antioch in the middle of the fourth century. The church of Milan under St. Ambrose first adopted it in the West. See Paulinus, *Vita S. Ambrosii*, 13; Augustine, *Conf.*, IX, 7; Gévaert, *La Mélopée antique dans le chant de l'église latine*, p. 82 et seq.; Ebert, *op. cit.*, I, pp. 178, 179. The melodies and chants of the liturgy, commonly known as the Gregorian Chants and attributed to Gregory the Great (590–604), were chiefly due to popes of the seventh and early part of the eighth century who were Greek by race or education (Gévaert, *Les Origines du chant liturgique de l'église latine; ib., La Mélopée antique*, etc., Introduction, and Chaps. IV and V). This view, however, is contested; see Gévaert, Introduction to *Mélopée antique*, for a list of his opponents and their arguments. Also, W. Brambach, *Gregorianisch. Bibliograph. Lösung der Streitfrage über den Ursprung des gregorianischen Gesanges*. Also regarding the influence of Greek hymns upon Latin sequences, see W. Meyer,

were many short and simple, yet doctrinally correct, devotional hymns, unlike any Greek compositions. Latin poetry has also lengthy compositions of a partly narrative and partly lyric character, presenting a general correspondence to the Greek hymns. But they were simpler in structure, and may be compared with the mediæval and modern ballad and elegy of which they were the forerunners. Latin poetry contained also long didactic or apologetic or polemic poems, as well as long poetical paraphrases of the Gospel story or of parts of the Old Testament.

The service of song and chant in Latin churches, as in the Greek, originated in Biblical phrases and translations. Some of the early Latin chants, however, like the *Gloria in excelsis*, may have been taken from Greek Church adaptations,[1] and not directly from the Scripture. There also existed in the fourth century translations of poetical passages from the Old Testament, into eleven-syllable phalaecian verse.[2] Aside from these early adaptations, Latin hymn writing begins apparently with St. Hilary of Poictiers, though the authenticity of the hymns attributed to him is not beyond dispute.[3] With St. Ambrose, we

---

"Anfang, etc., der lat. und griech. rhythmischen Dichtung," *Abhand. Bayer. Akad. Philos.-Philol. Classe*, Bd. XVII (1886), p. 357 et seq.; Bouvy, *Poètes et Mélodes*, pp. 376–378; Christ, *Anthol. Gr. Car. Chr.*, p. **xxv**; Krumbacher, *Gesch. byzantin. Lit.*, p. 682 (2d ed., 1897).

[1] *I.e.* from the ὕμνος ἀγγελικός of the Greek liturgy.

[2] *E.g.*, of Ex. xv., Num. xxi., Deut. xxxiii., to be found in Pitra's *Spicilegium Solesmensi*, I, pp. 187, 243, 253.

[3] Cf. U. Chevalier, *Poésie Liturgique*, pp. 56–66; Ebert, *Ges.*, etc., Vol. I (2d ed.), pp. 142 note, and 172–173; St. Hilary of Poictiers, in the *Library of Nicene Fathers*, 2d series, Vol. IX, Intro-

are on firmer ground, as he wrote at least four of the hymns attributed to him.[1]

These noble and dogmatically careful hymns have an antique clarity of phrase; they probably reflect the exigencies under which they were composed, to hearten the souls of the orthodox and keep them in the true faith, under the perils of Arian conflicts. They were written to be sung by the congregation, and have continued in liturgical use. The metre is iambic dimeter, one of the simplest of the antique, and is correct throughout.[2] Each hymn consists of thirty-two lines divided into four-line strophes.

Between the time of Ambrose and the tenth century, compositions in this most widely used hymn-form gradually changed from quantity to accent, and became rhymed. They afford a complete illustration

duction, pp. xlvi et seq. The hymns contained in the manuscript discovered by Gamurrini at Arezzo in 1884 (*S. Hilarii Tractatus de Mysteriis et Hymni*, Rome, 1887), which some think to have been written by Hilary, were doctrinally correct and polemically pointed against the Arians. They are not metrical (see Gévært, *La Mélopée antique*, etc., p. 64), and may be compared with Augustine's hymn, *Contra Donatistos*. This was alphabetical (as was the hymn attributed with greatest probability to Hilary) like an alphabetical psalm. It was written for the people, and is accentual and not in metre, each line ending in *e* and each strophe opening with the same refrain. Text in Du Meril, *Poésies Populaires Latines*, I, p. 120. Neither this hymn, nor the one attributed to Hilary, has poetic merits.

[1] To wit: *Veni redemptor gentium, Aeterne rerum conditor, Jam surgit hora tertia*, and *Deus Creator omnium.*

[2] As these ancient Latin hymns followed classic metre, they also adopted the current melodies of Greek and Roman lyric song, and gradually modified or transformed them. On this subject, see Gévært, *Les Origines*, etc., pp. 23–33, and *ib.*, *La Mélopée antique*.

of the change from quantity to accent within the same form of verse. The hymns of Ambrose rest altogether upon quantity and ignore the accent, which frequently falls on short syllables, and is in apparent conflict with the stress and movement of the verse. The next step is the retention of quantity combined with an attempt to observe the accent; *i.e.* to make the syllables which are long by nature or position coincide with the tonic accent of the words.[1] This stage is reached by the alphabetic hymn to Christ of Sedulius (circ. 450), in which, moreover, rhyme has become an element of the verse.[2] It is also noticeable that as this iambic dimeter changes to accent and acquires rhyme, the poems written in it contain more Christian emotion; with the disintegration of metre the emotional expression of the dawning Middle Ages is loosed. As an illustration of this, the *Deus Creator omnium* of Ambrose may be compared with a somewhat later hymn showing the beginnings of rhyme, and irregularities of metre through the encroachment of accent upon quantity.

> *Deus creator omnium*
> *Polique rector, vestiens*
> *Diem decoro lumine,*
> *Noctem soporis gratia,* —

---

[1] A tendency in this direction appears in the hexameters of two fifth-century pagan poets, the one writing in Greek, the other in Latin, Nonnos and Claudian. See Bouvy, *Poètes et Mélodes*, pp. 144–149.

[2] Printed in Clement, *Carmina*, etc., p. 175, and in Du Meril, *Poésies Populaires*, and in Humer's edition of *Sedulius*. It is composed of twenty-three four-line verses, beginning with the successive letters of the alphabet, and telling the important facts of the Saviour's life.

reverentially and with ordered thoughts, the hymn apostrophizes God the Creator and Ordainer. The fourth strophe delineates the religious attitude of the soul toward Him.

> *Te cordis ima concinant,*
> *Te vox canora concrepet,*
> *Te diligat castus amor,* ˎ
> *Te mens adoret sobria.*

The tone of this adoring strophe is given by the words *castus* and *sobria* — let *castus amor* wait on thee, *mens sobria* adore thee.   It is stately and contained, antique in mode of expression.

The other hymn, *In Ascensione Domini*, has been improperly ascribed to Ambrose, yet is prior to the seventh century.   It is more emotionally loving: —

> *Jesu, nostra redemptio,*
> *Amor et desiderium;*

how different in tone from the

> *Te diligat castus amor,*
> *Te mens adoret sobria.*

And the last strophe shows the coming of rhyme and its effect upon the tone: —

> *Tu esto nostrum gaudium*
> *Qui es futuris praemium,*
> *Sit nostra in te gloria*
> *Per cuncta semper saecula.*[1]

In the full Middle Ages, as with Adam of St. Victor, the accentual and rhymed iambic dimeter is found undergoing modifications which add to the emotional

---

[1] This hymn is in Clement, *Carmina e poetis Christianis*, p. 65.

quality or enable the poet to perfect the unison of sentiment and verse.[1] Thus a number of wonderful verse-forms and rhymes came into being, fitted to express the emotion which through the centuries had been gathering in Christian souls. A voice had thus been found for the feelings roused by the Gospel story, including those which might be attributed to Gospel personages, as in the *Stabat Mater*, through which wells the grief of the Virgin at the Cross. Similarly Christian hymns may tell the story of martyrs lyrically, and utter the feeling excited by their saintly heroism and blessed lot.[2]

We pass to the Latin poems which combine lyric with narrative or dramatic elements. The lyric element consists either in devotional feeling toward Christ or some martyred saint having power to aid, or in saddened loving sentiments touching the subject of the poem, living or dead. In the former case the poem is of the nature of a hymn, in the latter of the

[1] *E.g.*, in the *Heri mundus exultavit*, and other hymns in like metre.

[2] In these references to the change from metrical to accentual verse it is not intended to imply that the disintegration of metre was due to Christianity; for it was primarily due to the falling away of quantity from the Greek and Latin tongues, — and Latin may have always had its popular accentual verses. The Christian genius, seeking to express itself in poetry in the centuries when quantity was no longer observed in speaking, gradually availed itself of accent, which as the basis of actual speech was now the natural basis for living verse ; and, in fact, forms of accentual verse were evolved suited to the expression of Christian feeling. It is the writer's opinion that Christian feeling could not have been as adequately expressed in classic metres, which had been evolved in correspondence with the expression of quite different kinds of feeling.

nature of an elegy. The characters sometimes speak in the first person — dramatically. The narratives are not given such breadth and extent as to bring them into the category of epic poetry.

The greatest Christian poet of the fourth and fifth centuries was the Spaniard Prudentius, who was born in 348 and died sometime after 405. He and his amiable contemporary, Paulinus of Nola, unite classic culture with Christian sentiment. The resulting product is interesting, often charming, sometimes admirable. Rarely does either poet attain to great poetry or express feeling deeply and truly interpretative of Christ. Yet the feeling is as genuine as could exist under the limitations of classical verse-forms and a rhetorical literary epoch. Prudentius' hymns were literary, rather than adapted for worship, and none of them in its entirety was used as a church song.

The *Liber Cathemerinon* of Prudentius consisted of twelve hymns ranging in length from eighty to two hundred and twenty lines. The first six were written for the six daily hours of prayer. They contain much symbolism.[1] The facts are chosen with regard to their symbolical import, and are told briefly, symbolically as it were.[2] In the ninth hymn, *Hymnus omnis horae*, the deeds and incidents of Christ's life are told succinctly, or apostrophized somewhat as Jehovah's deliverances of Israel are narrated in the seventy-eighth Psalm. The twelfth hymn, for the feast of the Epiph-

---

[1] Thus in Hymn I, *Ad galli cantum*, the cock is a symbol of Christ, as the dawn is in Hymn II.

[2] One might make comparison with the conventionalized symbolical manner of catacomb paintings, as, *e.g.*, Noah in the ark.

any, tells of the Star and the Magi, and then gives a moving and dramatic story of Herod's fear and the Slaughter of the Innocents.

The hymns of the *Cathemerinon* are skilfully written. Sometimes they express sweet Christian feeling, and very beautifully.[1] Their metres seem well adapted to the contents. Iambic dimeter is most frequently used; also the trochaic tetrameter with good effect. These are the two simplest of classical metres; and the other metres used are also simple. But the poet's fine sense of metrical fitness is best shown in the *Peristephanon*, his hymn-book of martyr-legends. Some of these legends still existed in popular story, and some had been written in literary or rhetorical form. Likewise some of the hymns of the *Peristephanon* are popular, while others are not. The metres are suited to the character of the narrative. For example, the fourth hymn is a rhetorical pane-gyric on the martyrs of Saragossa, and is in sapphic strophes. Hymns IX and XI also are elevated and literary, and the poet uses in the one a couplet made of a hexameter and iambic tetrameter, and in the other the elegiac metre. The hymns of a popular character are of great interest. They are composed in the trochaic tetrameter[2] and the iambic dimeter.[3] Their contents were derived from the stories of the martyrs as told or sung on their festival days. They are beautiful illustrations of the finish of poetry set upon legend. First a martyrdom occurs. Then the legend rises, grows, and sometimes undergoes altera-

---

[1] See, *e.g.*, Hymn V, 149-161; X, 117-149; XII, 125-133.
[2] Hymn I.   [3] Hymns II and V.

tion of names, places, and incidents. At last a poet makes a poem from the matter. Prudentius' imaginative poetry fashions and universalizes events; whatever is unsuited to the type of man or occurrence is changed, and the narrative gains typical significance. For example, Hymn V tells the martyrdom of St. Vincent of Saragossa. The prætor, in order to persuade Vincent to abjure his faith, addresses him in words which give the poet's idea of what a Roman officer under such circumstances would say to a martyr. All halting details are omitted and the matter is universalized. Vincent's answering theological defiance is treated in the same way; it is given just as — to the poet's imagination — it must have been uttered. The poet may also sum up much fact and feeling in a line : *spes certat et crudelitas.* This was true, and, like the whole poem, conforms to the artistic verity of the Christian imagination fashioning its heroic past. In the prison cell the martyr knows that Christ and his angels are with him; and they cheer him; which is true also, universally and necessarily, like the rest of the poem. The tortures are told in full. The poem, in fine, is a typical picture of a martyrdom.[1]

The easy swing, the popular, spirited, and dramatic character of such a poem suggests the ballad form; and indeed the hymn to Vincent, like that to St. Laurence, is a precursor of the ballad, the spirited, popular narrative poem, which tells an occurrence with vivid detail, but not with the breadth and copiousness and dignity which make an epic. The ballad metre

[1] The last (XIV) hymn of the *Peristephanon*, in honor of St. Agnes, is another beautiful example of poetical recasting of legend.

or verse is quick and spirited, as the epic metre is
dignified and noble.   The iambic dimeter of the hymns
to Laurence and Vincent is not unlike the verse form
of English ballads.   The hymns of the *Peristephanon*
carry the feeling of the occurrence, and sometimes
seem to herald the emotional fulness of late mediæval
verse : —

> *O virgo felix, O nova gloria,*
> *Coelestis arcis nobilis incola —*

these lines truly sum up the feeling of the hymn to
St. Agnes.   One notices that they rhyme, and that
the rhyme adds to the surge of feeling.

St. Paulinus Nolanus was born at Bordeaux in 353,
and died in 431, at Nola in Campania, where he had
taken up his abode through devotion to the blessed
Felix, martyr and patron saint.   He was an affectionate and gentle person.   Nobly born, rich, and wedded
to a noble wife, he gave up the world and turned to a
life of gentle Christian asceticism.   His wife remained
his companion; and a sweet affection lasted to the end
between this husband and wife, who had become brother
and sister in Christ.   Many of his letters are in their
joint names : *Paulinus et Therasia peccatores.*

Paulinus had a heart lovingly turned toward Christ
and his saints.   But he was the pupil of the clever
rhetorician and *littérateur*, Ausonius, whose nominal
Christianity did not affect his pagan tastes.   The
pupil lacked originality to strike out new literary
paths.   The form of his poems is given by his education, and appears to limit their emotional contents.
In a poetic epistle to Ausonius he turns a grateful
compliment to his former teacher, which contained

more truth than Paulinus suspected. He is speaking
of his conversion to the religious life, and says: —

> *Mens nova mi, fateor, mens non mea, non mea quondam,*
> *Sed mea nunc auctore deo, qui si quid in actu*
> *Ingeniove meo sua dignum ad munera vidit,*
> *Gratia prima tibi, tibi gloria debita cedit,*
> *Cuius praeceptis partum est quod Christus amaret.*[1]

—"A new mind is put in me from God; if He sees anything in me worthy of His rewards, the thanks and
glory is thine (Ausonius), from whose precepts has
sprung whatever Christ would love." It was true
that a new spirit had come to Paulinus with his conversion; it was also true that his poetic skill was
rooted and nourished in his pagan culture, received
from his master, Ausonius; and that his poetic talent
could never break away from his early lessons. Yet,
so far as his manner of speech and forms of verse
permit, he feels as a Christian.

Two poems of Paulinus in elegaic metre are of
special interest. One is a most Christian epithalamion, in which purity is praised almost in monastic
tone, and all lust and folly exorcised: —

> *Concordes animae casto sociantur amore,*
> *Virgo puer Christi, virgo puella dei,*
> *Christe deus, pariles duc ad tua frena columbas*
> *Et moderare levi subdita colla jugo.*
> *Namque tuum leve, Christe, jugum est, quod prompta voluntas*
> *Suscipit et facili fert amor obsequio.*[2]

These are sentiments of Christian purity and obedience, virtues which, with patience and humility, were
to characterize Christian souls. The poem proceeds,

[1] Carmen X, 142–146.   [2] Carmen XXV, 1–6.

setting a rein to the young people's lust of the vain-
glory and pleasure of this world, and turning their
minds toward eternal joys. In tone and contents it
is the opposite of pagan epithalamia. It may be
compared with a sweet elegiac poem from husband to
wife, attributed to Tyro Prosper,[1] a poem of Christian
trust and marital consolation, written amid the terror
and ruin of the invasions. Tyro's poem closes with
these affectionate lines: —

> *Tu modo, fida comes, mecum isti accingere pugnae,*
> *　Quam Deus infirmo praebuit auxilium.*
> *Sollicita elatum cohibe, solare dolentem;*
> *　Exemplum vitae simus uterque piae.*
> *Custos esto tui custodis, mutua redde*
> *　Erige labentem, surge levantis ope;*
> *Ut caro non eadem tantum, sed mens quoque nobis*
> *　Una sit, atque duos spiritus unus alat.*

Thus husband and wife, with faces set toward Christ
and eternity, comfort and encourage each other on
the way. This noble view of marriage had scant
opportunity to develop in communities where monasticism was becoming the ideal of Christian life.

Like these elegiac marriage poems, Paulinus'
elegy upon the death of a boy [2] is distinctly Christian.
It suggests abnegation of temporalities, and shows
the mind set upon eternity. In spirit he passes with
the boy's departing soul to heaven, and there takes
joy in seeing the newcomer join company with the
soul of his own son, who had died before: —

> *Vivite participes, aeternum vivite, fratres,*
> *　Et laetos dignum par habitate locos.*

[1] Clement, *Carm.*, etc., pp. 67-71.　　[2] Carmen **XXXI**.

These poems are perhaps the first true elegies which
are Christian in point of view, in sentiment, and in
feeling. Devotion and lovingness also constitute the
most distinctive Christian elements in Paulinus' *Nata-
litia*, his lengthy series of poems written on the festal
days — the birthdays to eternity — of the martyr-saint,
Felix. They are poems of a panegyrical character,
mostly written in hexameters. We see in them how
the popular worship of the saints had supplanted the
cult of local pagan deities in Italy and other lands
which were becoming Christian. The departed saints
are potent through their relics, as local deities had
been potent at their shrines. The span of life being
short, the *omnipotens dominus* continues the healing
powers of the saints in their remains.[1] These are efficient in the place of their interment, or wherever they
may be moved. The period of *translationes* (removals)
is at hand, Constantine being the great inaugurator of
the custom, seeking to strengthen his new Constantinople with the mighty relics of Christian heroes.

In such superstitions there was little that was distinctively Christian. Paulinus' Christian feeling lay
in his humility and his love for the martyr-saint, such
as no keeper of a pagan shrine had felt. He feels his
unworthiness to serve Felix — but let this be punishment enough, the many years lived without thee : —

> . . . *tot iam quod te sine viximus annis,*
> *Sede tua procul heu ! quamvis von mente remoti.*[2]

---

[1] *Continuans medicos operosi martyris actus*, Carmen XVIII,
290. This poem bears interesting witness to the early worship of
saints and their relics.

[2] Carmen XII, 16, 17.

Now I have brought my life to anchor at thy shore : —

> *Hoc bene subductam religavi litore classem,*
> *In te compositae mihi fixa sit anchora vitae.*[1]

The didactic or polemic Latin poems remain to be noticed, and then the narrative. The two classes are not to be sharply set over against each other; for polemic and didactic poetry usually contained much narrative, and the narrative poetry frequently had a didactic or polemic purpose. Hexameter is the usual metre, and many of these poems have no other title to the name of poetry.

The last remark applies to the work of the earliest Latin Christian poet, Commodianus of Gaza, Syria, who wrote in the middle of the third century. He was the author of a book of *Instructiones*, consisting of eighty acrostics in unmetrical hexameters. The first part of the work is a polemic apology for Christianity, directed against the pagans; the second part contains ethical admonitions for the use of the various classes of Christians. The poet's *Carmen apologeticum* forms a sequel, in which he instructs as to the Trinity, attacks secular studies, also the Jews, and devotes much space to Antichrist[2] and the Last Times. He appears to have intentionally ignored quantity in his hexameters. The last acrostic in the *Instructiones*, read from below upward, is *Commodianus mendicus Christi ;* and it would seem as if one intending to be "poor in spirit" wrote, with a depreciation of classical culture, in order to impress

---

[1] Carmen XIII, 35.
[2] The first appearance of Antichrist in Latin Christian literature.

the people. He observes the cæsura after the second
foot; and the two final feet of the hexameters are
usually correct in quantity. The substance is dull
and unpoetical.

Prudentius, whose ballad-hymns have been noticed,
also wrote theological and controversial poems. The
first of these is his *Apotheosis*, a work in 1084 hexameters, directed against heresies, and especially against
those impugning the divinity of Christ. Though it
has spirited passages,[1] it is but a fiery rhetorical
polemic set in metre. The same in general may be
said of the poet's *Hamartigenia*, a poem on the source
of evil, fiercely polemic in character and directed
against the dualistic heresy of Marcion. Lucretius'
De Rerum Natura is poetry, where it is poetry, through
the intensity of its feeling. The mind of a Christian
poet might dwell on heresies and the ills springing
from them, until his thoughts fused to images and
visions embodying these evil results. This may be
poetry, and thus it is with passages in the *Hamartigenia*. In a prologue of iambic trimeters the poet likens
Marcion to Cain, and then begins his hexameters: —

> *Quo te praecipitat rabies tua, perfide Cain?*
> *Divisor blaspheme Dei!*

No! there is no second God, author of the Old Testament, as Marcion falsely says; we know the author
of evil, — no God, but the slave of hell; he is the *Mar-
cionita deus, tristis, ferus, insidiator*. There follows the
first great picture of the devil in Latin poetry. His
anguiferum caput and hairy shoulders covered with

---

[1] *E.g.*, lines 321–551 against the Jews.

snakes seem reminiscent of the Erynyes; but his character is his own — devilish : —

> *Liventes oculos suffundit felle perusto*
> *Invidia impatiens justorum gaudia ferre.*

Satan surrounds the soul with his evil ministers, to wit, sins, which beset it as the seven tribes of Canaanites beset the children of Israel : —

> *Serit ille medullitus omnes*
> *Nequitias, spargitque suos per membra ministros.*
> *Namque illic numerosa cohors sub principe tali*
> *Militat, horrendisque animas circumsidet armis,*
> *Ira, superstitio, moeror, discordia, luxus,*
> *Sanguinis atra sitis, vini sitis, et sitis auri,*
> *Livor, adulterium, dolus, obtrectatio, furtum.*
> *Informes horrent facies habituque minaces.*[1]

Here is the idea which the poet works out allegorically in his famous *Psychomachia*. That was a didactic allegory. The preface of iambic trimeters tells of Abraham with his three hundred and eighteen followers conquering the heathen kings; which means, allegorically interpreted, Faith aided by Christ conquering the representative sins of paganism. In the main poem, written in hexameters, the Christ-given virtues of the soul fight against the vices which threaten from out the soul itself and its proneness to temptation. The conflict is set forth allegorically as a succession of combats between champions. First, Fides conquers Idolatria; then Pudicitia conquers Libido and Patientia conquers Ira. Then Mens Humilis, together with Spes, and aided by Justitia, Hones-

[1] *Apotheosis*, ll. 392-399.

tas, Sobrietas, Jejunia, and Pudor, conquer the arch enemy Superbia. After this, Sobrietas overcomes Luxuria, among whose followers is Fugitivus Amor; and Operatio (charity) overthrows Avaritia. Concordia is now treacherously wounded by Discordia, surnamed Haeresis, whereupon Fides transfixes the latter. The victory won, Fides urges that a temple be built to Christ, in describing which the poet follows the twenty-first chapter of Revelation.

In form and structure Prudentius' *Psychomachia* seems to have been original; it was the first Western example of a purely allegorical poem.[1] The universal allegorizing spirit of the poet's time, and of the Christian centuries before him, led to it, and the continuing allegorizing spirit of the Middle Ages created many poems which drew substance or suggestion from it.

Prudentius may have drawn his personifications of the virtues from the works of the Fathers, especially Tertullian. The taste for allegory had also entered later pagan Latin literature. Terror and Fear in Apuleius are the servants of Minerva, and the story of

---

[1] The partly allegorical poem *De Phoenice*, attributed to Lactantius, is earlier than the *Psychomachia*. Cf. Ebert, *Ges.*, I, 97-101. The Phœnix, so important a symbol of immortality and resurrection in Christian art, illustrates the passing of an idea from paganism to Christianity. It is referred to in Ovid, *Metam.*, XV, 402, and Martial, *Epig.*, V, 7. The transition to Christian use appears in the poem *De Phoenice*, which is not distinctly Christian and retains the pagan tradition. Tertullian and Commodian refer to the Phœnix. There is an Anglo-Saxon poem founded on that of Lactantius; see Ebert, *Ges.*, III, 73-75. The legend of the Phœnix is told in the *Roman de la Rose*, 16,911 et seq. On the symbolism of the Phœnix in Christian art, see Evans, *Animal Symbolism in Ecclesiastical Architecture*, p. 68, etc.; 128, etc.

Psyche and Amor is an allegory, in the course of which appear many personifications, Sobrietas, Consuetudo, Sollicitudo, Tristities. The works of Prudentius' contemporary, Claudian, also contain many personifications.

The narrative poems, now to be noticed, consist of translations, transformations, or creations, from Old Testament or Gospel narrative. They form a class of poems of great magnitude, number, and variety; they do not stop with Latin, but branch out into the vernacular literatures of mediæval and modern Europe. If none of these poems reproduces the feeling and spirit of Biblical narrative, some of them have merits of their own.

The series begins with the *Historia Evangelica* of the Spanish priest Juvencus, written about the year 330. It is a close presentation of the Gospel story in four books of hexameters redolent of Virgil. The writer speaks in his prologue of the enduring fame of Homer and Virgil, who wove falsehoods; and he deems that the truth which he narrates shall bring him an eternal meed of fame. This is not a Christian thought. Juvencus tells the Gospel story with smooth mediocrity, quite unconscious of how his measures fail to reflect the spirit and feeling of the Gospel. To turn that story into hexameters meant a continual change of stress, with loss of point and emphasis. For example, Juvencus renders Christ's answer to the scribe, who said he would follow him: —

> *Olli Christus ait; quo me tu, scriba, sequeris?*
> *Vulpibus in saltu rupes excisa latebras*
> *Praebet, et aeriis avibus dat silva quietem;*
> *Ast hominis nato nullis succedere tectis*
> *Est licitum.*[1]

[1] *Hist. Ev.*, II, 14–18.

The flatness of this passage is partly due to its mediocrity, and partly is enforced by the metre. The poet
fails to give the feeling of the Gospel. A poem which
regularly speaks of God as *"summus tonans"* would
naturally have a Roman and Virgilian tone. The story
of Christ stilling the tempest closes thus : —

> *Inde procellis*
> *Imperat et placidam sternit super aequora pacem.*[1]

The last is a good line, but the feeling and reminiscence are Virgilian.

Mention may be made of the *Alethia*, or three books
of Commentaries on Genesis, written by Claudius
Marius Victor, near the middle of the fifth century.
They are an expository rendering in hexameters of
the Biblical story, with many didactic digressions.
Of greater interest and far wider influence was the
Paschale Carmen of Sedulius, composed at this time.
It comprised somewhat less than two thousand hexameters and was divided into five books. The name
would indicate some underlying thought on the part
of the poet, giving a unity to his work. It was a
poem of Christ our Passover, offered for men. The
first book sings the miraculous deliverances in the
Old Testament. The second book tells the birth and
childhood of Christ, and the three remaining books
sing the story of the saving *"miracula Christi,"* until
the final paschal sacrifice and redemption, consisting
of Christ's death, resurrection, manifestation of Himself, and His ascension. Sedulius' poem continued
to be widely read from his own century on to the

[1] *Hist. Ev.*, II, 38; cf. *Æneid*, I, 249.

time of Charlemagne, as well as in the later Middle Ages.

The closing years of the fifth century saw the production of the thoughtful and interesting poem of Dracontius, entitled *De Deo*. Its subject is God's mercy (*pietas*) which led Him to create and then redeem mankind, and which leads Him always to direct human affairs for good, despite the wickedness of men. The poem served as an argumentative consolation to the author, cast into prison by the Vandal King Gunthamund. The first book celebrates God's mercy as revealed in the creation of the world. It is a spirited and poetic account of the six days' creation, and was reproduced by itself, under the title of *Hexaemeron*, before the seventh century. As a narrative, it was the best part of the work, and continued widely read, while the other two books of the poem were neglected, filled as they were with expression of the poet's feeling and thoughts springing from his sad lot. They contain disconnected narratives, passing from the miseries of the poet's time to the salvation brought by Christ, and again to the heroes of pagan antiquity.

Contemporary with Dracontius lived Avitus in Gaul, his life extending through the first quarter of the sixth century. He died as bishop of Vienna in Auvergne. His poem, the most original of the early Latin poems based on Biblical story, was called *De spiritalis historiae gestis;* its special divisions received the following titles: De origine mundi, De originali peccato, De sententia dei, De diluvio mundi, De transitu maris rubri. The first three constitute a veritable poem, having a definite subject imaginatively treated

— the fall of man, or "Paradise Lost." Avitus was a precursor of Milton, who appears to have used the Latin poet.

Book the first sings of God moulding man from dust, which He transforms to living flesh and blood. In the night succeeding the sixth day, God formed Eve from the side of Adam, as the Church sprang from the pierced side of Christ. The Creator bids them live together in concord and fill the earth. A description of Paradise follows, and then the Almighty's prohibition. The second book, — " The Fall," — opens with a picture of the happy life in Paradise. Then comes a description of the Devil's nature, and of his jealousy, his utter pride,[1] and his elation, in misery, at the power left to him of working evil — *summa virtus nocendi.* He takes on the Serpent's form and, "terrible in his fearful beauty," he seeks Eve, whom he deceives with serpentine address. The poet pictures Eve toying with the apple, till she tastes. Then Adam tastes. After two digressions on Lot's wife and Astrology, the book closes with the Serpent's song of triumph — "God made you," he cries to the guilty pair; "I taught you; you are as much mine as His."

The third book tells the shame which leads Adam and Eve to clothe themselves, then Adam's proud plaint to God — better had he remained wifeless! — and then the sentence, and the expulsion to the world without, which seems so ugly after Paradise, the day

---

[1] Both Avitus and Milton, in the character of Satan, have been true to the common Christian conception of pride as chief of sins.

so pale and the heavens so far away.   The book ends
with the lines : —

> *Livida quos hostis paradisa depulit ira,*
> *Fortior antiquae reddat tua gratia sedi.*

The fourth book, on the Flood, is hardly connected with
the preceding ones ; the story is told with spirit, but
with much symbolism.   The Ark naturally is the
Church; the ravens remaining without to tear the
dead are the Jews; and the rainbow is the type of
Christ.   In the fifth book, the poet treats freely and
symbolically the story of the Exodus.

IV. *The Transition to Mediæval Latin Poetry*

The early Christian Latin poets, as inheritors of
antique culture, used antique metres and made such
use of the forms of antique poetry as their own faculties and the novelty of their subjects permitted.   Pagan commonplace and reminiscence survived in their
poems.   With the approach of the Middle Ages, the
antique metres decayed or were transformed to accentual rhythms; the appreciation of antique forms of
poetry passed away; the antique pagan phrases no
longer flowed so naturally and abundantly.

As has been seen, Christian Latin poets of the fourth
and fifth centuries chose the simpler classical metres.
A few accentual hymns were written even then, and
a tendency to preserve the force of accent in metrical
verse had already appeared.   After the fifth century,
rhymes became more frequent.   Then, very gradually,
accent took the place of quantity as the determinant
of the rhythm, and with this change rhymes devel-

oped strikingly. Of the old metres, the hexameter, the elegiac, and the sapphic did not lend themselves readily to the change from quantity to accent. Though continuing in rude use in mediæval Latin poetry, they did not become a medium for the evolution of accentual verse forms. On the other hand, the simple iambic and trochaic metres readily passed through the change and emerged from it to new life as accentual verse, with the added element of rhyme.[1] From this accentual and rhymed verse novel verse-forms were developed with more impressive rhymes. This poetry reached its zenith in the hymns of Adam St. Victor and other great hymn writers of the twelfth century.[2] Latin hymns composed through the twelfth and thirteenth centuries still constitute living verse, though life had departed from other forms of poetry in Latin, and was flowering in the lyric and narrative poetry of the Teutonic and Romance tongues.[3]

---

[1] See *ante*, p. 265. A collection like that of E. du Méril, *Poésies populaires latines*, shows how the life of Latin poetry passes into accentual rhymed verses formed from these metres, and does not remain in the metrical poetry. The *Waltharius* is an exception to this rule. It was composed in hexameters by Ekkehard I, abbot of St. Gall (d. 973), and rewritten by Ekkehard IV between 1021 and 1031. The substance of this famous poem was Teutonic legend, and Ekkehard composed it in hexameters apparently as a school exercise (Ebert, *Allge. Ges.*, III, p. 266). It is one of the most spirited pieces of mediæval narrative poetry.

[2] There was in the Middle Ages a mass of popular Latin songs which frequently reflect or parody the versification and phraseology of Latin hymns. These *Carmina Burana*, or Goliardic poems, as they are called, have life and sometimes beauty, and like the hymns are characterized by effective rhymes.

[3] The verse forms of the Romance tongues, with their assonance and rhyme, came from Latin accentual verse. Early Teutonic

Naturally, no date can be set for the change from quantity to accent and rhyme in Latin poetry. Between the eighth and the tenth centuries a mass of accentual poetry was composed. Herein were hymns and other religious poems; also poems of a secular character. Among the latter were laments (*planctus*),[1] poems upon battles[2] or other striking events,[3] poems of a satirical or polemic character,[4] narrative poems with subjects taken from Scripture or from antiquity. At the same time there was an academic use of metre. For these were the centuries of the Carolingian revival, which was necessarily a revival of the antique. In that time of endeavor after a higher order of culture, men could turn only to the antique world. Alcuin, Charlemagne's minister of education, wrote poems in metre, as did others of his time and the times after him.[5] In fact, there was no period of

(Anglo-Saxon, Norse, Old German) verse depended on the alliteration of strong syllables; it gradually modified its rhythm and adopted rhyme under the influence of Latin and Romance poetry.

[1] *E.g.*, " Planctus de obitu Karoli," Dümmler, *Poet. Lat. Aev. Car.*, I, 434–436.

[2] *E.g.*, " De Pippini regis victoria avarica," Dümmler, *op. cit.*, I, 116; *The Battle at Fontanetum* (841 A.D.), Dümmler, *op. cit.*, II, 138.

[3] *E.g.*, on the destruction and restoration of the cloister at Glonna, Dümmler, *op. cit.*, II, 146.

[4] *E.g.*, against the town of Aquilegia and its claims, Dümmler, *op. cit.*, II, 150.

[5] *Alcuini Carmina*, printed in Dümmler, *Poet. Lat. Aev. Car.*, I, 161–351. His contemporary, Paulus Diaconus, wrote both metrical and accentual verses, see Ebert, *Allge. Ges.*, II, 48–56; poems printed in Dümmler, *op. cit.*, I, 27–86. The *Martyrologium* of Wandalbert, completed cir. 848, shows considerable knowledge of classic metres and skill in their use; Dümmler, *op. cit.*, II, 569–

the Middle Ages when metrical Latin verse was not produced.

The early Christian Latin poets followed the usual forms or genres of antique poetry, yet with deviations caused by the novel character of Christian topics as well as by the declining literary taste of the period in which they wrote. The classical world had always been familiar with epic poems, *i.e.* heroic narratives in hexameters; and from the times of Hesiod and Xenophanes that metre had been used in didactic and philosophic compositions. The general conception of a large narrative poem occupied with a lofty theme passed into classically educated Christendom. The substance of the Christian attempts at epic poetry was taken from the Pentateuch and the Gospels. Pale reproductions of Gospel story were Juvencus' *Historia Evangelica* and Sedulius' *Carmen Paschale*. Small literary gain came to the narratives of Genesis from the *Commentaries* of Claudius Marius Victor. Dracontius' *Hexaemeron* was a more spirited production; and in the poem of Avitus emerges at length an epic of the Fall of Man.

There was little epic quality in these poems; characters as well as narratives were paraphrases rather than creations. The poems lacked unity and heroic action. Their lofty themes constituted religious narratives in which the action was not wrought out through the greatness and energy of the charac-

603; Ebert, *op. cit.*, II, 185–189; so does the *Vita S. Germani* by Heiricus (Traube), *Poet. Lat. Aev. Car.*, III, 432–517; Ebert, *op. cit.*, II, 289–291 (cir. 873). Cf. also Norden, *Antike Kunstprosa*, 721–724, as to metrical poems in the eleventh and twelfth centuries.

teṛs.[1] In epic spirit and heroic action these Latin poems are surpassed by the Anglo-Saxon and old German paraphrases of Scripture.[2]

Lengthy narratives in hexameter or in elegiac couplets continued to be written by clerical hands through the Carolingian period and the time of the German Ottos. Among them were *Vitae Sanctorum*. An example of these is the *Vita Sancti Germani* written (cir. 876) by Heiricus.[3] It consisted of six books of hexameters, each preceded by a *prefatio* written in some other metre. The poem was founded on an older prose *Vita*, and tells the story of the saint's entire life. The subject was not epical, nor was its treatment heroic.[4] Of somewhat greater epic possibilities was the subject of Ermoldus Nigellus' poem (cir. 827), *In honorem Hludovici*, consisting of four books of elegiac couplets.[5] But again, it is the whole life of the hero that is told, and the narrative is not made to revolve around a central event, so as to give it an epic unity. In this respect, the unknown author of the *Gesta Berengarii Imperatoris*[6] did better; his five books tell the career of Berengarius in gaining the imperial crown, and stop when the crown is won. On the other hand, the poem of the famous nun of

---

[1] Avitus' Devil is exceptional in this respect.

[2] *E.g.*, the Saxon Genesis and the Old German Heliand.

[3] Traube, *Poet. Lat. Aev. Car.*, III, 432–517; Ebert, *Allge. Ges.*, II, 289.

[4] A similar life in metre is Milo's *Vita S. Armandi*, Traube, *op. cit.*, III, 567–609. Fortunatus, about three centuries before, wrote a Life of St. Martin in four books of hexameters, based on the Life by Sulpicius Severus.

[5] *Poet. Lat. Aev. Car.*, II, 1–79.

[6] *Ib.*, IV, 354–403; see Ebert, *Allge. Ges.*, III, 138–143.

Gandesheim, *De gestis Oddonis I imperatoris,* is a sort
of family history.[1] Of the Latin poems of the early
Middle Ages, the poem of Abbo (cir. 896), *De bellis
Parisiacœ urbis,*[2] rude as it is, approaches nearest to
an epic. The subject of its three books of hexameters
is the attack of the Normans upon Paris, a topic having
national importance. As the poem treats of a central
event, so it also has a proper hero, Odo, and the barbarous Latin narrative is spirited. Ekkehard's *Waltharius* was an equally spirited and far more polished
production. But the successful escape and adventures
of Waltharius and Hildegarde hardly make a subject
of epic breadth, and lack the epic element of national
importance which is possessed by the subject of Abbo's
poem.

As the successors of antique didactic, philosophic,
and scientific poets — classical Greek, Alexandrian,
and Roman[3] — Prudentius and others used both the
hexameter and the elegiac metre in polemic and
religiously didactic poetry. The plaintive or com-
memorative elegiac poems, which make the proper
Christian elegy, had also their pagan predecessors.[4]

---

[1] This poem of Hrotsvith is printed in *Mon. Germ. Hist. Scriptores,* IV, p. 317, etc.

[2] Printed in *Mon. Germ. Hist. Scriptores,* II, 776–803, and in
Poet. Lat. Aev. Car., IV, 72–121. See also Ebert, *op. cit.,* III,
129–138.

[3] The ancient classic line of poets would be Hesiod, Xenophanes,
Parmenides, Empedocles; the Alexandrians, Aratos (*Phaenomena,*
translated by Avienus last part of fourth century A.D.) and Era-
tosthenes; the Romans, Lucilius, Lucretius, Virgil (*Georgics*),
Ovid (*Fasti*).

[4] One might look as far back as to the ancient elegiac poets,
Solon, Theognis, etc.; then Antimachus of Colophon (see Couat,

On the other hand, novel subjects, a new feeling, and different social conditions evoked novel forms of poetry. Prudentius' *Psychomachia* was a novelty, and his ballad hymns of the *Peristephanon* had no pagan predecessors; though possibly a certain relationship may be felt between the jaunty hexameters of the Greek *Hymn to Hermes* and the Latin Christian poet's ballad-hymn in honor of St. Laurence. Pagan poetry had its songs or "hymns" in honor of gods and heroes. But the substance, more especially the feeling, of the veritable Christian hymns of worship was so different from anything in pagan literature or life that new forms of composition were evolved as the Christian spirit attained the power of self-expression.

The drama is an exception to the general fact of the continuity between the antique and mediæval forms of Latin literature. Long before the time of Constantine the pantomime and the arena had destroyed the theatre. The people cared for neither tragedies nor comedies. In the fourth and fifth centuries there was no drama to pass over into Christian literature with the other antique forms of composition. The rhetorical tragedies ascribed to Seneca are the latest extant Latin pagan plays; and probably they were not written to be acted. We know of no further dramatic compositions until the middle of the tenth century, when Hrotsvith of Gandersheim wrote her pious imitations of Terence. Hrotsvith does not

---

Poésie Alexandrine, p. 62); then the Alexandrians, Philetas, Hermesianax, Callimachus; and then the Latins, Tibullus, Propertius, and Ovid. Love was the usual theme of the Alexandrian and Latin elegiac poets.

appear to have been an influence in the subsequent mediæval development of either liturgical or comic plays. The antique drama was dead before the rise of Christian Latin Literature, and there seems to be no connection between it and mediæval plays.[1]

Naturally Christian Latin poems reflect classic phrase and pagan commonplace and reminiscence. Plagiarism has been frowned on only in modern times. Classic Latin poets borrowed from the Greeks or from each other. The habit passed to Christian writers. A man seeking to express what he has created or what he has felt and made his own with power, is likely to say it in his own words. Thus it was with some of the early devotional productions of Christian poets; there is no borrowed phrase or definite classical reminiscence in the hymns of Ambrose. But it was otherwise when a Christian came to reset the Gospel story in hexameters, or, like Paulinus of Nola, occupied his pious leisure writing folios of elegiac verse. The words and phrases of the great poets who

---

[1] That is to say, the antique drama is not connected with the origin of Easter and Christmas plays or "Mysteries" or mediæval pantomime. See Petit de Julleville, *Hist. de la Langue et de la Lit. Française*, Vol. II, pp. 399–445; *ib.*, *Les Mystères;* Froning, *Das Drama des Mittelalters;* Ebert, *op. cit.*, III, 314–329. The Middle Ages even lost the original meaning of the words "comedy" and "tragedy"; by comedy was understood a poetic narrative beginning in horrors and ending joyfully, and using lowly language, while tragedy begins quietly and ends in horror, and uses sublime language, — so Dante thinks in the letter to Can Grande, Dante's *Ep.*, X, 10. The definition in this letter was taken from Uguccione da Pisa, see Toynbee, *Dante's Obligations to the Magnae Derivationes of Uguccione da Pisa*, Romania, XXVI (1897), 537. For post-mediæval Aristotelean conceptions of the drama, see Spingarn, *Literary Criticism in the Renaissance*, p. 60 et seq.

had written in these metres would certainly come to him. Modern education offers no analogy to the many ways in which the Latin-speaking youth were saturated with Virgil. They almost wrote Virgil as they spoke Latin.

Thus classical reminiscence and, above all, Virgilian phrase entered Christian Latin poetry. Even Commodianus, writing with intentional illiteracy, has Virgilian phrases, and shows knowledge of Horace, Lucretius, and Terence.[1] Juvencus and Sedulius are Virgilian in phrase and tone, so far as mediocrity can reflect greatness. Paulinus of Nola, educated in pagan rhetoric, with some faculty of diction and no originality, never thought to avoid classical phrases. His Carmen VII, an adaptation of the first psalm, begins with Horace's

> ' Beatus ille qui procul ' vitam suam
> Ab impiorum segregavit coetibus;

and again in Carmen XIII he plays devotionally with the name of Felix in the words of Virgil: —

> Sis bonus o felixque tuis.

Prudentius, also, shows his classic education, though not borrowing so profusely. The following lines from his *Apotheosis* curiously echo Horace and Lucretius: —

> O nomen praedulce mihi ! lux, et decus, et spes,
> Praesidiumque meum ! requies ô certa laborum,
> Blandus in ore sapor, fragrans odor, irriguus fons,
> Castus amor, pulchra species, sincera Voluptas.

---

[1] See Dombart's edition (Vol. XV of *Vienna Corpus*), Pref., pp. iii–vi.

Phrases classically reminiscent carried hallowed
associations, and gave tone and feeling to the lines
in which they fell.   But a misuse might be ridiculous.
In one so much a poet as Avitus it is a little pause-
giving to find the Almighty setting his marriage
admonition and blessing of our first parents in words
borrowed from Jupiter's promise to Venus that empire
without end should be the lot of Æneas' race:

> *Vivite concordi studio, mundumque replete;*
> *   *   *   *   *
> *Progenium sine fine dedi. . . .*[1]

Besides these veritable Christian poets, there were
nominal Christians whose poetry discoursed of pagan
themes.   Such was Ausonius, friend and master of
Paulinus; Apollinaris Sidonius (430–480) of Lyons, a
rhetorician-poet of noble birth, ability, and bravery,
whose panegyric on the shadow emperor Anthemius
was rewarded with the office of præfectus urbi; and
Ennodius (473–521) of southern Gaul.   One may
hardly speak of pagan reminiscence in poetry which
is pagan by descent, and frankly pagan in spirit and
in theme.   These writers fill their poems with mythology as naïvely as the pagan poets Claudianus and
Rutilius.

A partial change was not far off.   In the fifth and
sixth centuries Teutonic barbarians were entering
the Empire in great masses; they were learning the
Latin language and gaining some knowledge of the
literature.   The barbarians received Christianity upon
a foundation of German mood and feeling, and not,
as the Latin Christians had received it, upon a foun-

[1] Avitus, I (*De origine mundi*), 173.

dation of classical culture; they received Christianity more as a "little child"; and through it they also received civilization and Latin culture. The effect of Christianity upon the German character, language, and institutions was revolutionary.[1] But the German character was never Latinized, though greatly altered in those countries where Germanic speech was abandoned for a Romance tongue. Even there German mood and tradition long endured, though deeply Christianized. A poet who writes for Franks, Goths, and Thuringians, is not writing for people who have drawn in classical culture with their mother's milk. And the tendency will be for Latin poetry, written within the sphere of influence of the Christianized German mood, to change in feeling, if not to find new themes.

An illustration of this is afforded by Venantius Fortunatus, whose divers works are curiously heterogeneous. He was a Latin, born in upper Italy about the year 530. He spent his youth and early manhood at Ravenna. Then he left his home, to pass through Germany into France, and first stayed at the court of the Austrasian Sigebert, where he wrote a poem upon the marriage of that prince with Brunhild. Some time afterward at Poictiers he won the patronage and friendship of St. Radagunda, a Thuringian princess, who on the overthrow of her father's kingdom by the Franks had been forcibly married to Clotaire I, the son of Chlodowig.

Fortunatus was a voluminous and versatile writer.

[1] From the time of Ulfilas say to the year 1000 by far the greater part of the extant German literature is religious, as may be noticed by glancing through Piper's *Die älteste Literatur.*

He had a classical education and a command of the ancient metres. Quite naturally his poems contain pagan allusions. For instance, he brings in all the paraphernalia of Venus and Cupid in his epithalamion on the marriage of Sigebert and Brunhild. But in other poems, written under the inspiration of his friendship with the deep-hearted German woman Radagunda, there enters a new Germanic feeling as well as a deeper Christian spirit. An example is his long elegy on the marriage and death of Gelesvintha, sister of Brunhild. The poem was written for Radagunda, who loved the young bride. It has much feeling; deep grief is expressed, the grief of a mother for a daughter torn from her to foreign wedlock, the grief of a daughter forced to leave her home to go among strangers — then comes premonition, then the violent death, and then lamentation of nurse and sister and mother for the murdered girl. A deeper feeling has entered Latin elegiac verse than it had previously possessed in these decadent centuries. This is also shown by other elegies of Fortunatus upon the troubles of Radagunda, — *De Excidio Thoringiae.* In these writings, classic reminiscence and commonplace have given way to a genuine expression of the poet's own feelings and the feelings of those surrounding him.

Likewise with his hymns. Although they are metrical and observe quantity, they belong to the coming time, rather than the past. His famous *Vexilla regis prodeunt* is in iambic dimeters, but assonance and rhyme help to express the new spirit with which it glows. His equally famous *Pange, lingua, gloriosi proelium certaminis* is in the popular trochaic tetrameter.

It utters the mediæval feeling for the Cross, so different from that of the early Church in the Roman Empire. From the fourth century the Cross was becoming an object of deep devotion. No longer connected with shame, it was the emblem of the Saviour's glory. Fortunatus approaches it with reverence and adoration, also with a new spirit of love for the sacred wood: —

> *Crux fidelis, inter omnes arbor una nobilis*
> (*Nulla talem silva profert flore fronde germine*)
> *Dulce lignum, dulce clavo dulce pondus sustinens.*

This hymn has caught the mediæval spirit.

Fortunatus' poems are representative of the modes in which the antique survived in mediæval Latin poetry as well as of the ways in which it was superseded: antique phrases and the references to pagan tradition and mythology never cease; they are of course more common in some writers than in others.[1]

---

[1] We find abundant classic phrase and reminiscence in the poets who lived in the midst of the Carolingian revival, when learned men turned to antiquity for their guidance. For example, the hexameters of Hibernicus Exul reflect Virgilian phrase (Dümmler, *Poetae Lat. Aev. Car.*, I, 395, etc.). Likewise the *Vita Aegili*, by "Candidus" (Brunn), in its versified portions is full of Virgil and Ovid (Dümmler, *op. cit.*, II, 94–117). The phrases of the great classics do not flow as copiously in the later Middle Ages, and yet never entirely fall from the memory of scholars. For example, in a long rhyming poem on St. Thomas à Becket occurs this line, almost out of Horace: —

> *Coelum non animum mutat transmarinus.*

(E. du Méril, *Poésies Populaires Latines du Moyen Age*, II, p. 76.) Only the last word varies from Horace's line. So the popular Goliardic *Latin Poems commonly attributed to Walter Mapes* (ed. by Wright) have quantities of classical allusions, which is also true of the drinking and love songs in the collection of *Carmina Burana*. Others of the *Carmina Burana* have the Tale of Troy as their subject.

On the other hand, the antique spirit ceases utterly; it is replaced by the more completely Christianized genius of the Middle Ages. Speaking more particularly, the antique sense of form and proportion, the antique observance of the mean and avoidance of extravagance and excess, the antique dislike for the unlimited or the monstrous, the antique feeling for literary unity, and abstention from irrelevancy, the frank love for all that is beautiful or charming, for the beauty of the body and for everything connected with the joy of mortal life, the antique reticence as to hopes or fears of what was beyond the grave, the antique self-control and self-reliance,—these qualities cease in mediæval Latin poetry. The analogy is clear between poetry and the arts of sculpture and painting; in those also, antique theme and reference survived, as well as antique ornament and design; but the antique spirit ceased and was superseded by the mediæval genius, which within general lines of homogeneity showed itself so diversely according to the characters of the different peoples of the Middle Ages.

The traits of the various peoples of Western Europe soon began to appear in their Latin verse and prose, as through a veil, in no wise as clearly as they were to show themselves in the vernacular literatures. Incipient French traits, for example, appear in the balance and moderation, the neatness or deftness of form, of the poems of Paulinus of Nola. In a different way they also appear in Gregory of Tours' *Historia Francorum*, a work in which the Latin is taking the French order of words and acquiring some of the vivacity and picturesqueness of Froissart. Again, we seem vaguely

to discern Irish traits in the almost burlesque fulsome-
ness of the inscriptions of Columbanus' letters to the
Popes Boniface IV and Gregory the Great: *Pulcher-
rimo omnium totius Europae, ecclesiarum capiti, papae
praedulci, praecelso praesuli, pastorum Pastori, reveren-
dissimo speculatori: humilissimus celsissimo, maximo,
agrestis urbano, micrologus eloquentissimo, extremus
primo, peregrinus indigenae, pauperculus praepotenti,
mirum dictu! nova res! rara avis, scribere audet Boni-
facio Patri Palumbus.*[1] Likewise a certain Irish extravagance seems discernible in the *Hisperica famina,* a curious grammatical treatise of the ninth or tenth century.[2]
Perhaps, also, one can discern an Irish flavor in the
poems of the founder of scholastic philosophy, the Irish-
man Erigena, or in other Latin verses written by Irish-
men in the later Carolingian period. The following lines
read like a lament of a " poor exile from Erin " : —

> *Nocte dieque gemo, quia sum peregrinus et egens ;*
> *Attritus febribus nocte dieque gemo.*
> *Plangite me, juvenes, animo qui me colebatis ;*
> *Rideat hinc quisquis ; plangite me, juvenes.*[3]

More clearly the characteristics or tastes of Anglo-
Saxon literature appear in the Latin poetry written
by Anglo-Saxons. For example, the alliteration so
marked at the beginning of Aldhelm's poem *De laudi-
bus Virginum*[4] recalls that cardinal element of Anglo-

[1] Migne, *Patr. Lat.*, Vol. 80, col. 274; also *ib.*, col. 259, the letter
to Gregory.

[2] A. Mai, *Auctores Classici*, V, p. 479 et seq.; and see *ib.*, Introd.,
pp. xlviii–l.

[3] Traube, *Poet. Lat. Aevi Caroli.*, III, p. 688; see also *ib.*, passim, pp. 685–701.

[4] Migne, *Patr. Lat.*, Vol. 89, col. 239

Saxon versification. Also the many Latin *aenigmata* composed by Anglo-Saxons reflect their taste for riddles so pronounced in their vernacular literature. Apparently this kind of writing was not original with them; for a book of *aenigmata* existed, ascribed to one Symposius, of whom nothing is known except that he lived before the seventh century and was not an Anglo-Saxon. But Anglo-Saxons cultivated these riddles in Latin; Tatwine, Aldhelm, Winfried-Boni-fatius, wrote many of them. The Anglo-Saxon way of enduing inanimate objects with life and feeling strikingly appears in Aldhelm's *aenigmata*. He borrowed a little from Symposius, but not this habit; and his *aenigmata* form a link between the earlier writer and the riddles of Cynewulf.

That portion of the Teutonic race which afterward became German and dwelt in German territory acquired Latin culture as brought to it by Anglo-Saxons (Boniface) and their scholars (Luidger), or by Gallo-Franks. But as the Germans begin to write in Latin German feeling shows itself; as, for example, in the elegiac *Dialogus Agii*, written by the noble Saxon monk Agius (cir. 875) to commemorate the virtues of his sister Hathumod.[1] A brother's heartfelt love finds voice in this poem, which also echoes the dear memories of a loved home. Again, rude German banter and rough-handed valor appear in the famous *Waltharius*. Not that German sentiments and feeling were to find as clear expression in these poems as in the mother tongue. In the German translations or adaptations of Scripture the German spirit rings as true as the Anglo-

[1] Traube, *Poet. Lat.*, etc., III, pp. 369–388.

Saxon in Anglo-Saxon poetry. Otfried's *Evangelien Buch* and the *Heliand* unveil the tender loves of German home life and the race's love of fight; even as the pathetic elegiac Anglo-Saxon soul and its high devotions find clear expression in the *Christ* of Cynewulf.

General traits of mediæval humanity might show themselves in mediæval Latin prose and verse. But the use of a single academic language could not but give a certain common tone to everything composed in it. Mediæval Latin retained something of the genius of the Latin language. No man could altogether free himself from its influence when writing Latin, or free himself from his clerkly Latin education, which everywhere consisted of the trivium and quadrivium, and in Italy, France, Spain, England, and Germany, made like use of classic or transitional Latin authors. Moreover, the great majority of mediæval Latin writers were monks or priests, and so had undergone the levelling influence of ecclesiastic training. Hence through all mediæval Latin literature a like course of study, and the common language with its still surviving, though barbarized and antiquated, genius, lessens and obscures distinctive racial or national traits. But in the vernacular literatures — so largely the creation of uneducated and unpriestly men — individual and race characteristics show themselves clearly and with power. Thus in the *Byrthnoth* and the *Beowulf* appears the stubborn Anglo-Saxon heroism; in the Eddic poems and the Sagas appears the Norseman's love of fight — so different from Greek and Roman valor — and the tremendous energy of the Norse character; in the *Cid* we recognize the valor of the chivalry of Spain, also its hate and unforgetting vengefulness. The rashness, the fire, and devotion of the crusading Frank find expression in the *Chanson de Roland*, that epic of Germanic spirit and Romance form. The common hard barbarian Teuton nature is found in the old *Hildebrandslied;* then, after some centuries of growth, clear German traits are seen at their zenith in two utterly different, yet typical, expressions of the German spirit, the *Nibelungenlied* and the *Parzival*, Wolfram's thoughtful poem. How utterly different from all these, and how masterfully and inclusively and finally Italian, is the *Divina Commedia*, which is no whit Latin, and yet distinctly Italian in that it bears transformed within itself the classic Latin heritage.

CHAPTER X

I. *The Transition from Antique to Mediæval Architecture*

THE course of architecture from antiquity to the Middle Ages shows a gradual transition from classical forms to a style based upon other principles of construction, embodying other elements of beauty, using other modes of decoration, — a style suggesting what its colored and sculptured ornament expressed, the universal plan, the spiritual scope, the infinite yearning, the extreme and mystic emotion, of the Christian faith. This completely Christian style was the Gothic.

Perfect classical types are the Doric, with its masculine strength, its definite proportion, its absolute unity; and the Ionic, in its limpid grace forming the complementary feminine style. The Doric and Ionic styles present temperance, reverence, and beauty, the one in modes proper to man, the other in modes proper to woman. They both embody Greek intellect; and they disclose complementary modes of Greek feeling which might, however, exist together in the complete Greek personality. Plato is Ionic as well as Doric. The younger sister of the Ionic was the Corinthian, a style less strictly classical, more pliant, and touched with the possibilities of Romanticism.

The Romans used the Greek orders in the construction of colonnades, or combined them with the arch, which may have come from Etruria. The arcade formed from this combination represented a Roman style, distinguishable from later forms taken directly from contemporary Greek designs, as the fashion was at Pompeii. In temples and basilicas, the Romans followed foreign traditions; while their own constructive genius displayed itself in baths, aqueducts, amphitheatres, fortifications, and roads. It was chiefly for architectural ornament that they looked to the Greek orders, just as they sought for pleasure in Greek literature. They found no pleasure in Æschylus or Sophocles, nor did they find decoration in Doric. The exclusively supporting function of a Doric column was too manifest to permit its use as mere ornament. The Ionic was less austere; but the Corinthian was most richly ornamental. The Romans ordinarily used this to support the architraves of basilicas, or when the piers of an arcade were to be ornamented with engaged columns. The general plan of the basilica was taken from the Greeks, and consisted, according to Vitruvius, of one central and two lateral naves, the latter having two stories, and the whole roofed in wood.

If there were any general survival of Roman buildings of the third and fourth centuries, the antecedents of Christian basilicas would not have become a special subject of archæological dispute. They would have been recognized as part of the usual Roman styles of construction, having architecturally neither origin nor development peculiar to themselves. No attempt would have been made to trace the Christian church to the interior arrangement of the Italian dwelling-house, or to the *scholae* of the clubs, or to any parts of the underground construction of the catacombs, or to the memorial *cellae* which may have stood before their entrances. All these had features common to the structures of the time; and the same features may be found in the Christian basilica. The latter shared its name with the variously shaped private basilicas in the palaces of the emperors and nobility, and with the splendid basilicas used as law courts and for other business occasioning the assembling of many persons. These forensic basilicas presented most of the structural elements of the antique Christian church. Yet there may have been no relationship of parent and child between them, even though in some instances forensic or other basilicas were taken for ecclesiastical uses. When a Christian basilica was built, it was built to serve the purposes of Christian worship; when a forensic basilica was built, it was built for the transaction of legal affairs. Both were constructed to meet quite similar requirements; and sometimes a pagan structure may have served as model for the Christian.

Christian worship had begun in an " upper room," and was carried on in private houses until the increasing numbers of worshippers required other buildings. There were probably churches in the third century;[1] but we do not know their plans or sizes. The buildings used for Christian worship were destroyed in the persecution under Diocletian; and

[1] Cf. Dehio and Bezold, *Die Kirchliche Baukunst des Abendlandes*, Chap. I.

to-day no Christian structure exists antedating Constantine.[1] It was a momentous change from a persecuted faith to a State religion; clergy and laity were safe; indefinitely greater resources were at their disposal, and their organizations were sustained by the dignity and power of the Empire. Constantine's Christianity was Roman and imperial, differing from the lowliness of the Gospel as the basilicas of S. Pietro in Vaticano and S. Paolo Fuori differed from an "upper room." The closest architectural relationship of these two churches is with the Basilica Julia of Cæsar and the Basilica Ulpia of Trajan.

An architectural revival followed the triumph of Christianity. Forms of pagan building were modified to meet the requirements of Christian worship. Architecturally there was little that was specifically Christian in these early basilicas. Nor does the subsequent history of the Roman Christian basilica show an organic architectural development. Italy, disturbed and threatened, smitten with invasion and pestilence, had neither the peace, the resources, or the faculties for architectural progress. Basilicas from the fourth to the tenth century are architecturally indistinguishable. Their columns were usually taken bodily from pagan basilicas and temples. The story of these Christian basilicas is the last chapter of the history of antique architecture in the West.

On the other hand, the Hellenic East produced a Christian style called Byzantine. The chief home of this achievement was Constantinople, the final for-

[1] Except the catacombs and their memorial structures above ground.

tress of antique culture as well as of the Græco-Roman Empire. Besides the basilica form, the Greek circular temple had passed to Rome in pre-Christian times. The Pantheon, built, as it stands, under the Antonines, is the great example of a circular temple crowned with a dome of concrete constructed in the Roman method. This dome is set directly upon a circular drum and therefore needs no pendentives. These are rare and rudimentary in Roman dome construction, for the Romans never set a dome upon a square base, and only in a few secondary instances upon an octagon.[1] Byzantine domes are not "cast" with concrete, but are constructed out of layers of brick or tiles. Hence they are not held together by the cohesion of the material. They rest either upon a circular base, an octagon, or a square. The first are related to the Pantheon. The second are represented by St. Sergius at Constantinople and St. Vitale at Ravenna, both built in Justinian's time, and employing pendentives. The great church representing the third group stands for the climax of Byzantine architectural achievement. In the latter part of Justinian's reign, the Greek architects of St. Sophia solved most beautifully the problem of setting a dome upon a square, by the use of pendentives in the form of spherical triangles resting upon arches.[2]

[1] An instance is afforded by one of the smaller halls in the Baths of Caracalla.

[2] This means of adjusting a dome to a square base is quite different and far more beautiful than the ancient (originally Persian) mode of conical vaults — "trompes" — rising from the corners of the square and joining with the sphere of the main dome (Choisy, *L'histoire*, etc., I, 125, II, 8). An interesting modification of the

St. Sophia represents a new style of edifice. The skill of its construction, the excellence and beauty of its interior, are known to all. The genius of Christianity was here operative, and yet did not reach complete expression of itself. The lack of sculpture prevented the building from declaring its end and aim in the speech most germane to architecture. There was an aversion in the Greek Church to statuary smacking of idolatry. Byzantine carving is decorative rather than expressive. Yet architecturally St. Sophia .was as truly a Christian creation as the stately hymns of Romanos, who may have lived while its domes were rising. Like those hymns, St. Sophia was a Christianizing of art through the strength and genius of the civilized and mature Greek race, and with no infusion of young blood; and, like those hymns, St. Sophia was not unaffected by the formalism of an over-mature civilization in which the culture and principles of the great classic past had become lifeless conventions. In the West, meanwhile, the old basilica style of antique Christian building continued its unprogressive existence, and antique metres remained supreme in Latin Christian poetry. It required centuries for the religious genius of the North to free itself from metre, and create true heart-expressing Christian hymns; likewise centuries passed before the Germanic genius attained the power and knowledge to create a Christian architecture. The West

latter method may be seen in the church of S. Giovanni dei Eremiti or in the Capella Palatina, at Palermo. The juncture between the square base and the dome is effected — not very gracefully — by three advancing arches springing from the corners of the base.

had first to quiet its wild barbarism; but when its genius had cleared, Western hymns voiced Christian feeling more simply and directly than the hymns of Romanos, and Gothic cathedrals told their Christian story, and even expressed Christian emotion, with an adequacy making St. Sophia in comparison seem Hellenic and oriental rather than Christian.

The styles and methods by which the young races of the West passed from the antique Christian basilica to Gothic are called Romanesque. Between these and the Byzantine there was a cardinal difference: Byzantine art was the work of a civilized and mature people, before whom lay no further growth; Romanesque was the work of young peoples who were themselves to advance, and with their progress perfect their art. Byzantine architecture in the sixth century reached its culmination in the perfection of dome construction. This was the final architectural achievement of the Greek genius, creative still even in the transformation and perfecting of adopted forms. The past, changed, yet still the past, was triumphantly renewed in St. Sophia, quite as much through finished knowledge as through originative faculty, and all under the inspiration of Christianity. But Romanesque architecture, instead of a last creation, was a growth of what was immature and crude; it had neither perfected knowledge nor a great inheritance of building tradition; its varied progress in different Northern lands was homogeneous in this, that everywhere it represented continually widening departure from the antique, and increasing knowledge of new principles of construction.

Roughly speaking, the period of Romanesque extends from the breaking up of Charlemagne's Empire to the end of the twelfth century. It was a time when Germanic peoples collectively were rapidly advancing in civilization; but as yet there was no large growth of towns. Monasteries contained the largest and wealthiest assemblages of people. Their needs, and the endeavor to replace the perishable wooden roofs of the antique basilica with a roof of stone, determined the development of Romanesque. The parts of the basilica used by the clergy were extended, the ground plan reaching the form of a Latin cross; the choirs were enlarged, or sometimes doubled, and likewise the transepts; crypts and clock towers were added; piers and pillars began to replace the antique columns. Toward the end of the period, pillars and piers were breaking into clusters corresponding to the strains which they supported. They had still a twofold function, that of a pier supporting a vertical weight and that of a buttress counteracting a thrust. Yet the spirit of architectonic analysis is beginning to distinguish these two functions, and is approaching a corresponding division of these structural elements into pillars and buttresses.

The Roman vault was cast, a rigid block of brick and concrete. The Romanesque vault was to be a living arch built of stones. The antique basilica had always a vaulted apse, which first of all the Romanesque architects constructed in their manner with a vault of stone. Next, in order to replace the flat wooden roof of the antique basilica, they succeeded in vaulting the side aisles and then the central nave,

which had to be raised above the lateral vaulting in
order to receive sufficient light. The next step was to
substitute cross-vaulting for the barrel vault. One
school of Romanesque architects stopped at one point
of incomplete attainment of these ends, another at
another. But it was in the progressive development
of methods entailed by the endeavor to vault the nave
perfectly that Romanesque was to reach its apotheosis
in Gothic.

Although the progress of Romanesque architecture
came through the energies and growing experience of
the northern peoples, the style was a continuance of as
well as a departure from architectural forms existing
in the western or eastern portions of what had been
the Roman Empire. The point of departure was the
Western antique Christian basilica, from which the
Romanesque church took its general arrangement, its
vaulted apse, and the arches connecting the piers
which supported the nave. On the other hand, the
mode of vaulting the naves was influenced rather by
the East than by antique Roman principles. A
spherical vault upon a square base was unknown in
the West until it appeared in Romanesque churches
at the crossing of the nave and transept; nor did the
Romans employ cross-vaults of stone. The presence
of these forms in Romanesque churches betrays the
influence of Byzantine and other oriental modes of
building.[1]   Different oriental influences, operating

[1] See Choisy, *Histoire d'Architecture*, II, pp. 134–138, 200–202,
240–257, for a statement of the sources and paths by which came the
Eastern influences. Cf. also Hittorff. *Architecture Moderne de la
Sicile* (1835).

with different degrees of strength, affected Sicily, southern France, and the Rhine countries, a circumstance leading to a divergence of Romanesque styles in France and Germany as well as England. Yet this divergence was due still more to the different characteristics of the several peoples, and the various conditions under which the Romanesque developed in these countries.

In Gothic the possibilities of Romanesque reach their logical conclusions. More analytically and completely the vault determines the rest of the structure. Downward stress and lateral thrusts have been analyzed; they have been gathered up and then distributed in currents of pressure exerted along the lines of the ribs of the vaulting. Each thrust or stress is met by separate support of pillar or colonnette, or by directly counteracting pressure of pier and flying buttress. Through these the weight and lateral thrusts of the building are conducted downward and outward in channels as definite as the gutters which lead the rain-water from the roof. More especially the devices of rib and flying buttress have facilitated the use of the pointed arch, and have lifted Romanesque from the earth; while the confinement of stresses to definite channels has enabled the architect to replace opaque walls with a many-colored translucency of glass, in which the Christian story is painted in the light of heaven.

The architectural ornament emphasizes the structure of the building as determined by the requirements of the vault. Constructively, artistically, and symbolically, the ornament of a Gothic church completes and

perfects it and renders it articulate. The strength of
the building is in its ribs and arches, columns, piers,
and flying buttresses. Their sustaining forms render
this strength visible. The lines and points of sculptured ornament show forth these forms of power distinct and excellent in beauty. Leaves of veritable
plants crown the columns, making them as living
branches. Beasts and birds live enforested in the
capitals of the great pillars; and the pinnacles of the
flying buttresses, which are the final fastenings of
the giant structure, are exquisitely chiselled, so that
their beauty may be equal to the importance of their
function.

The sculpturesque ornament is also strong in truth-
fulness. For the workman has broken away from the
old conventions; he has opened his eyes and has seen
living plants with living foliage; and he has wrought
in stone their life-giving and life-emblematic beauty.
Gothic sculptors rival nature's exhaustlessness of design. Festoons and clusters grow and hang in infinite
variety. Likewise in the grouping of living figures.
Byzantine art had been formal and conventional. For
real grouping, the artist must look to life, where the
Byzantines did not look, nor with much confidence
the hesitating Romanesque artists. But the Gothic
sculptor follows life and evokes it in his statuary as
in his leaf decoration.[1]

---

[1] A prodigious realism enters some of the fantastic animal creations of Gothic, often the realism of caricature, which consists in
the unreal and impossible combination of elements that, separately,
actually exist. This gives the fantastic reality to the devils and
other evil beings in Gothic sculpture.

An art which has gone back to nature and drawn upon her unfailing newness is a new art. Gothic sculpture is not altogether ignorant of lessons which it might learn from Rome or Constantinople. It has had these lessons, but has gone forth from the school-room to the world without; where it has become itself. And this art is Christian, not only in theme, but in its style and feeling. It has grown up among young peoples who received Christianity as little children. It can tell the Christian story, and can express Christian feeling as far as that may be carved in stone.

Christianity is utter love, with its reasonable justification. Christian love is absolute, and its reasons compass the verities of earth and heaven from the beginning to all eternity. A Gothic cathedral is a great piece of reasoning, analytically logical from its highest keystone to its foundations. Its ornaments, its wealth of love and beauty, spring from its structure, adorn and emphasize that. And they tell the whole tale of Christianity and include the story of the world, sometimes directly and again in symbols. Christianity is infinite; Gothic follows, as far as stone may follow. The cathedral building is unlimited, unmeasured, if not actually in size and intricacy, at least in its suggestions and intent. And over all of it is thrown the mystery of the beauty of great art —like the mystery of the living union between Christian love and its reasons.

Limit, the mean, nothing too much, these were principles which the Greeks followed in the contours and proportions, as well as in the dimensions, of their temples. The Gothic cathedral strives for the immense. Its builders were too intelligent to seek this effect merely by the barbarous means of enormous dimensions. The immensity of a Gothic cathedral is in every way enhanced by the architecture. If actually a Greek temple was large, there was nothing to indicate its size. It was a perfectly proportioned whole. The architectural proportionment of its members was absolute. Each feature was enlarged or lessened with the general dimensions of the building; nothing marked the scale. Doors and steps, as well as columns, were proportioned to the size of the temple, larger and higher in a larger temple, proportionally diminished in a smaller one. A temple was not devoted to practical purposes; it was rather dedicated to the Greek love of proportion.[1]

Certain features of Gothic churches have the same dimensions whatever the size of the building. In a cathedral, as in a small church, the height of the doors and of the steps corresponds to the size of human beings. Likewise the height of the galleries and their balustrades remains nearly the same. These comparatively unchanging dimensions at once afford a scale which renders the size of the building apparent. This is also indicated by the Gothic and Romanesque practice of making the height of every architectural member, for example the capital of a pillar, a certain multiple of the courses of stones of which the pillars and the rest of the building are built. Moreover, in Gothic construction the materials are palpably sub-

---

[1] This absolute proportionment probably did not hold in Greek civic and domestic buildings; see Choisy, *op. cit.*, I, 400–422.

jected to stress and pressure approaching their limit of resistance, and the eye at once judges the size of a structure by the massiveness of its supports.[1] Thus the scale is marked. But, beyond this, the size of the cathedral is enhanced and made evident by the many divisions of the interior, and the dimensions grow as unseen spaces are disclosed to one moving beneath the bays of nave and pillared aisle and choir. The height is raised by the prominence of perpendicular or oblique ascending lines. Not infrequently the arcades are lowered as they recede from the entrance; and sometimes the lines of the choir are converged. Thus the effect of perspective is enhanced and the length of the building exaggerated.

Gothic symmetry also is different from the Greek or Byzantine. Instead of a succession of like members the symmetry of a Gothic cathedral may consist in regular recurrence of dissimilarity. A general balance of masses is preserved, while more diversity of architectural design and decorative detail is admitted within this general balance than in a Greek temple or a Byzantine church. Here the Gothic building is nearer to the symmetry of natural growth.[2] But its single statues and groups of statuary rarely equal the Greek artist's consummate symmetry of life. Gothic

[1] Neither the Romanesque nor the Gothic columns lessen toward the top, nor have they entasis; they are cylindrical. There is no proportionment of diameter to height, as in the antique, but the diameter depends on the weight to be supported. Corinthian was the only classical order imitated in Romanesque, and the imitation was free.

[2] On these matters, see Choisy, *op. cit.*, II, 167-170, 397-415; Dehio, *op. cit.*, p. 198.

statuary is often realistic, and the grouping sometimes is natural. Yet, quite as frequently the figures are arranged in hierarchic manner, as, for instance, within the recessed arch of a doorway.

Finitude and, within it, perfection characterize Greek creations. To these qualities Christianity opposes its infinitude. The Greek temple is structurally a unit; and the themes of its sculpture have limit as well as interrelation. Structurally a Gothic cathedral is a dynamic organism. Each of its parts is a factor in the equilibrium of the whole. Yet its many and diverse divisions prevent it from presenting the striking unity of a Greek temple. The themes of its sculpture and painting extend from the beginning to all eternity, and include the wicked and grotesque in man and devil, as well as the holy and sublime in man and God. Their principle of unity lies in their relation to the Christian scheme of salvation.[1] Greek sculpture is as clear and open as the natural life of man; Greek architecture is apparently as simple as in reality it is intellectual. Gothic sculpture tends toward mystic symbolism; and the structure of a Gothic cathedral discloses subtleties of balance which are sheer unrest as compared with the classic poise.

II. *Antique Christian Painting and Sculpture*

From apostolic times, gentile Christians lived in an environment of art, pictorial, statuesque, or merely decorative. The fact that they were Christians

---

[1] Cf. Didron, *Iconographie chrétienne* (1843), Introduction: Kraus, *Geschichte der christlichen Kunst*, II, 360–384. Besides subjects that could possibly be regarded as sacred (*i.e.* related to sal-

brought no change in matters apparently irrelevant
to the Faith and to the purer social morality demanded
by it. Those who were in a servile position continued
to live in the establishments of their patrons; those
who were of independent station did not change the
style of their houses; nor did they object to the common modes of decoration, except when containing
palpably idolatrous images. The decoration of Christian houses and tombs becomes distinguishable by the
omission of these and by the gradual substitution of
Christian themes. For example, in the fresco on the
ceiling of the lower entrance to the catacombs of S.
Genaro dei Poveri at Naples (cir. 100 A.D.) there is
nothing to shock the Christian conscience, and yet
nothing distinctly Christian.[1] Christian themes, however, begin to appear on the somewhat later ceiling of
the upper catacombs.[2] It may be said that the position of Christians toward art made part of their attitude toward matters of this world, and there would
be individual differences of opinion.[3]

vation or damnation), topics from popular mediæval literature
were represented in cathedral sculpture; see R. Rosières, *L'évolu-
tion de l'architecture en France*, Chap. X (*Petite Bib. d'art*, etc.).
Cf. E. Male, *L'art religieux du XIII*ᵉ *siècle en France*.

[1] Garucci, II, Tav. 90 ; cf. Schultze, *Archaeologie der Altch.
Kunst.*, p. 164.

[2] Garucci, II, Tav. 95 et seq. These paintings are now scarcely
visible.

[3] Tertullian, *De Idolatria*, VI, VII, VIII, inveighs against Christians helping to make idols. In Lib. II, Cap. 22, of *Adversus Marcionem*, he distinguishes between images prohibited by the Mosaic
law, *causa idolatriae*, and those *quae non ad idolatriae titulum
pertinebant*, or which were *simplex ornamentum*. Likewise the
Passio sanctorum quattuor coronatorum speaks of these martyrs of
Diocletian's time who were artificers, as willing to carve an image

Pagan mythological figures and decorative motives occur throughout the Roman catacombs, and upon the Christian sarcophagi of the fourth and fifth centuries found at Rome and in the south of France.[1] Sometimes the pagan design is modified and given a Christian significance; for example, the pagan type of Hermes carrying a sheep is transferred to Christ as the Good Shepherd. Again, the pagan subject appears to have become a Christian allegory;[2] and a number of personifications pass on from the pagan antique into the Roman and Byzantine Christian art, an example of which is the mode of representing the river Jordan under the form of a river-god in mosaics in the churches of S. Giovanni in Fonte and S. Maria in Cosmedin at Ravenna. Perhaps most frequently the pagan image or pattern is retained as mere decoration.

The early Christian paintings in the Roman cata-

of the Sun in his chariot and also *conchas sigillis ornatas, conchas et lacus cum sigillis*, which *sigilla* were Victories and Cupids, but as refusing to make an *Asclepii similacrum* (De Rossi, *Roma Sott.*, III, 578–579). Cf. Müntz, *Études sur la Peinture*, etc., p. 2. Sometimes the same workmen made objects with pagan as well as Christian images upon them. Le Blant, *Revue Archéologique*, 1875, Vol. 29, p. 1; and *Rev. Arch.*, 1876, Vol. 31, p. 378; Müntz, *Études*, etc., p. 3.

[1] The vintage and seasons of the year designed in the usual pagan style appear upon Christian sarcophagi in the Lateran Museum; cf., generally, Ficker, *Die Altchristlichen Bildwerke im Christlichen Museum des Laterans;* and for pagan themes upon Christian sarcophagi in Gaul, see Le Blant, *Sarcophages chrétiens de la Gaule*, Introduction, pp. iv–vii.

[2] As in the representation of the myth of Cupid and Psyche and of Orpheus in the catacombs. See, generally, Kraus, *Geschichte der christlichen Kunst*, I, 203–224.

combs range from the end of the first to the middle of
the fourth century, when the catacombs ceased to be
used as burial-places.[1] The subjects are largely Biblical. The Old Testament scenes most frequently represented are: The Fall (Adam and Eve) (13 times);
Noah in the Ark (26 times); Sacrifice of Isaac (15
times); Moses smiting the Rock (47 times); the Three
Young Men in the Fiery Furnace (19 times); Daniel
among the Lions (32 times); the Story of Jonas (45
times). From the New Testament: Adoration of the
Magi (12 times); the Healing of the Paralytic (12
times); Miracle of the Loaves (23 times); Raising of
Lazarus (39 times); also a number of representations
of Christ and the Twelve. Less frequent Biblical
subjects are: Moses receiving the Tables of the
Law, Moses taking off his Shoes; and among others
from the New Testament, the Healing of the Blind
Man, and Christ and the Woman of Samaria. Repasts
are frequently represented, and family scenes, and a
large number of female figures praying (Orantes).
Most frequent of all is the figure of Christ as the
Good Shepherd (85 times) carrying a sheep.[2]

Besides the foregoing there are many paintings of
objects animate or inanimate, as the fish, dove, lamb,
peacock, lamp, ship, palm. These were symbols of
the Christian faith. But were the Biblical scenes,
especially those of the Old Testament, intended as
allegorical? Probably no single categorical answer
will correctly cover this question.

[1] There are also pictures in them painted by pious hands in the
three or four centuries following.
[2] Hennecke, *Altchristliche Malerei*, p. 123.

Mentem mortalia tangunt: the incidents of one human life present analogies to the actual or imaginative experience of others. Whatever happens to man has something of the universal in it, and may be typical of analogous experiences coming to other men under different circumstances. Occurrences most palpably presenting elements which may be verified in common human experience are best suited for literature and art. The features of a story that fire the artist's imagination are those which are most readily verifiable in his own life or spiritual experience; he is likely to represent these and omit the rest. The story is thus freed from its special circumstances and becomes more widely typical. All human events, and still more their presentations in art, have something of the symbolical in them, and may be taken as allegories of other human situations and spiritual experience.

The stories of the Old Testament were of wide religious application, that is, were widely representative of relations between God and man; so they contained elements of the universal. The story of Jonas, of Moses striking the rock, or of Daniel among the lions, might be taken as a partly allegorical presentation of the universal truth of divine rescue of trusting humanity. This, however, is different from treating those stories as symbolical of certain subsequent events, to wit, the facts and import of Christ's life on earth. But Jesus had thus specifically applied the story of Jonas to his own death and resurrection; and again had said, " As Moses lifted up the brazen serpent in the wilderness, so shall the Son of Man be lifted up;" Paul made an allegorical application of the incident of Moses and the rock — " and the Rock was Christ." [1] After apostolic times, the Fathers set out upon that course of allegorical interpretation which resulted in treating the whole of the Old Testament as prefigurative of Christ and the events of his earthly life. This mode of interpretation reached general acceptance in the Christian Church.

The question is: Were the Old Testament incidents in the catacombs depicted for what they were and for their comforting assurance of God's unfailing deliverance of His faithful servants; or were they intended as allegorical representations of the incidents and import of Christ's life and the specific elements of the Christian faith? Catacomb painters, and sculptors of Christian sarcophagi after them, selected — or were given — scriptural events which most strikingly set forth the miraculous saving power of God. It was largely this same series that Christian writers most frequently refer to from the time of Roman Clement [2] on through every successive generation of men. [3] They contained a wealth of significance and hope. Christians drew such consolation from them as accorded with their faith. The fact that they were so frequently represented in the catacombs affords evidence, which is confirmed in early Christian literature, of the

[1] 1 Cor. x. 4.

[2] Cf. Hennecke, *op. cit.*, pp. 158–180; Schultze, *Archaeologie*, etc., pp. 180–185.

[3] In especial they were also the occurrences referred to in ancient funeral liturgies; Le Blant, *Étude sur les sarcophages Chrétiennes antiques de la ville d'Arles*, Introduction, §§ 4 and 5; Pérate, *L'Archéologie Chrétienne*, pp. 70–74.

novel and spiritualized import which they had for
Christians. The ancient Jewish religion held scant
expectation of a future life; divine deliverances
related to the earthly fortunes of the chosen people.
Not so with Christians. Their faith did not deliver
them from human enemies and earthly torment. The
faith of Christ delivers from the bondage of death,
and raises up the believer unto eternal life. Naturally the Christian interpreted Old Testament deliverances and also the miracles of Christ as symbolical
of this. The first cause of its need, the sin of our
first parents, was frequently shown in the catacombs.[1]
On the other hand, habits of allegorical interpretation prevailed in both pagan and Christian literature;
allegory and symbolism were common in pagan sculpture and painting; and sheer symbols are frequent in
the catacombs. When symbolism and allegory were
common·in art, and when that system of allegorical
interpretation which made the Old Testament prefigurative of Christ was coming to universal acceptance,
many Christians must have thus interpreted these
Old Testament scenes. Such allegorical significance
may also have been in the minds of the painters, or
at least of those who directed them.

This mention of subjects and these suggestions as
to their interpretation are far from exhausting the
range or significance of the paintings in the Roman
catacombs. There occur Christian themes not readily
falling within the topic of the saving power of God,

[1] Perhaps the teachings of Paul — as in Adam we all died, so in
Christ are we made alive (Rom. v) — had something to do with the
frequency of this subject in the Roman catacombs.

as well as figures and designs taken from the common decorative painting of the time. In style and technique the entire painting of the catacombs is part of the Græco-Roman antique. The work was carried on with dim light; Christians were not rich enough to employ the best artists; hence, this painting never surpasses, and is often inferior to, contemporary pagan decoration. Its best performances are figures like Psyche, frankly taken from the pagan art. The Christian compositions are inferior.[1] Frequently they rest with a bare indication of the subject, with slight detail or setting.[2] The many palpable symbols bespeak a child's need to make a sign for what it cannot express. Indeed, the more distinctively Christian paintings in the catacombs are just childlike compositions, inadequate, unfinished, immature. Yet they suggest the furthest hopes of man, and with quiet assurance of their realization beyond the grave. There is no reference to the persecutions which occasionally, or to the hatreds which continually, beset the Christian folds. No martyrdom is drawn, but palms and lilies are painted on the tombs of those who sweetly, sometimes through fire and blood, passed to immortal life.[3] The catacombs are at peace with all the world; in them is naught but hope assured, and joy and love.[4]

[1] Moses striking the Rock, or Daniel among the Lions, or Noah in the Ark exhibit utter inferiority in composition compared with the Psyche or some of the pictures of the Good Shepherd.

[2] Noah in the Ark is an illustration of this.

[3] Not that the palm or lily is to be taken as evidence of a martyrdom, but generally of the victory over death.

[4] In this there was no total departure from the pagan antique; for in Roman and Greek paganism there is peace in the tomb, and sometimes cheerfulness, but little hope.

Little Christian sculpture can be placed before the time of Constantine. Possibly the statue of Christ as the Good Shepherd, in the Lateran Museum, belongs to the third century, to which belong a very few carved Christian sarcophagi. There are at Rome many Christian sarcophagi of the fourth and fifth centuries. Their reliefs present mainly the circle of Biblical subjects painted in the catacombs, and may be interpreted in the same way. Their style is the Græco-Roman antique of the time; and, as with the paintings in the catacombs, the Christian compositions are inferior to those borrowed from pagan designs.

Outside of Rome, the sarcophagi of these centuries have sometimes the same characteristics as the Roman, and sometimes show deviations. For example, the sarcophagi of the southeastern part of Gaul (Provence) resemble the Roman in style, while those of the southwest (Aquitaine) show local peculiarities and perhaps barbarisms. The former, and still more the latter, group of sarcophagi present some new Biblical subjects, and omit certain subjects carved upon the Christian sarcophagi of Rome. The Ravenna sarcophagi show Eastern influences, and some of them are altogether Byzantine.

The course of antique Christian sculpture was comparatively unimportant. After Hadrian's time the technique of Italian sculptors rapidly deteriorated. By the fourth century they could not carve the human figure correctly, whether nude or draped. The new stimulus which came to art with the free expansion of Christianity in the fourth century revived painting and mosaic, rather than sculpture. Much of the artistic impulse came from the East, from the new thriving capital, Constantinople, where sculpture was itself to become unsculpturesque. Nevertheless, even the Roman sarcophagi disclose a certain extension of the circle of subjects in the catacombs, and a certain modification in the mode of presentation, indicative of the new stage upon which Christian painting entered in the reign of Constantine.

When the imperial government became Christian, and Christianity was made the State religion, imposing edifices were at once erected for the purposes of Christian worship. These required decoration with subjects belonging to the Christian faith and according with the exultation of the faithful. A whole circle of novel religious compositions was demanded; and the demand was met with an energy giving to this novel creation of Christian pictures the appearance of a revival of art in a decadent time. And so it was; but this revival was limited to sacred art, and, in Italy and the West, was to succumb to the calamities of barbarian invasion, famine, and pestilence. At Constantinople the Christian revival of art was more lasting, and passed through vicissitudes before its final mummification.

With respect to the impermanence of this Christian revival, one should bear in mind that the arts depend on technique, and are otherwise subject to the artistic and intellectual limitations of the period. In literature and philosophy the greatness of the fourth and fifth centuries was confined to the writings of men inspired by Christianity and moved by ecclesiastical and apologetic needs. Outside of these Christian writings and the inspiration of the Christian situation, the West saw no intellectual progress and little human growth. The same conditions limited the Christian revival of art. There had come fresh inspiration with novel and exhaustless topics; but the living forces which make a period one of catholic human advance were either too crude, or too confused and wavering, to unite with the new inspiration and move onward in the whole strength of human faculty to the creation of a clear new style.

The new situation of the Church in the fourth century caused a change in the purposes and character of Christian art, which had now to illuminate the triumphant edifices where henceforth the Christians were to worship. Upon the walls of the new-built basilicas the Christian faith was to be set forth prophetically, in its Old Testament types, historically, in the miraculous scenes of the life of Christ, and finally, in the victory of the cross and the afar-descried realization of the visions of the Apocalypse. The faith was to endure forever, and the most everlasting artistic means should be employed to illustrate it.

Mosaics were a well-known mode of decoration. Most common was the use of marble mosaics for pavements. This continued in churches. But the grand endeavor of the Christian decorator was to glorify the walls of the churches with monumental compositions in glass and enamel setting forth Christian themes. The Romans had used mosaics of this kind for mural decoration, as Pompeian remains testify; the catacombs can also show some specimens of the art. But in the Christian revival of art these mosaics were

used with a new glory and unparalleled success.
They became the chief mode of church decoration,
and illustrate most markedly the change in the character and style of Christian art and the extension
of its range of subjects in the fourth and fifth
centuries.

Early Christian preaching frequently referred to
the striking and prefigurative incidents of the Old
Testament and to the prophets who foretold Christ;
also to the events of Christ's life and the miracles
wrought by Him. Thus many of the most impressive
incidents of the Bible became familiar. The artists
whose task it was to fill the new-built churches of the
fourth and fifth centuries with Christian pictures
would naturally have chosen these same subjects,
many of which were eminently pictorial. But doubtless it was the Church authorities who selected them
for the churches. Thus the events approved by authority, emphasized in preaching, familiar to the
people, and described by poets,[1] were painted on the
church walls for the beautifying of the churches and
the edification of the faithful.

These scenes do not fall within narrow limits. They
include the most pictorial events of the Old Testament
and its Apocrypha, and also representations of Biblical personages; they reproduce the life of the Saviour
in those incidents which have been familiar to all gen-

---

[1] Prudentius and Paulinus of Nola have described series of these
scenes as these poets saw them on the walls of basilicas; Prudentius, *Dittochaeon;* Paulinus, *Poemata*, XXIV, XXV. Cf. Von
Schlosser, *Quellenbuch zur Kunstgeschichte des abendländischen
Mittelalters;* Kraus, *op. cit.*, I, 383–398; Ficker, *Die Bedeutung der
altchristlichen Dichtungen für die Bildwerke.*

erations.   Then these pictures extend beyond the
Bible, and draw subjects from the Apocryphal Gospels and Acts; they tell the whole story of the Virgin's life and parentage, and complete the circle from
the stories of the great company of angels, saints, and
martyrs.   The fourth and fifth centuries made the
beginning.   Thereafter the series continued to expand,
while custom and authority tended to order it and
to keep the methods of representation in accord with
tradition.

The most impressive of these church mosaics are
the symbolic scenes from the Apocalypse which regularly glorify the apse and the triumphal arch.   The
scenes of the nave were taken from the Old Testament
or from the earthly life of Christ; they represent
prophets or other Church heroes in the guise in which
they lived on earth.   Whenever these appear in the
apse, they are shown in their state of future glory, and
so harmonize with the apocalyptic character of apse
decorations.   The central figure of the apse and the
triumphal arch is Christ represented in human form
or under the symbol of the Lamb.   But the lamb is
not the symbol of the Saviour's earthly life, nor in
any way related to the Good Shepherd of the catacombs; it is the Lamb of the Apocalypse.   And in
general, while the symbolism of the catacombs sets
forth the saving power of Christ as exerted through
the believer's earthly life and in the hour of death,
this symbolism sets forth the triumph of the Lamb
that was slain and the final coming of the Kingdom
of God.

No less marked than the extension of the circle of

subjects was the change in the character and the elevation of the style of Christian painting in the fourth and fifth centuries. In catacomb paintings, figures and features were indeterminate; now they have become clear in type and individuality; St. Peter, St. Paul, Christ, have all reached their typical individualities. In the catacombs, scenes or objects were occasionally depicted for their own sake, and not because of their religious significance. An example of this is the figure of Diogenes the Fossor (digger) in S. Domitilla. But the usual purpose of catacomb painting was to typify the saving power of God, which should raise the Christian alive at the Last Day. Symbols like the fish and anchor were used in hieroglyphic fashion. Even in Biblical scenes the composition appears as a sign or a suggestion rather than a complete picture of the subject. It is different with the mosaics of the churches. They are grand and elaborate compositions; the apparent intention is to set forth the subject adequately and with a pictorial sufficiency of detail. The lowly simplicity of the former time, with its gentle other-world calm, is changed to stately triumph; the dignity of Rome, the ceremony of Byzantium, are entering these mosaics. Naturally the naïve symbolism and suggestion of catacomb paintings make way for a larger historical rendering and a stricter dogmatic presentation of Christian topics. Many of the simpler symbols disappear;[1] those elements of symbolism and allegory which are retained are dogmatically perfected in forms some of which became canonical

[1] *E.g.*, the Fish.

in Christian art;[1] and in this new art of the victory
of the Church the topics symbolized are chiefly taken
from the Apocalypse.

The productiveness of the fourth and fifth centuries
in Christian compositions was extraordinary. Many
of the subjects had never been treated. And when we
consider that the greatest art owes to the art preceding
it the full debt of child to parent, and that its noblest
compositions borrow much from prior designs, then we
shall realize how great was the work of these mosa-
icists. Was the artistic source of this art Greek or
Latin; did it flow from the East or rise in the West?
Most of the extant monuments are in Italy — because
there they have been preserved. In the fourth century, as previously, in dogma and the ascetic ideals of
Christian living, the initiative was from the East; the
West accepted it. In art also the initiative was from
the East, and was apparently Hellenic. The allegorism
which was to dominate the Latin Fathers came from
the Greeks, and the early symbols, like the Fish, occurring in the Roman catacombs. It would also appear
from the few scattered remains of early Christian art
in the eastern portions of the Empire, as well as from
descriptions of pictures in the works of Basil, Cyril of
Alexandria, and Gregory of Nyssa, that from the Hellenic East came the Christian compositions of the
fourth and fifth centuries.[2] Even in Italy the artists
probably were Greeks.

[1] An example of this formal and dogmatic symbolism is afforded
by the mosaics of the choir of St. Vitale in Ravenna, which cele-
brate the sacrifice of the Eucharist.

[2] See Bayet, *Récherches pour servir a l'histoire de la Peinture
et de la Sculpture chrétiennes en Orient*, Part I, Chaps. I and II;

Antique Christian art, in so far as it was Christian, differed in its subjects from pagan art as the antique Christian literature differed from pagan. But it was slow to develop new æsthetic motives or elements of ornament, and it continued to use the common decorative designs of pagan art; nor did it evolve new ideals of human beauty, though it wrought a certain desensualizing and spiritualization of Greek and Roman types of the human form. Yet this modification of types was but inchoate.

Some of the fourth and fifth century compositions were of great excellence, and were to constitute the type-pattern which Christian artists were to follow through the Middle Ages and the Renascence. Yet the incitement and directing influence in their production was largely ecclesiastical and dogmatic. Theological elements in them outstrip the human. The poetry, the feeling, the sentiment, encircling objects long thought upon and loved, have not yet come. These will germinate and flower in the course of centuries, and pass over into art, which will thereby be completed in the veritable tragic elements of love and pity and terror.[1] As in art, so in literature. The

ib., *L'art Byzantin*, p. 11. In the *Anthology*, Bk. I, are to be found a number of epigrams addressed to portraits of Christ and the archangel Michael; also epigrams upon the series of scenes so frequently represented in painting. These epigrams date from the beginning of the sixth to the ninth century.

[1] The fulness of feeling and the charm of poetry enter Western Christian art in the thirteenth century. The beginning may be traced in the Roman mosaics of the twelfth and thirteenth centuries. For example, the mosaics in the apse of S. Maria in Trastevere (1140) and in the apse of S. Clemente (cir. 1150) show a little sentiment, a little poetic feeling, which was not theological. Yet

fourth and fifth centuries were the great creative period
of dogma and doctrine; again, hundreds of years of
human growth are told before the Christian heart
expresses itself in poetry with a fulness and power
corresponding to those truths of man and God which
those early centuries had rendered definite to the
Christian mind.   In the fourth and fifth centuries the
genius of Christianity had not achieved full mastery
over the arts of painting and poetry; it had not fully
penetrated and transformed them; as yet it could not
adequately express itself and the sentiments and
emotions of the Christian soul through these noble
mediums of human expression.

III. *Byzantine Painting*

The history of Christian painting and sculpture in
Italy and the West after the fifth century cannot easily
be divided into periods.   But the processes can be distinguished, through which emerged the art of the
thirteenth century, Christian in style, feeling, and
sentiment, as well as in contents.   These processes

these elements are still very faint. They become more pronounced
in Torriti's "Coronation of the Virgin," in the apse of S. Maria
Maggiore (1295), and still more in the lovely mosaics depicting the
Virgin's life, in the lower zone of the apse of S. Maria in Trastevere
(cir. 1290), by Cavallini. One may say as to these mosaics, that the
stags which drink the waters of life have become eager for them;
the angels are not only decorative, but have love and tears and pity;
and the flowers have become lovely, have become even the "seintes
flurs" of Paradise, on which the soul of Roland may repose. The
same growth of appropriate feeling and poetic sentiment may be
followed in the Gothic sculpture of France and in the great advance
of painting in Italy with Giotto.

are, on the one hand, those of decay and barbarization as well as of intentional discarding; while, on the other, they consist in modes of human growth — the development of intellect, sentiment, and emotion, the acquisition of faculty and knowledge, the maturing of artistic thought, and the clarification of ideals.

The Christian revival of art in the fourth and fifth centuries has been spoken of. In the East, the artistic centre being Constantinople, this revival resulted in an art distinct in style from the antique. In Italy and the countries of the West, having part in Roman civilization, the Christian revival of art yielded to advancing barbarism and the prevailing decadence. The influences of Byzantine art tended to preserve the art of Italy from barbarization and to stamp a certain impress upon it, until the artistic capacities of the emerging Western culture were sufficient to conquer antique and Byzantine lessons, and move on to the great religious art of the Middle Ages with its essential oneness and manifold local differences.

The antique style, which is retained and ennobled in the great mosaics of S. Pudenziana in Rome (fourth century) and the mausoleum of Galla Placidia in Ravenna (fifth century), cannot properly be called Roman or Italian.[1] One may speak of Roman archi-

[1] The same may be said of the oldest Christian mosaics in Italy, those of S. Costanza, a circular memorial church built and decorated in Constantine's time. Those remaining in the vault are taken from pagan decorative designs. The decorations of the apses are Christian: in one, God gives the Old Law to Moses; in the other, Christ gives the New Law to Peter (De Rossi, *Musaici Cristiani*, Fasc. XVII, XVIII). These two compositions have been

tecture; but painting and sculpture at Rome were
rather Græco-Roman. They had come from Greece
and were practised by Greeks.[1] In the latter years
of the Republic and through the first centuries of
the Empire, these arts, as practised by Greeks in
the service of Romans, tended toward the production
of types differing from those of the classical art of
Greece and from those of the contemporary art of
the eastern portions of the Empire. Greek sculpture
at Rome would be subject to special influences and
would undergo modifications. These influences are

barbarized through restorations; they may never have been as
good as the conventional pagan compositions on the vault. Artists
of the fourth century, struggling with new subjects, might commit
faults not found in earlier, frequently repeated designs, which were
merely decorative and contained no large drawings of the human
form. Cf. E. Müntz, *Revue Archéologique*, 1875, Vol. 30, pp. 224–
230, 273–284.

[1] Were there ever any Roman sculptors or Roman sculpture
properly speaking? In early days at Rome there was Etruscan influence. Then came the Greek wave, and sculpture was carried on
by Greeks, some of whom, however, may have been born in Italy.
Maxime Collignon, in the concluding pages of the second volume
of his *Histoire de la Sculture Grecque*, speaks of sculpture at
Rome at the beginning of the Empire as being entirely in the hands
of Greeks. See also Ernest Gardner, *Handbook of Greek Sculpture*,
Vol. II, Chap. 6. Pliny in his lists of sculptors has only Greek names,
Naturalis Historiae, Lib. XXXVI, §§ 9–44; cf. Jex-Blake and Sellers,
Pliny's Chapters on the History of Art (1896). Schnaase, *Geschichte
der Bildenden Kunste*, Vol. II, Chap. 4. Nor was there any specifically Roman painting; that was also Greek. See Schnaase, *op. cit.*,
II, Chap. 4; Woltmann and Woermann, *History of Painting*, Bk. II,
Chap. I et seq. Yet the opposite view of Wickhoff, *Roman Art*, is
of interest. There were Roman names among the painters at Rome,
from the time of the curious example of the noble Fabius Pictor
(303 B.C.) onward. Cf. Friedländer, *Sittengeschichte Roms*, 6th ed.,
III, 300.

plain in historical relief work like that on Trajan's
column, which was a careful record of a conquest,
and again they are pronounced in portrait sculpture.
The subjects being Romans, the portraits naturally
showed Roman features.   Moreover, the Romans preferred to be portrayed clothed in the toga, or in
armor, rather than nude, which would have suited
the Greek taste: *Graeca res est nihil velare, at contra
Romana ac militaris thoraca addere,* says Pliny.[1]   In
the East these influences would rarely operate, or these
Roman modifications occur.

An artist tends to reproduce what he sees and what
he is; what he is, is affected by his environment.   At
Rome and in Italy painting as well as sculpture, by
whomsoever practised, tended to differ from the art
of the East, where scenes and people were Greek and
oriental.   The Pompeian frescoes afford an example.
They are Greek works, yet are touched by the Italian
landscape and by Italian taste and the Italian type of
human form and feature.   The subjects were taken
from myth and legend; often the pictures were reproductions of classic Greek compositions.   But the human types in them seem to differ generically from the
group of Greek portraits discovered at Fayoum in
Egypt.[2]   In fine, during the first centuries of the
Empire, painting in Italy was Greek, yet affected by
the influences of its environment.

[1] *Nat. Hist.*, XXXIV, 18.   The imperial statue of Augustus in
the Vatican is an example of this.

[2] Certain pictures at Pompeii seem to have been portraits.   See
Marriott, "Family Portraits at Pompeii," *The Archæological Journal*, 1897.   These also are Roman in type.

Making allowance for these differences in types, in the fourth and fifth centuries painting was still one art, having substantially one and the same style throughout the Empire. There is no reason to suppose that in Italy it did not continue in the hands of Greeks, who would there have produced the same kinds of religious pictures as at Constantinople.[1] These were the centuries when Christian mosaics reached the zenith of their excellence, as for instance in the church of S. Pudenziana and the mausoleum of Galla Placidia. Nothing in these compositions distinguishes them stylistically from paintings previously executed in Italy under pagan patronage, save their great excellence due to the revival of art under Christian inspiration. However, in tracing the course of that revival in those seats where it longest endured and produced most distinctive results, we shall also be tracing the development of Byzantine art. Rome was no longer the centre of power; and after Alaric captured the city in 410, her great name gave no sense of security to her inhabitants. The safest place in Italy was Ravenna, lying surrounded by marshes near the Adriatic. There Honorius fixed the imperial court of the West in 404. Ravenna, being the seat of government, was the city in closest touch with Constantinople, the Eastern seat of empire. In consequence of all these circumstances the most beautiful mosaics of the fifth century are to be found at Ravenna, adorning the mausoleum of that same energetic princess whose beneficence adorned with mosaics

[1] The reliefs of the doors of S. Sabina on the Aventine were probably executed in the fifth century by Greek artists.

the triumphal arch of S. Paulo Fuori at Rome.   And
it is at Ravenna that this art most distinctly discloses
the development of a definite style which gradually
shows itself Byzantine.   Yet artistically Ravenna was
less than Constantinople.   If the Adriatic city was
wealthy, powerful, and secure, the city on the Bosphorus surpassed her in safety, power, and wealth.
And Constantinople was more fully Greek than Ravenna, and was possessed of a store of Greek art with
which her founder had endowed her.   But the evolution of the Byzantine style in mosaics can no longer
be traced in the plundered city of the Bosphorus ;
while in grass-grown Ravenna may yet be seen the
progress from the renewed and ennobled antique art of
the fifth century to the Byzantine style of Justinian's
time, which later will show Byzantine characteristics
hardening to faults.

The decorations of the Mausoleum and of S. Giovanni in Fonti represent the culmination at Ravenna
of the Christian revival of art, which in Rome fifty
years before had culminated in the great mosaic of
S. Pudenziana.   As yet the Ravenna mosaics show
no specific Byzantine traits.[1]   A next stage is represented by the mosaics of S. Apollinaris Nuovo, built
by Theodoric about the year 500.   Those in the upper
part of the nave narrate the miracles and incidents of
Christ's life.   They are better compositions than the

[1] Besides the noble composition of Christ as the Good Shepherd
amid his sheep, the Mausoleum contains (among other pictures) an
early and idealized representation of a martyrdom.   St. Lawrence
bearing a cross advances toward the gridiron set on a bed of flames ;
the picture shows no torture, suggests no pain, but only the triumph
of the martyr's faith.

historical series from the Old Testament in the nave of S. Maria Maggiore at Rome; and they show some slight tendency toward the formal symmetry which was to characterize Byzantine art. This is more pronounced in the procession of saints and angels which moves along the architraves above the columns of the nave to meet in the triumph of the tribuna. In this grave and stately composition appears moreover the ceremonialism which also was to be characteristic of Byzantine art. Yet a third stage is represented by the mosaics of S. Vitale, the work of the first years of the Exarchate (cir. 550) in Justinian's time. These magnificent decorations develop certain Byzantine types, as, for instance, of angels; in the choir the sacrifice of the eucharist is represented in the Old Testament incidents prefiguring it. A ceremonial and dogmatic symbolism appears, while ceremonialism of another kind is shown in the representation of the Emperor Justinian and the Empress Theodora. These characteristics — dogmatic symbolism, ceremonialism, formal symmetry — stiffen and become monotonous, while the figures lose their beauty, in the incipient decadence of the mosaics in S. Apollinaris in Classe.[1]

At Rome, also, certain mosaics of the fifth, sixth, and seventh centuries show traces of the style which is becoming Byzantine, though this evolution is less clearly marked than at Ravenna. Possibly the mosaics on the triumphal arch of S. Maria Maggiore of the first part of the fifth century show a *Byzantinismo incipiente*,[2]

---

[1] The church was built soon after S. Vitale; but the extant mosaics referred to in the text date from the seventh century.

[2] De Rossi.

which does not appear in the somewhat earlier mosaics of the nave. In the impressive apse mosaic of SS. Cosmo and Damiano (sixth century) there is something not inherited from the antique style, something which possible traces of the lineaments of the northern barbarians will hardly account for. The draperies of the individual figures are not so very hard, nor their attitudes so very stiff; but a symmetry like the Byzantine controls the composition as a whole.[1] Possibly the mosaics in the arch of S. Lorenzo (578-590) and in the apse of S. Agnese Fuori, of about the same time, show clearer traces of the transition from the antique to the Byzantine. The calamities of Italy from war, pestilence, and famine in the seventh century were contemporary with a lessening of Eastern influence. In consequence, art rapidly declined, sinking to its lowest level in the eighth century. The ninth brings a renewed activity at Rome, yet the mosaics show ignorance and incapacity,[2] and a barbarism which seems just touched by the Byzantine style.

Apart from the influences which may be called Byzantine, no new style of sculpture, painting, or

[1] De Rossi, *Musaici Cristiani*, in the text accompanying the reproduction of this mosaic, says: " Esso segna un passo notabile del processo più o meno lento, che l'antica arte cristiana transformò nella così detta bizantina. La monotona e dura simmetria della composizione è difetto dominante . . ."

[2] This decay appears strikingly upon comparing the apse mosaic of SS. Cosmo and Damiano (sixth century) with the degenerate imitation of it in the Church of S. Praxede (ninth century). The mosaics on the triumphal arch of SS. Nereo ed Achilleo (cir. 800) and in the apse of S. Cecilia in Trastevere (ninth century) also show art at a low level.

mosaics was developed in Italy during the centuries under consideration. The analogy of architecture bears indirect testimony to this. Under the Republic and during the first two centuries of the Empire, the Roman genius was creative in architecture, but not even then in painting or sculpture. Upon the conversion of the Empire the basilica type, which had become Roman, maintained itself in Italy. But Roman Christian basilicas show no architectural development from the time of their first construction. The East, however, can show the evolution of a distinct Christian architecture culminating in S. Sophia.

Thus the influences which promote the development of a distinct style in Italy, and also tend to retard the barbarization of art, are Greek, and are continually recruited from the East. Naturally they reflect the course of art at Constantinople and other Eastern cities. The general features of Byzantine art in its Eastern home may be summarized as follows: The antique survived, potent and moulding; Christian schools of painting and mosaic appropriated the antique, and also departed from it in modes which do not represent decadence, but the evolution of a distinct style — a style, however, not original and new, for the race was mature, and the classic heritage was overpowering. This art shows no spontaneity of youth and scant faculty of drawing new artistic truth from nature. Non-Hellenic elements from Syria, from Persia, from the East indefinitely, seem also to have affected the development of Byzantine art. That art took to itself the ceremony of the Byzantine court, which sought to elevate the Emperor above mankind. If this was Asiatic in part, it had begun with Diocletian. At all events, ceremonialism, passing into art, conduced to the hardening of certain inherited Hellenic principles, — for example, the principle of symmetry. Classical art had reached the pliant symmetry of life. In Byzantine art the symmetry of life gives place to a formal arrangement of figures.

In harmony with its ceremonialism, and following the spirit of the Greek formulation of Christianity in dogma, Byzantine art presents a dogmatic orthodoxy. This appears in its symbolism, which is systematized and made strictly to conform to the doctrines of the Church. It also appears in the representations of Christ and the Virgin. There is no mistaking the divine nature of the Byzantine Christ — he is ever ὑπερούσιος, as in the great hymn of Romanos; and the Virgin is ever θεοτόκη, the mother of God. Byzantine images of Christ and his mother differ from those of mediæval Western art as the same poet's *Hymn of the Virgin at the Cross* differs from the Stabat Mater. One may not seek in them the humanity of the God-man. The Sufferer is not in Byzantine art, nor does the Madonna weep for a crucified Son. The symbols attached to the images of Christ signify unmistakably the God. No nature less than absolute divinity might bear the great crossed nimbus, whereon the letters Alpha and Omega declare that this is He who was before all time and is eternal — in whose eternity the earthly episodes of Jesus' life are but a point. These are images of God the Son rather than of the Son of God.

Byzantine art has greatness. Its stately mosaic compositions are magnificently decorative, harmonizing with the forms and functions of the architecture they adorn, admirably suited for the sufficient ornamentation of edifices containing little sculpture. Their grace is not that of Nature's lithe pliancy, but the gracious stateliness of forms that move without movement, rhythmic elements of great church decoration. Beautiful colors are combined in balanced schemes showing a genius for color values, which may have come from the East and not have been a classic heritage. The drawing and coloring of the figures display the architecturally beautifying effect of colored composition to a degree which Gothic stained glass windows surpass only through their sun-lit translucency. Each figure is religiously appropriate and decoratively beautiful. The majesty of Christ is unimpeached, the gracious dignity of God's mother unexcelled. Angelic forms are not debased by any striving after naturalism in the representation of what is not of this earth. Their wings are of surpassing beauty, not made to fly with, but drawn to symbolize the celerity with which the angelic nature does the will of God.[1]

In the sixth century Byzantine art develops its characteristics and reaches the summit of its excellence. This is true in miniature painting, in mosaics (S. Vitale), in architecture (S. Sophia), even in sculpture. A few existing Byzantine capitals of this period

---

[1] See the *Celestial Hierarchy*, Chap. XV. Bayet, *Récherches*, etc., says that the Byzantine type of angel was formed at the time when the writings of the Areopagite became known in the East.

show sculpture truly sculpturesque, as well as natural
in its reproduction of vine leaves and animals, although
the aversion to human images has weakened the carving of the human figure.[1]   Byzantine sculpture, however, soon ceased to observe nature; its foliage became
conventional, its animals fantastic.   Except in ivory
work, sculpture did not flourish with the Byzantines.
Even in the best period, the characteristic type of the
Byzantine column is that of S. Sophia or S. Vitale,
where the carving is mainly designing by incision.[2]

In the century after Justinian's death, disasters be-
fell the Eastern Empire, and a decline in art set in.
Leo the Isaurian inaugurated the iconoclastic conflict
in 726; that lasted with varying fortunes till the middle of the ninth century.[3]   Sometimes the reform-
ing iconoclasts were in power; again the monks and
all the hosts of image-worshippers gained ascendency.
The latter finally won the day, and, soon after, the
line of Macedonian emperors came to the throne, to
retain it for two centuries (867–1057), during which
the Eastern Empire prospered and art flourished.   But
this period is less progressive than that of the first
development of Byzantine art, which culminates in
Justinian's reign.   Many typical sacred compositions

[1] Strzygowski, *Byzan. Zeitschrift*, 1892, p. 574, etc., especially
pp. 582 and 589.

[2] Strzygowski, *Byz. Denkmäler*, I, p. 10, says that the Byzantine
basket capital is evolved from Theodosian capitals (eine Umbil-
dung); the basket takes the place of the acanthus leaves, and animals replace the volutes.

[3] A barren period (650–850 A.D.) in Byzantine literature corresponds to this period of decline in Byzantine art, Krumbacher, *Ges.
der Byz. Lit.*, 2d ed., p. 12.

had become fixed by the time of that Emperor's death;[1] and between the sixth and the ninth century artistic precedent, ecclesiastical precept, and the decrees of councils[2] had combined to render sacred painting immutable.[3] At length all sacred compositions were arranged and embodied in manuals from the injunctions of which the artists ceased to have the will or power to depart.[4]

These remarks suggest the modes in which Byzantine art declined after the eleventh century. Its originative power decayed; its technique and decorative qualities survived for a period; then they also declined. Decline became irretrievable ruin when the

[1] For example, the painting of the Arian baptistry in Ravenna (S. Maria in Cosmedin) of Theodoric's time copies that of the orthodox baptistry (S. Giovanni in Fonti).

[2] The second Nicene council, held under the auspices of the Empress Irene in 787, decreed the adoration of images. It recognized the eighty-second canon of the council of Trullo (692 A.D), directing that Christ should be represented under his human form rather than by a symbol (see Labbe, *Concilia*, ed. by Coletus (Venice, 1729), Vol. VIII, col. 813, 814, 881, 882). The second Nicene council also recognized that these sacred images should not be regarded as the design of the artist, but as embodying the authoritative tradition of the Church. Of course, if images were to be adored, — as they were through the Middle Ages in the East and West, — their fashioning could not be left to the caprice of the artist.

[3] Miniatures naturally preserved more freedom than church mosaics; see Kondakoff, *op. cit.*, Chap. VI.

[4] The reference is to the famous manuscript discovered by Didron at Mt. Athos, and frequently described and referred to in works upon Byzantine painting. It may be as late as the sixteenth century, and may describe compositions unknown to the earlier art. But on the whole its directions correspond to the remains of Byzantine painting, and probably embody traditions from the times when typical compositions first became recognized conventions.

Crusaders captured the Capital in 1204. Up to the eve of that destruction Constantinople was incomparably the most splendid city of Europe, a city marvellous, incredible, in art and splendor greater than all other cities, according to Villehardouin, who participated in its destruction.[1] Before then its art had done its work of instruction in Italy and the West, carrying its suggestions of technique and skill, and offering as models its conventional and stately, its beautifying and somewhat lifeless compositions.[2]

In Italy, as already noticed, in the seventh and eighth centuries, when Byzantine influences are weakest, art touches its lowest level. Yet traces of Byzantine work or suggestion at no time entirely disappear. With the eighth century, especially in northern Italy, special barbaric (Lombard) elements enter, which do not represent mere barbarization of the existing styles, but the beginnings of new styles. For example, the Baptistry at Cividale in Friuli (cir. 750) is one of the first instances of animal carving which was to characterize Romanesque sculpture; and in the tenth century the vaulted Lombard architecture takes its beginning under the influence of the Italo-Byzantine style.[3]

Magna Græcia of old had included Apulia, the

[1] See *Conquête de Constantinople*, § 128; in one of the conflagrations of the siege more houses were burnt than there were in the three largest cities in France; *ib.*, § 247.

[2] " Dans l'histoire de la civilisation au moyen âge avant le XIe siècle, Byzance a eu un rôle analogue à celui d'Athènes et de Rome dans l'antiquité, à celui de Paris dans les temps modernes. Elle a rayonné sur le monde entier; elle a été *la Ville* par excellence." Bayet, in Lavisse et Rambaud's *Histoire Générale*, Vol. I, p. 682.

[3] Cf. Cattaneo, *L'architettura in Italia*, Chaps. I, II, and III.

Terra d'Otranto, and Calabria. These Greek countries were conquered by the Romans in the third century before Christ, and thereafter were thoroughly Latinized. They remained Latin for centuries. From Justinian's time they formed part of the Eastern Empire; but the Latin and Italian character of their civilization was not affected before the iconoclastic conflict. Its opening found them under the ecclesiastical jurisdiction of the Roman See. Leo the Isaurian transferred them to the jurisdiction of the Patriarch of Constantinople. The Emperor made slight effort to suppress images in his Italian provinces; but he and his successors zealously pressed the adoption of the Greek language and the ritual of the Eastern Church. Quite as effectively the re-Hellenization of these lands was promoted by the bitterest opponents of the iconoclastic emperors, the Eastern monks who fled in multitudes to provinces where images were not suppressed. They brought their ritual, their language, customs, and painting with them. Not many generations passed before the Greek language and ritual, as well as Byzantine painting, gained ascendency in Calabria and Otranto, if not in Apulia. In the eleventh century the Greek governors were driven out by the Normans. These masters of Hellenized subjects were themselves among the last of many conquerors captivated by captive Greece.[1]

[1] The Saracenic influence is also marked; see Choisy, *Histoire de l'architecture*, II, 134-138; Clausse, *Basiliques et Mosaiques*, II, 524. In Sicily — at Palermo, Monreale, and Cephalù — the architecture (twelfth century) is Norman and Saracenic as much as Byzantine, but the mosaics (twelfth century) are mainly Byzantine. The sculpture of animals and human beings, as in the capitals of the

Not until the middle of the thirteenth century, the time of Frederic II, does Hellenism — and Orientalism — finally disappear before the Italian spirit.[1] Southern Italy still contains many Byzantine paintings executed between the ninth and the twelfth century.

Byzantine art is dominant in the south of Italy, and also in the northeast, where Venice and Torcello succeed Ravenna.[2] Yet even in southern Italy quite another art appears, barbarized and yet incipiently Italian. The superiority of Greek workmen was recognized. In the year 1070 Abbot Didier of Monte Cassino imported a colony of them. But again, as in the days of the Cæsars, Greek art in Italy becomes partially Italianized. The artists who revived mosaics at Rome in the eleventh and twelfth centuries kept to Byzantine types of composition and yet clothed their sacred figures, except the Virgin, in Roman costume and according to the Roman ritual. Their purely decorative designs imitate the ancient mosaics of the fourth to the sixth century. But in the twelfth century, art in Italy was not, as in the days of the Cæsars, to stop with a mere Italianizing of the Greek. Italy was reawakening; she was to renew her youth and then her manhood; but it was a new youth and a new manhood. New racial elements now made part

cloister of the Monreale cathedral, may perhaps be regarded as Norman; but there are many carved Saracenic and Byzantine designs.

[1] A considerable knowledge of Greek continued in these countries through the Middle Ages to the Renaissance, and in sections of Calabria and the Terra d'Otranto, Greek is still spoken. See Fr. Lenormant, *La Grande Grèce*, Vol. II, pp. 372–433.

[2] Ravenna was lost to the Eastern Empire in the eighth century.

of the Italian people; new inspirations had come to them, and new faculties were ripening. Pictures having more distinctive Italian traits were painted. Italy was now to be the sun of art herself, and no mere mirror to the Greek. Her own genius had reached the stage where, having used its Byzantine lessons, it could overcome and pass beyond them. Her art remembers its past knowledge, yet turns from precedent to life. The artists begin once more to bring nature into art. With Cimabue art is neither barbarous nor Byzantine. With Giotto and Ducio art is Italian; it is national and great, as once had been the art of Greece.[1]

IV. *The Antique in Mediæval Art*

The art of pagan antiquity is carried over to the Middle Ages through the Christian antique art of Italy and the Romanized countries of western Europe, and through the art called Byzantine. Aside from its novel subjects, the antique Christian art is first an humble branch, then a revival and ennoblement, and finally a barbarization of pagan art. In the East, pagan art is distinctly altered in its Christian use, and there results a definite new style, the Byzantine. As may readily be imagined, the question of the debt and relationship of mediæval to antique art is complicated

[1] Speaking of Torriti's mosaics (1295) in the apse of S. Maria Maggiore, and of the contemporary work of Cavallini in the lower zone of the apse of Sta. Mar. in Trastevere, De Rossi says both represent " la scuola italiana ancora pregna dello tradizione dell' arte greca, ma nella sua transizione al nuovo stile, del quale Giotto era allora famoso maestro ed iniziatore."

by many considerations. Yet definite antique influences upon mediæval art may be pointed out, as well as the survival of antique themes in the art of the Middle Ages. The evolution of mediæval sculpture and painting is analogous to that of mediæval architecture, and the three branches of art present some broad analogies to the history of mediæval literature.

From the time of their first appearance the northern races possessed certain artistic faculties, they built primitive structures, they carved and they painted. As they came in contact with Roman civilization and were converted to Christianity, their building, their carving and painting, were brought into comparison with the art and methods of the antique. They adopted the antique forms of church architecture. But the antique Christian basilica at Rome was constructed according to Roman methods out of material at hand in Rome and the vicinity. The northern peoples did not have the materials for concrete, and could not apply Roman methods, although they adopted the plan of the basilica. Hence an initial modification in methods of construction, while the plan of the basilica was adopted. Through the needs of mediæval churches and the necessities and possibilities of northern methods of construction, the partly borrowed and transitional Romanesque styles were developed, and at last the full originality of the Gothic.

In sculpture and painting, as in architecture, the native traits and faculties of these northern peoples affected their appreciation and appropriation of the Christian-antique and the Byzantine styles. Their own methods of decoration were not entirely abandoned; but the art and civilization to which they were being introduced were so much greater than their own, that their own art tended to succumb. North and west of the Alps, in the early Middle Ages, the antique was imitated and modified according to the character of the people and the capacities of the artist. New styles developed as the builders and artists of France, Germany, and England reached the level of what they had borrowed from antiquity and passed on along paths of their own invention.

Italy was the home of the antique and was more generally subject to Byzantine influence than any northern land. In spite of foreign admixtures, its inhabitants were largely descendants of the antique races. Naturally the antique and Byzantine maintained a longer and more complete dominance in Italy than in the north, just as the Italian language was slower than the French in asserting its literary dignity as against the Latin.

The Carolingian period represents in the north the dominance of the antique and the Byzantine in art. Charlemagne's reign was a titanic labor for order and civilization, and for the extension of Christianity and the suppression of superstitious practices attached to it. The antique literature and knowledge, the antique arts, the Roman civil and political forms, were the quarry whence the Emperor and his ministers could draw. Rome was also the preëminent source of Christianity for all the peoples of the north. Any struggle for order and civilization in this period had to draw upon the only civilization and order then

known in western Europe, that of the Roman Empire.
But Charlemagne did not ignore the elements of culture and strength in his own peoples.   He had the
German poems collected and preserved.   Nevertheless, the literature of the time was Latin, and showed
a distinct striving after antique metre and form.   In
fine, Charlemagne's struggle for a better culture and
civilization could hardly avoid taking the form of an
attempted revival of the antique.   This was recognized
by the Emperor and by those familiar with his policy.
Eginhard writes that Charlemagne's ceaseless endeavor was to restore the supremacy of Rome; [1] like
thoughts are prominent in the poetry of the period;

Aurea Roma interum renovata renascitur orbi. [2]

These ideas were probably vague and confused; Eginhard's Latin does not convey a clear meaning, and
the poet's . line expresses but a fancied ideal.   Yet
such thoughts reached their reality in the actual domi-
nation of the antique in the literature and art of the
ninth century.

At this time the interiors of churches were covered
with paintings, a custom coming from the antique
Christian mosaic and fresco decoration.   Charlemagne's Capitularies provide for the renovation of
churches, including their decorations.   The imperial
decrees suggest an artistic activity, which, in fact,
existed.   The Emperor, however, expressed himself
with no uncertain voice against the worship of images.
Carolingian architecture consisted in the use and ex-

---

[1] *Vita Caroli*, Cap. 27.
[2] *Nasonis Ecloga*, Dümmler, *Poet. Lat. Aev. Car.*, I, 385.

tension of antique Roman Christian or Byzantine forms; for example, the royal chapel at Aix-la-Chapelle was built upon the model of S. Vitale. No large sculpture comes down from the time of Charlemagne; but the ivory carving copies or imitates Byzantine or antique Christian models. The painted church decoration followed the antique, and continued and also extended the cycle of antique Christian subjects. In this church decoration, as well as in the miniatures, Byzantine and Syrian influence made itself felt through the ninth century. In at least one respect, however, miniature painting significantly departed from the antique. Instead of antique idyllic motives, it shows a veritable Teutonic and mediæval interest in war and fighting. Also Celtic (Irish) and German motives appear in the purely decorative patterns of the manuscript illumination.

Thus the architecture, sculpture, and painting of the Carolingian age are in the main a continuance or reproduction of the Christian antique and the Byzantine. The influence of these styles affected Carolingian art in a catholic manner, moulding the form and largely supplying the substance. There resulted that general uniformity which marks the art of the early Middle Ages. After the ninth and tenth centuries the effect of the antique and Byzantine, though still clearly marked, is less catholic; and the early mediæval uniformity is broken by the growth of national individuality, which shows a different character in the various countries of northern Europe.

Some of the antique influences and survivals in mediæval art may be mentioned. An example of the survival of the antique is afforded by the habit of personifying the subjects represented. In all periods of mediæval art are to be found personifications of natural objects, like rivers, of human vices and virtues,[1] of the arts and sciences, of the months and signs of the Zodiac and the seasons of the year. Many creatures of pagan myth and legend, monsters, human personages and demi-gods, survive in mediæval art,[2] — Satyrs and Centaurs, Sirens and Sibyls. These figures may be simply ornamental, or the myth may carry a moral and Christian significance. For example, Ulysses and the Sirens symbolize temptation,[3] and the Sibyls appear among those who prophesied of Christ. Throughout the Middle Ages the representation of animals, realistically or conventionally or fantastically, was universal, and the influence of the *Physiologus* is continually encountered, a work apparently first composed in Greek in Alexandria. Not infrequent in mediæval art were representations of antique themes of legend and history which were

[1] The Christian virtues and vices, personified so frequently through mediæval art, were not the virtues and vices of paganism — quite the contrary. Nor were the human qualities which they represented subjects of pagan antique art, with some few exceptions. It was this general habit of personifying human qualities that came from the antique.

[2] The *Libri Carolini*, Lib. III, Cap. 23 (Migne, *Patr. Lat.*, Vol. 98), express themselves strongly against the representation of rivers and other natural objects by means of human figures, and against other untruthful creations of pagan art, but such personifications appear in Carolingian miniature painting. See Leitschuh, *op. cit.*, pp. 32 et seq., 274 et seq.

[3] Ulysses and the Sirens appear as a symbol of temptation in the twelfth century *Hortus Deliciarum* of Abbess Herrad, of Hohenburg in Alsace.

popular in mediæval literature; prominent among them
was the legend of Alexander the Great.

Most of the foregoing themes of art were pagan as
well as antique. It is different with the antique influences still to be mentioned. Quite plain is the survival
of antique and Byzantine designs and motives of decoration in church sculpture[1] and painting, in the miniature illustration of manuscripts, and in ivory carving.
Somewhat less tangible, and yet real, was the survival
of antique and Byzantine ways of ordering and composing the subject of the painting or sculpture. A
plain example of this is afforded by the Bernward
column in Hildesheim (eleventh century), which in
its spiral ordering of the composition follows Trajan's
column.[2] Again the general arrangement of figures
in the tympanums over the Romanesque church doors
at Vézelay, Autun, Moissac, and on the capitals of
Moissac and of St. Trophime at Arles recall the panels
of antique Christian sarcophagi, while movement and
drapery suggest the Byzantine style.[3] Finally, the

[1] See, generally, Viollet-le-Duc, *Dictionnaire*, article " Sculpture." On the Romanesque capitals in the south of France appear
the acanthus of antique capitals and the fantastic animals observed
in works from the Orient. In Provence, Roman ornamentation is
copied, and in Poitou, Byzantine ornament (Choisy, *Hist. de l'architecture*, II, 169, 180). The capitals of St. Michael's and St. Godehard's
at Hildesheim likewise show the antique acanthus leaf, as do many
other Romanesque churches of Germany.

[2] Also the Bernward doors to the cathedral at Hildesheim seem
to imitate the doors of S. Sabina at Rome. See Bertram, *Die
Thüren von S. Sabina*, etc. Hence they are indirectly related to
Byzantine art, to which the doors of S. Sabina (fifth to sixth
century) are related.

[3] Choisy, *Histoire de l'architecture*, Vol. II, pp. 180–181; Viollet-
le-Duc, *Dictionnaire*, article " Sculpture," pp. 104–116.

antique and Byzantine survive in drapery and costume and in types of form and feature.[1]

The survival of the antique does not represent the more positive and original side of the development of mediæval art, which advances by using the antique and in friendly competition with it. Between the twelfth and the fourteenth century mediæval art culminates in styles organic in their growth, and novel and original. This art, being no copy, has mastered and transformed the suggestions from the past which it has used. But the victory over the antique is not the victory of native northern traits, or methods of decoration, existing in early times and apart from the influence of Roman culture. Such traits and ways of decoration had existed; they showed themselves in early Irish and Anglo-Saxon miniature painting. They even affected the art of the Carolingian period. Here they came in conflict with the antique styles, and the latter won the day. Generally these original elements in their unmodified state neither come to dominance in mediæval art nor constitute its greatness. Its growth and greatness spring rather from faculties and capacities, tastes, conceptions, and ideals, evolved and matured in the course of mediæval progress and development, from which the general educational and evolutionary influence of the antique was never absent. Under the Christian dispensation and the tutelage of the antique, the growing faculties and advancing conceptions of mediæval peoples evolve styles of art in which antique and Byzantine elements are superseded or transformed.

[1] This is plain in Carolingian art.

These transformations and changes may be roughly grouped. In the personifications there takes place a mediæval Christianizing of the human figures. Hosts of angels and demons are carved or painted in a style that is completely Christian and mediæval, and neither antique nor Byzantine. The pagan antique monsters and personages become relatively unimportant, except the Sibyl. Instead of one Sibyl, the later Middle Ages and the Renaissance have many; and the representation of them becomes frequent. Yet it is to be remembered that, although Christian literature took the Sibyl from paganism, the Sibyl in mediæval art was an original Christian creation. The legends of the saints and martyrs are represented in untold numbers, and the legend of Charlemagne and his paladins vies with the legend of Alexander. Gothic ornamentation drawn from living plants and foliage supplants antique and Byzantine conventions.[1]

In the composition of single figures, and in their grouping, the antique and the Byzantine give way to the mediæval. In Italy, with Giotto and Ducio, the formal hieratic symmetry of arrangement yields to compositions in which the grouping seen in nature and in actual events is harmonized and idealized. An analogous revolution takes place in the north. The antique compositions of Romanesque sculpture are changed in Gothic compositions. The grouping of the latter is often natural and easy. Above all, it

[1] This revolution from its beginning in the Romanesque period can best be seen in France. See, for a fine statement of it, Louis Gonse, *La Sculpture Française*, introductory chapter, especially p. 7. Also *ib.*, *L'art Gothique*, p. 410, etc.

is architectural, germane to the structure of the building, which it makes plain and emphasizes. From the
twelfth century, moreover, the cycle of subjects in
church painting and sculpture enlarges, and becomes
a mirror of universal life, as known and ordered in
the Christian science of the Middle Ages. The creation and ordering of this gigantic whole was the
supreme achievement of the Middle Ages in artistic
composition. In certain subjects the general lines of
antique Christian or Byzantine compositions might be
retained as sacred; but the elements which were preserved were modified, and then engulfed in this new
world of Gothic sculpture.

The antique types of form and feature pass away;
their place is taken by types which are not abstract
and conventional, but formed from observation of
mediæval humanity. These become real, national,
individual, conforming to the characteristics of the
peoples creating them.[1] There is, however, another
supreme fact regarding them. In the north the races
among whom they arise have been Christian from the
times of their barbarian childhood, and these types
have been matured under the Christian dispensation.
In Italy the new art of Giotto has also grown out of
the barbarism and decadence of the preceding Christian centuries. It, too, is Christian, and according to
its different national style will be found expressive of
Christian sentiments, emotions, and ideals, even as the
sculpture of the north expresses them. These per-

[1] Respecting the evolution of these true local types in French
Gothic, see Louis Gonse, *La Sculpture Française* (1895), pp. 9–15;
ib., *L'art Gothique*, Chap. XII.

fected mediæval types, as they may be seen on the
Church of the Arena at Padua, or on the Cathedral
of Rheims, are stamped with the racehood and artistic
genius of their creators, and yet they have also a
Christian character constituting a common element
which becomes stronger in them the more strongly
their different racial individuality is marked.   Hence,
these types differ from the antique Greek and Roman,
first, in that they are the true types of later times
and races, and secondly, in that they are Christian
and represent the expression in art of the distinctly
Christian emotions, — love, fear, grief, reverence, humility, and beatific joy, as well as the evil opposites of
these, — pride, anger, hatred, and disdain.   The genius
of Christianity has achieved full mastery over the
arts of painting and sculpture, it has penetrated and
transformed them, and can express itself and utter
the sentiments and emotions of the Christian soul
through these two noble means of human expression.
How completely the genius of Christianity mastered
architecture, sculpture, and painting, may be learned
from the long history of Christian art.   In scope and
purpose, in tone and feeling, Christian art has proved
equal to its great task of setting forth Christianity
as well as the joys and sorrows, the loves and abhor-
rences, of the Christian soul; it has been historical
and dogmatic, instructive and edifying, dignified and
formal; it has been symbolical and mystical; it has
been devotional, loving, joyful, and full of tears — as
many things as Christianity has been.

BIBLIOGRAPHY

Prepared for the Torchbook edition by Kenneth M. Setton, Henry C. Lea Professor of History, University of Pennsylvania.

The following lists of books are designed to identify for the reader some of the more important and more recent works relating to the various aspects of early medieval intellectual and cultural history with which Henry Osborn Taylor has dealt in *The Classical Heritage of the Middle Ages*. Often the most significant studies are to be found in the periodical literature, and the following learned journals are devoted solely or largely to the middle ages: *Bibliothèque de l'École des chartes*, 1839 ff.; *Le Moyen-Age*, 1888 ff.; *Byzantinische Zeitschrift*, 1892 ff.; *Revue d'histoire ecclésiastique*, 1900 ff.; *Byzantion*, 1924 ff.; *Speculum*, 1926 ff., Mediaeval Academy of America; *Archives d'histoire doctrinale et littéraire du moyen-âge*, 1926 ff.; *Medium Aevum*, 1932 ff.; *Classica et mediaevalia*, 1938 ff.; *Medieval Studies*, 1939 ff.; *Medieval and Renaissance Studies*, 1941 ff., Warburg Institute; *Traditio*, 1943 ff.; *Medievalia et humanistica*, 1943 ff.; and the *Revue du moyen-âge latin*, 1945 ff. The *Revue d'histoire ecclésiastique* and the *Byzantinische Zeitschrift* are especially noteworthy for their bibliographies.

For the last thirty-five years helpful bibliographical reports have been published in the successive bulletins of the *Progress of Medieval Studies in the United States and Canada*, 1923 ff., and for guidance among the many hundreds of journals in which articles on the middle ages may occur, see P. Caron and M. Jaryc, eds., *World List of Historical Periodicals and Bibliographies*, Oxford, 1939, and H. Kramm, ed., *Bibliographie historischer Zeitschriften, 1939–1951*, 2 vols., Marburg, 1952–3. There are national bibliographies to assist in the study of particular countries, such as Charles Gross, *Sources and Literature of English History from the Earliest Times to about 1485*, 2 ed., London, 1915. of which a new edition is needed; Dahlmann-Waitz, *Quellenkunde der deutschen Geschichte*, 9 ed. by H. Haering, Leipzig, 1931; Francesco Cognasso, *Avviamento agli studi di storia medievale*, Turin, 1951; B. Sánchez Alonso, *Fuentes de la historia española e hispanoamericana*, 3 ed., vol. I, Madrid, 1952, chaps. I–V on ancient and medieval Spain; and the *Bibliographie annuelle de l'histoire de France,* which appears each year and covers all topics and periods in French history. L. J. Paetow, *Guide to the Study of Medieval History,* 2 ed., New York, 1931, is still useful but obviously rather antiquated now (Gray C. Boyce is preparing a new edition). Another most helpful book is C. P. Farrar and A. P. Evans, *Bibliography of English Translations from Medieval Sources,* New York, 1946.

Few encyclopaedias are sufficiently trustworthy for serious reading in the history of medieval culture, but the following are all very valuable adjuncts to study: *Dictionnaire d'archéologie chrétienne et de liturgie,* Paris, 1903 ff.; *Dictionnaire de théologie catholique,* 15 vols. in 30, Paris, 1908–50, which ranges much more widely than its title suggests; *Dictionnaire d'histoire et de géographie ecclésiastiques,* Paris, 1912 ff.; *Dictionnaire de droit canonique,* Paris, 1924 ff.; and T. Klauser and others, *Reallexicon für Antike und Christentum,* Stuttgart, 1950 ff.

The general background of ancient and medieval history may be explored in the *Cambridge Ancient History,* 12 vols., Cambridge, 1923–39, and the *Cambridge Medieval History,* 8 vols., 1911–36, of which vol. IV on the Byzantine empire is being redone and should appear soon. Much less extensive general works include C. W. Previté-Orton, *The Shorter Cambridge Medieval History,* 2 vols., Cambridge, 1952; C. G. Crump and E. F. Jacob, eds., *The Legacy of the Middle Ages,* Oxford, 1926; and G. G. Coulton, *Life in the Middle Ages,* 4 vols., Cambridge and New York, 1928, also 1930, 1935, which contains selections from the sources in translation.

More specialized general works on late antiquity and the early middle ages are: Michael Rostovtzeff, *Social and Economic History of the Roman Empire,* Oxford, 1926; Julius Beloch, "Der Verfall der antiken Kultur," *Historische Zeitschrift,* LXXXIV (1900), 1–38; R. Laqueur, H. Koch, and W. Weber, *Probleme der Spätantike,* Stuttgart, 1930; Otto Seeck, *Geschichte des Untergangs der antiken Welt,* 2 ed., 6 vols., Berlin and Stuttgart, 1897–1920, a brilliant work in which the author's imagination sometimes complicates problems gratuitously; Ernst Stein, *Geschichte des spätrömischen Reiches,* vol. I: *Vom römischen zum byzantinischen Staate (284–476),* Vienna, 1928; vol. II: *Histoire du bas-empire . . . à la mort de Justinien (476–565),* Paris, 1949, solid; and Alfons Dopsch, *Wirtschaftliche und soziale Grundlagen der europäischen Kulturentwicklung,* 2 ed., 2 vols., Vienna, 1923–4, trans. in one vol., condensed, by M. G. Beard and Nadine Marshall, as *The Economic and Social Foundations of European Civilization,* New York and London, 1937, very significant and suggestive, covers the period from Caesar to Charlemagne.

Also André Piganiol, *L'Empire chrétien, 325–395,* Paris, 1947; Sam-

uel Dill, *Roman Society in the Last Century of the Western Empire*,
2 ed., London, 1899, and often reprinted, easy to read and fascinating;
J. B. Bury, *History of the Later Roman Empire*, 2 vols., London,
1923 (repr. 1931), excellent; Margaret Deanesley, *A History of Early
Medieval Europe, 476–911*, London, 1956; Ferd. Lot, Chas. Pfister,
F. L. Ganshof, *Les Destinées de l'empire en occident, 395–888* (in G.
Glotz, ed., *Histoire générale: Histoire du moyen-âge*), 2 vols., Paris,
1940–1; F. Lot, *La Fin du monde antique et les débuts du moyen-âge*,
Paris, 1927, trans. Philip and Mariette Leon, London and New York,
1931; Henry St. L. Moss, *The Birth of the Middle Ages, 395–814*,
Oxford, 1935; Christopher Dawson, *The Making of Europe*, repr.
New York, 1945, and *Religion and the Rise of Western Culture*, London, 1950; R. W. Southern, *The Making of the Middle Ages*, London,
1953; E. S. Duckett, *The Gateway to the Middle Ages*, New York,
1938; Louis Halphen, *Les Barbares, des grandes invasions aux con-
quêtes turques du XI⁰ siècle*, Paris, 1926, repr. 1930; Samuel Dill,
Roman Society in Gaul in the Merovingian Age, London, 1926, not so
good as his *Last Century* (listed above); E. Salin, *La Civilisation
mérovingienne*, vol. I, Paris, 1949; L. Halphen, *Charlemagne*, Paris,
1947; A. Kleinclausz, *Charlemagne*, Paris, 1934; H. Fichtenau, *The
Carolingian Empire*, trans. P. Munz, Oxford, 1957; Erna Patzelt, *Die
karolingische Renaissance: Beiträge zur Geschichte der Kultur des
frühen Mittelalters*, Vienna, 1924; H. Naumann, *Karolingische und
Ottonische Renaissance*, Frankfort, 1926; K. Strecker, *Einführung in
das Mittellatein*, 2 ed., Berlin, 1929, of which there is also a French
translation (Geneva, 1948), an important book; Geoffrey Barra-
clough, ed., *Medieval Germany, 911–1250*, 2 vols., Oxford, 1938;
W. W. Goetz, Paul Kirn, and August Heisenberg, *Das Mittelalter bis
zum Ausgang der Staufer, 400–1250*, Berlin, 1932; Percy Ernst
Schramm, *Kaiser, Rom, und Renovatio*, Leipzig, 1929; Edmond
Pognon, *L'An mille*, Paris, 1947; and H. Focillon, *L'An mil*, Paris,
1952.

Christianity underlies the intellectual and cultural transformation
of society which Taylor describes in this book. From an immense
bibliography a few titles may be cited: M. Goguel, *Origines du
christianisme*, 3 vols., Paris, 1946–7; J. R. Palanque, G. Bardy, P. de
Labriolle, G. de Plinval, and Louis Bréhier, *The Church in the Christian Roman Empire*, trans. Ernest C. Messenger, 2 vols., New York,
1953 (actually a translation of A. Fliche and V. Martin, eds., *Histoire
de l'église*, Paris, 1934 ff., vols. III–IV, with excellent bibliographies);
Hans Lietzmann, *From Constantine to Julian*, trans. B. L. Woolf,
New York, 1950, and *The Era of the Church Fathers*, New York,
1952 (being vols. III–IV of Lietzmann's *History of the Early Church*),
brief, readable, valuable books; George LaPiana, "Foreign Groups

in Rome during the First Centuries of the Empire," *Harvard Theological Review*, 1927, pp. 183–403, illuminating. There is a very large literature on the Emperor Constantine, in whose time Christianity received final official recognition as a state religion, a momentous development which was to bring with it thorny problems of the relations of Church and State: Eduard Schwartz, *Kaiser Constantin und die christliche Kirche*, Leipzig, 1913; Norman H. Baynes, "Constantine the Great and the Christian Church," *Proceedings of the British Academy*, XV (1929), 341–442, fundamental; André Piganiol, *L'Empereur Constantin*, Paris, 1932; András Alföldi, *The Conversion of Constantine and Pagan Rome*, trans. Harold Mattingly, Oxford, 1948; Heinz Kraft, *Kaiser Konstantins religiöse Entwicklung*, Tübingen, 1955; and cf. Joseph Bidez, *La Vie de l'empereur Julien*, Paris, 1930, and K. M. Setton, *Christian Attitude Towards the Emperor in the Fourth Century*, New York, 1941. See also Carl Schneider, *Geistesgeschichte des antiken Christentums*, 2 vols., Munich, 1954; Pierre de Labriolle, *La Réaction païenne*, Paris, 1950; Louis Duchesne, *L'Église au VIe siècle*, Paris, 1925; and special reference should be made to Charles N. Cochrane, *Christianity and Classical Culture*, Oxford, 1940; M. L. W. Laistner, *Christianity and Pagan Culture in the Later Roman Empire*, Ithaca, 1951; Chester G. Starr, *Civilization and the Caesars: The Intellectual Revolution in the Roman Empire*, Ithaca, 1954; and Edward M. Pickman, *The Mind of Latin Christendom*, London and New York, 1937, which handle some of the same themes as Taylor in this book.

On the intellectual background and development of Christianity, see further: George Foot Moore, *Judaism in the First Centuries of the Christian Era: The Age of the Tannaim*, 3 vols., Cambridge, Mass., 1927–30; Frank S. B. Gavin, *The Jewish Antecedents of the Christian Sacraments*, New York, 1928; Christian D. Ginsburg, *The Essenes: Their History and Doctrines*, New York, 1956; Erwin R. Goodenough, *Religious Tradition and Myth*, New Haven, 1937; and *An Introduction to Philo Judaeus*, New Haven and London, 1940; Harry A. Wolfson, *Philo: Foundations of Religious Philosophy in Judaism, Christianity, and Islam*, 2 vols., Cambridge, Mass., 1947, and *The Philosophy of the Church Fathers*, Cambridge, Mass., 1956; Philip Merlan, *From Platonism to Neo-Platonism*, The Hague, 1953; W. R. Inge, *The Philosophy of Plotinus*, 3 ed., 2 vols., London, 1948: Philippus V. Pistorius, *Plotinus and Neo-Platonism: An Introductory Study*, Cambridge, 1952; L. J. Rosán, *The Philosophy of Proclus*, New York, 1949; Edwin Hatch, *The Influence of Greek Ideas and Usages upon the Christian Church*, London, 1888, and new ed., New York, 1921, and Harper Torchbooks, 1957, the last edition containing a good bibliography on the background and early history of the

Church by F. C. Grant; Franz Cumont, *The Oriental Religions in Roman Paganism*, Chicago, 1911, *Astrology and Religion among the Greeks and Romans*, London, 1912, and *After-Life in Roman Paganism*, London, 1922; Samuel Angus, *The Mystery Religions and Christianity*, New York, 1925, and *The Religious Quests of the Graeco-Roman World*, New York, 1929; W. W. Hyde, *From Paganism to Christianity in the Roman Empire*, Philadelphia, 1946; Ernest Gottlieb Sihler, *From Augustus to Augustine*, Cambridge, 1923; J. Geffcken, *Der Ausgang des griechisch-römischen Heidentums*, Heidelberg, 1920, excellent; Adolf Bauer, *Vom Griechentum zum Christentum*, 2 ed., Leipzig, 1923; Arthur Darby Nock, *Conversion, the Old and the New in Religion from Alexander to Augustine*, Oxford, 1933, and his informative essay on "Early Gentile Christianity and its Hellenistic Background," in A. E. J. Rawlinson, ed., *Essays on the Trinity and the Incarnation*, London, 1928; E. Schwartz, *Charakterköpfe aus der antiken Literatur*, Leipzig, 1912.

There are several essays pertinent to the general interests of the *Classical Heritage* in J. T. McNeill, Matthew Spinka, and H. R. Willoughby, eds., *Environmental Factors in Christian History*, Chicago, 1939. Also U. Fracassini, *Il misticismo greco e il cristianesimo*, Città di Castello, 1922; B. Heigl, *Antike Mysterienreligionen und Urchristentum*, Münster, 1932; Albert Schweitzer, *The Mysticism of Paul the Apostle*, trans. William Montgomery, New York, 1956; W. David Stacey, *The Pauline View of Man in Relation to its Judaic and Hellenistic Background*, London, 1956; J. V. Langmead Casserley, *The Christian in Philosophy*, New York, 1951; H. R. Niebuhr, *Christ and Culture*, New York, 1951; R. C. Petry, *Christian Eschatology and Social Thought*, New York, 1956; and J. Westbury-Jones, *Roman and Christian Imperialism*, London, 1939.

On the church fathers there is a huge literature, made generally manageable, however, by such patristic manuals as those of Fulbert Cayré (2 vols., Paris, 1936–40), Berthold Altaner (2 ed., Freiburg, 1951), and Johannes Quasten (Westminster, Md., 1951 ff.). Also A. von Harnack, *Geschichte der altchristlichen Literatur bis Eusebius*, 3 vols., Leipzig, 1893–1904; O. Bardenhewer, *Geschichte der altkirchlichen Literatur*, 2 ed., 5 vols., Freiburg i. B., 1913–32; Wilhelm Schmid and Otto Stählin, *Geschichte der griechischen Litteratur*, II, pt. 2: *Von 100 bis 530 nach Christus*, 6 ed., Munich, 1924; Aimé Puech, *Histoire de la littérature grecque chrétienne depuis les origines jusqu'à la fin du IVᵉ siècle*, 3 vols., Paris, 1928–30; M. Schanz, *Geschichte der römischen Literatur*, vols. III–IV, i and ii, Leipzig, 1914–22. On a few significant individual fathers, cf. C. Mondésert, *Clément d'Alexandrie*, Paris, 1943; E. de Faye, *Origène*, 3 vols., Paris, 1923–8; J. Daniélou, *Origène*, Paris, 1948; F. Homes Dudden, *The*

Life and Times of St. Ambrose, 2 vols., Oxford, 1935; Ernesto Buonaiuti, *Sant' Ambrogio*, Milan, 1941; Alcuin F. Coyle, "Cicero's *De Officiis* and the *De Officiis Ministrorum* of St. Ambrose," *Franciscan Studies*, n. s., XV (1955), 224–56; Whitney J. Oates, ed., *Basic Writings of Saint Augustine*, 2 vols., New York, 1948; Étienne Gilson, *Introduction à l'étude de St. Augustin*, Paris, 1949; E. Buonaiuti, *Sant' Agostino*, 2 ed., Rome, 1923; H. I. Marrou, *St. Augustin et la fin de la culture antique*, 2 ed., 2 vols., Paris, 1950; H. Combès, *La Doctrine politique de St. Augustin*, Paris, 1927; H. X. Arquillière, *L'Augustinisme politique*, Paris, 1934; Harald Fuchs, *Augustin und der antike Friedensgedanke: Untersuchungen zum neunzehnten Buch der Civitas Dei*, Berlin, 1926; V. Giorgianni, *Il concetto del diritto e dello stato in S. Agostino*, Padua, 1951; and F. Homes Dudden, *Gregory the Great*, 2 vols., London, 1905.

Eduard Norden, whose *Antike Kunstprosa* (2 vols., Leipzig, 1898) Taylor used extensively in the *Classical Heritage*, also wrote a fine synthesis of *Die lateinische Literatur im Übergang vom Altertum zum Mittelalter* (*Die Kultur der Gegenwart*, I, viii), Leipzig, 1912. Also J. F. D'Alton, *Roman Literary Theory and Criticism*, London, 1931; A. G. Amatucci, *Storia della letteratura latina cristiana*, 2 ed., Turin, 1955; F. A. Wright and T. A. Sinclair, *A History of Later Latin Literature*, London, 1931; R. Pichon, *Les Derniers écrivains profanes*, Paris, 1906; E. S. Duckett, *Latin Writers of the Fifth Century*, New York, 1930; Pierre de Labriolle, *Histoire de la littérature latine chrétienne*, 2 ed., Paris, 1924 (and better, 3 ed., 2 vols., Paris, 1947), trans. Herbert Wilson, *History and Literature of Christianity from Tertullian to Boethius*, London and New York, 1924; Paul Monceaux, *Histoire littéraire de l'Afrique chrétienne depuis les origines jusqu'à l'invasion arabe*, 7 vols., Paris, 1901–23; Ernesto Buonaiuti, *Il Cristianesimo nell' Africa romana*, Bari, 1928; M. L. W. Laistner, *Thought and Letters in Western Europe, A. D. 500–900*, 2 ed., London, 1957, and (selected essays of Laistner, edited by C. G. Starr) *The Intellectual Heritage of the Early Middle Ages*, Ithaca, 1957; Pierre Courcelle, *Les Lettres grecques en occident de Macrobe à Cassiodore*, Paris, 1943, thorough and interesting; Max Manitius, *Geschichte der lateinischen Literatur des Mittelalters*, 3 vols., Munich, 1911–13; J. de Ghellinck, *Littérature latine au moyen-âge*, 2 vols., Paris, 1939; M. Hélin, *A History of Medieval Latin Literature*, New York, 1949; F. J. E. Raby, *A History of Secular Latin Poetry in the Middle Ages*, 2 ed., 2 vols., Oxford, 1957, and *A History of Christian Latin Poetry from the Beginnings to the Close of the Middle Ages*, 2 ed., Oxford, 1953; Ernst Robt. Curtius, *Europäische Literatur und lateinisches Mittelalter*, Bern, 1948, trans. Willard R. Trask, *European Literature and the Latin Middle Ages* (Bollingen Series, XXXVI),

New York, 1953; C. Pascal, *Poesia latina medievale*, Catania, 1907, and *Letteratura latina medievale: Nuovi saggi e note critiche*, Catania, 1909; Albert Dresdner, *Kultur- und Sittengeschichte der italienischen Geistlichkeit im 10. und 11. Jahrhundert*, Breslau 1890.

On medieval Latin and vernacular literatures there is an almost unending bibliography: E. Ronca, *Cultura medievale e poesia latina nei secoli XI e XII*, 2 vols., Rome, 1891; J. de Ghellinck, *L'Essor de la littérature latine au XIIᵉ siècle*, 2 vols., Paris, 1946; F. Novati, *L'influsso del pensiero latino sopra la civiltà italiana del medio evo*, Milan, 1897; W. P. Ker, *The Dark Ages*, London, 1904; Philip Schuyler Allen, *The Romanesque Lyric, 50–1050 A. D.*, Chapel Hill, 1928, and *Medieval Latin Lyrics*, Chicago, 1931; Rudolf Teuffel, *Individuelle Persönlichkeitsschilderung in den deutschen Geschichtswerken des 10. und 11. Jahrhunderts*, Leipzig, 1914; Wilhelm Kosch, *Deutsches Literatur-Lexikon*, 2 ed., 3 vols., Bern, 1949–56 (incomplete); and for medieval German literature and intellectual history in general, see the invaluable work edited by Wolfgang Stammler and Karl Langosch, *Die deutsche Literatur des Mittelalters: Verfasserlexikon*, 4 vols., Berlin and Leipzig, 1933–53, to which Langosch added a supplementary volume of addenda (Berlin, 1955). Also Reto R. Bezzola, *Les Origines et la formation de la littérature courtoise en occident (500–1200)*, pt. I: *La Tradition impériale de la fin de l'antiquité au XIᵉ siècle*, Paris, 1944; G. Chiri, *Poesia cortese latina*, Rome, 1954; P. Lehmann, *Pseudo-antike Literatur des Mittelalters*, Leipzig, 1927; H. R. Patch, *The Goddess Fortuna in Medieval Literature*, Cambridge, Mass., 1927; James S. Beddie, "The Ancient Classics in the Mediaeval Libraries," *Speculum*, V (1930), 3–20; Domenico Comparetti, *Vergil in the Middle Ages*, trans. E. F. M. Berrecke, London, 1895; Giovanni Pansa, *Ovidio nel medioevo e nella tradizione popolare*, Sulmona, 1924; Angelo Monteverdi, "Orazio nel medio evo," *Studi medievali*, n. s., IX (Turin, 1936), 162–180; A. Biese, *Die Entwicklung des Naturgefühls im Mittelalter*, 2 ed., Leipzig, 1892, English trans., London, 1905; Stephen Gaselee, *The Transition from the Late Latin Lyric to the Medieval Love Poem*, Cambridge, 1931; C. S. Lewis, *The Allegory of Love*, Oxford, 1936; John A. Symonds, trans., *Wine, Women and Song: Mediaeval Latin Students' Songs*, London, 1925, 1931, and other editions; Helen Waddell, *Medieval Latin Lyrics*, London, 1929, and *The Wandering Scholars*, 6 ed., London, 1932; K. Bojunga, *Lieder fahrender Schüler aus der Stauferzeit*, Leipzig, 1922; H. Brinkmann, *Geschichte der lateinischen Liebesdichtung im Mittelalter*, Halle, 1925; and Edgar de Bruyne, *Études d'esthétique médiévale*, 3 vols., Bruges, 1946, and *L'Esthétique du moyen-âge*, Louvain, 1947.

See further N. K. Chadwick, *Poetry and Letters in Early Christian*

Gaul, London, 1955; Clifford H. Moore, "Rome's Heroic Past in the Poems of Claudian," *Classical Journal*, VI (1910–11), 108–15; John C. Rolfe, "Claudian," *Transactions and Proceedings of the American Philological Association*, L (1919), 135–49; A. Baudrillart, *S. Paulin, évêque de Nole*, 3 ed., Paris, 1914; O. Chadwick, *Cassian, a Study in Primitive Monasticism*, Cambridge, 1950; O. M. Dalton, trans., *The Letters of Sidonius*, 2 vols., Oxford, 1915; C. E. Stevens, *Sidonius Apollinaris and his Age*, Oxford, 1933; A. Loyen, *Sidone Apollinaire et l'esprit précieux en Gaule*, Paris, 1943; H. R. Patch, *The Tradition of Boethius*, New York, 1935; Pierre Courcelle, "Boèce et l'école d'Alexandrie," *Mélanges d'archéologie et d'histoire*, LI (1934), 185–223; H. M. Barrett, *Boethius*, Cambridge, 1940; William Bark, "Theodoric vs. Boethius," *American Historical Review*, XLIX (1944), 410–26, and "The Legend of Boethius' Martyrdom," *Speculum*, XXI (1946), 312–17; A. van der Vyver, "Cassiodore et son oeuvre," *Speculum*, VI (1931), 244–292; Leslie W. Jones, "The Influence of Cassiodorus on Medieval Culture," *Speculum*, XX (1945), 433–442, and cf., *ibid*, XXII (1947), 252–56; and especially Arnaldo Momigliano, "Cassiodorus and the Italian Culture of his Time," *Proceedings of the British Academy*, XLI (1955), 207–245, with an excellent bibliography. Also O. M. Dalton, trans., *Gregory of Tours, History of the Franks*, 2 vols., Oxford, 1927; R. Köbner, *Venantius Fortunatus*, Leipzig, 1915; D. Tardi, *Fortunat*, Paris, 1927, and "Fortunat et Angilbert," *Bulletin DuCange*, II (Paris, 1925), 30–38; Ernest Brehaut, *An Encyclopedist of the Dark Ages, Isidore of Seville*, New York, 1912; H. B. Workman, *Evolution of the Monastic Ideal*, 2 ed., London, 1927; Edw. L. Cutts, *Scenes and Characters of the Middle Ages*, 6 ed., London, 1926; Dom David Knowles, *The Monastic Order in England, 943–1216*, Cambridge, 1949.

Ireland and England are important in the early middle ages not only in themselves but also for the influence they exerted upon the continent: J. Ryan, *Irish Monasticism*, Dublin, 1931; H. Zimmer, "Ueber die Bedeutung des irischen Elements für die mittelalterliche Kultur," *Preussische Jahrbücher*, LIX (1887), 27–59; L. Gougaud, "L'Oeuvre des Scotti dans l'Europe continentale," *Revue d'histoire ecclésiastique*, IX (Louvain, 1908), 21–37, and 255–77; and "Les Scribes monastiques d'Irlande au travail," *ibid.*, XXVII (1931), 293–306, and *Christianity in Celtic Lands*, London, 1932; L. Bieler, "The Island of Scholars," *Revue du moyen-âge latin*, VIII (1952), 213–234; and cf. V. Gardthausen, "Die griechische Schrift des Mittelalters im Westen Europas," *Byzantinisch-Neugriechische Jahrbücher*, VIII (1931), 114–35. Also Samuel J. Crawford, *Anglo-Saxon Influence on Western Christendom (600–800)*, London, 1933; W. Levinson, *England and the Continent in the Eighth Century*, Oxford, 1946; J. D.

Ogilvy, *Books Known to Anglo-Saxon Writers (670–804)*, Cambridge, Mass., 1936; and cf. E. Lesne, *Les Livres, scriptoria et les bibliothèques, VIIe–XIe siècles*, Lille, 1938; J. J. Laux, *Der heilige Kolumban*, Freiburg i. B., 1919; M. Dubois, *Un Pionnier de la civilisation occidentale: S. Colomban, c. 540–615*, Paris, 1950; J. M. Clark, *The Abbey of St. Gall as a Centre of Literature and Art*, Cambridge, 1926; A. H. Thompson, ed., *Bede, his Life, Times, and Writings*, Oxford, 1935; G. F. Browne, *Venerable Bede*, London, 1930; A. L. Maycock, "Bede and Alcuin (735–1935)," *Hibbert Journal*, XXXIII (1934–5), 402–12; E. S. Duckett, *Alcuin, Friend of Charlemagne*, New York, 1951; A. Kleinclausz, *Alcuin*, Paris, 1948; Eva M. Sanford, "Alcuin and the Classics," *Classical Journal*, XX (1924–5), 526–33; A. Jundt, *Walafrid Strabon*, Cahors, 1907; T. Schieffer, *Winfrid-Bonifatius und die christliche Grundlegung Europas*, Freiburg, 1954; G. F. Browne, *Boniface of Crediton*, London, 1910; E. Dinkler and E. Wissmann, *Gottschalk der Sachse*, Stuttgart, 1936; and H. Bett, *Johannes Scotus Erigena*, Cambridge, 1925.

See also W. Harster, *Walther von Speier, ein Dichter des X. Jahrhunderts*, Speyer, 1877; J. Kempf, *Froumond von Tegernsee*, Munich, 1900; H. Christensen, *Das Alexanderlied Walters von Chatillon*, Halle, 1905; G. Cary, *The Medieval Alexander*, Cambridge, 1956; John R. Williams, "Godfrey of Rheims, a Humanist of the Eleventh Century," *Speculum*, XXII (1947), 29–45, and "William of the White Hands and Men of Letters," in *Anniversary Essays by Students of Chas. H. Haskins*, Boston, 1929, pp. 365 ff.; A. Boutemy, *Gautier Map, conteur anglais*, Brussels, 1945; C. C. Webb, *John of Salisbury*, London, 1932; H. Liebeschütz, *Medieval Humanism in the Life and Writings of John of Salisbury*, London, 1950; Chas. H. Haskins, *The Renaissance of the Twelfth Century*, Cambridge, Mass., 1927, and *Studies in Medieval Culture*, Oxford, 1929; E. K. Rand, "The Classics in the Thirteenth Century," *Speculum*, IV (1929), 249–69; and Leslie W. Jones, *Classical and Medieval Studies in Honor of Edward Kennard Rand*, New York, 1938.

Two recent books bearing upon the subject of the *Classical Heritage* but extending much further in time are: Gilbert Highet, *The Classical Tradition: Greek and Roman Influences on Western Literature*, Oxford, 1949, and R. R. Bolgar, *The Classical Heritage and Its Beneficiaries*, Cambridge, 1954. Note also Paul Shorey, *Platonism Ancient and Modern*, Berkeley, 1938; Raymond Klibansky, *The Continuity of the Platonic Tradition during the Middle Ages*, London, 1939, on which see the review by Ernst Kantorowicz, "Plato in the Middle Ages," *Philosophical Review*, LI (1942), 312–23. Various selections from Vincent of Lérins, Ratramnus of Corbie, Gregory the Great, Alcuin of York, Agobard of Lyons, Rabanus Maurus, and others are translated, with introductions, in G. E. McCracken, *Early Medieval Theology* (Library of Christian Classics, IX), Philadelphia, 1957; Alois Dempf-Bonn, *Metaphysik des Mittelalters*, Munich and Berlin, 1930, and *Christliche Philosophie*, Bonn, 1938; R. L. Poole, *Illustrations of the History of Medieval Thought and Learning*, 2 ed., London, 1920; E. Gilson, *The Spirit of Medieval Philosophy*, trans. A. H. C. Downes, London and New York, 1936; H. O. Taylor, *The Medieval Mind*, 4 ed., 2 vols., London and Cambridge, Mass., 1938; Sydney H. Mellone, *Western Christian Thought in the Middle Ages*, Edinburgh and London, 1935; A. C. McGiffert, *History of Christian Thought*, 2 vols., New York, 1932–3; Martin Grabmann, *Mittelalterliches Geistesleben*, 2 vols., Munich, 1926–36; Gustav Schnürer, *L'Église et la civilisation au moyen-âge*, trans. from the German by G. Castella and M.-Th. Burgard, 3 vols., Paris, 1933–8; G. G. Coulton, *Five Centuries of Religion*, 4 vols., Cambridge, 1927–50 (vols. were not published consecutively), interesting, learned, and frequently polemical; Henry Adams, *Mont-Saint-Michel and Chartres*, Boston and New York, 1913, also 1933; K. Vossler, *Mediaeval Culture: An Introduction to Dante and his Times*, trans. W. C. Lawton, 2 vols., New York, 1929; E. Gilson, *Dante et la philosophie*, Paris, 1939, and *Dante the Philosopher*, New York, 1949; also by Gilson, *La Philosophie au moyen-âge, des origines patristiques à la fin du XIVe siècle*, 2 ed., Paris, 1944, and *History of Christian Philosophy in the Middle Ages*, New York, 1955; and N. Lenkeith. *Dante and the Legend of Rome* (Warburg Institute), London, 1953. Also F. von Bezold, *Das Fortleben der antiken Götter im mittelalterlichen Humanismus*, Bonn and Leipzig, 1922; Jean Seznec, *La Survivance de dieux antiques*, London, 1940, and *The Survival of the Pagan Gods*, New York, 1953; and Arthur O. Lovejoy. *The Great Chain of Being: Study of the History of an Idea*, Cambridge, Mass., 1936.

The history of education may be brought into alignment with the main topics of Taylor's *Classical Heritage* by reading: Werner W. Jaeger, *Paideia, the Ideals of Greek Culture*, trans. Gilbert Highet, 3 vols., Oxford, 1934–5, also New York, 1939, which surveys the whole classical period of Greek civilization from the standpoint of education (*paideia*); Glanville Downey, "Education in the Christian Roman Empire: Christian and Pagan Theories under Constantine and his Successors," *Speculum*, XXXII (1957), 48–61; also Downey, "The Emperor Julian and the Schools," *Classical Journal*, LIII (1957), 97–103. and "Justinian's View of Christianity and the Greek Classics," *Anglican Theological Review*, XL (1958), 13–22; M. Lechner, *Erziehung und Bildung in der griechisch-römischen Antike*, Munich, 1933; T. Haarhoff, *Schools of Gaul: Pagan and Christian Education in the Last Century of the Western Empire*, Oxford, 1920; M. Roger, *L'En-*

seignement des lettres classiques d'Ausone à Alcuin, Paris, 1905; Erich Weniger, "Das deutsche Bildungswesen im Frühmittelalter," *Historische Vierteljahrschrift*, XXX (1935–6), 446–92; E. Lesne, *Les Écoles de la fin du VIIIᵉ siècle à la fin du XIIᵉ siècle*, Lille, 1940; L. Maître, *Les Écoles épiscopales et monastiques en occident avant les universités (768–1180)*, 2 ed., Paris, 1924; G. Paré, A. Brunet, P. Tremblay, *La Renaissance du XIIᵉ siècle: les écoles et l'enseignement*, Paris and Ottawa, 1933; Stephen d'Irsay, *Histoire des universités françaises et étrangères*, vol. I, Paris, 1933, extending through the medieval period into the 16th century; Hastings Rashdall, *The Universities of Europe in the Middle Ages*, eds. F. M. Powicke and A. B. Emden, 3 vols., Oxford, 1936; and cf. J. W. Thompson, *The Literacy of the Laity in the Middle Ages*, Berkeley, 1936; G. H. Hörle, *Frühmittelalterliche Mönchs- und Klerikerbildung in Italien*, Freiburg i. B., 1914; F. Fuchs, *Die höheren Schulen von Konstantinopel im Mittelalter*, Leipsig, 1926; J. Ebersolt, *Orient et occident*, Paris, 1928; and J. E. Sandys, *History of Classical Scholarship*, vol. I, 3 ed., Cambridge, 1920, a small mine of accurate information with careful references to the sources.

See also William W. Buckland, *A Textbook of Roman Law from Augustus to Justinian*, 2 ed., Cambridge, 1932; Paul Vinogradoff, *Roman Law in Medieval Europe*, 2 ed., Oxford, 1929; Simon Stein, "Lex Salica," *Speculum*, XXII (1947), 113–34, and *ibid.*, 395–418; Jos. Declareuil, *Histoire générale du droit français des origines . . .*, Paris, 1925; K. Voigt, *Staat und Kirche von Konstantin bis zum Ende der Karolingerzeit*, Stuttgart, 1936; G. Tellenbach, *Church, State, and Christian Society at the time of the Investiture Contest*, Oxford, 1940; Fritz Kern, *Kingship and Law in the Middle Ages*, trans. S. B. Chrimes, Oxford, 1939; Walter Ullman, *Medieval Papalism*, London, 1949, and *The Medieval Idea of Law*, London, 1946 (on Lucas de Penna in the 14th century); and especially R. W. and A. J. Carlyle, *History of Medieval Political Theory in the West*, 6 vols., New York, 1909–36; Chas. H. McIlwain, *The Growth of Political Thought in the West*, New York, 1932; and George H. Sabine, *History of Political Theory*, New York, 1937.

On art the following titles may be selected from many hundreds that might be regarded as pertinent to the *Classical Heritage:* Jos. Strzygowski, *Origin of Christian Church Art*, Oxford, 1923, and *Early Church Art in Northern Europe*, London, 1928; Emerson H. Swift, *Roman Sources of Christian Art*, New York, 1951; Walter Lowrie, *Art in the Early Church*, New York, 1947; Chas. R. Morey, *Early Christian Art*, 2 ed., Princeton, 1953, deals with sculpture and painting from antiquity to the eighth century; Émile Mâle, *La Fin du paganisme en Gaule et les plus anciennes basiliques*, Paris, 1950;

Marguerite van Berchem and Étienne Clouzot, *Mosaïques chrétiennes du IVme au Xme siècle*, Geneva, 1924; H. Jantzen, *Ottonische Kunst*, Munich, 1947; H. Focillon, *Art d'occident, le moyen-âge, roman et gothique*, Paris, 1938, and *Vie des formes*, Paris, 1939; M. Aubert, *La Sculpture au moyen-âge*, Paris, 1947; Joan Evans, *Art in Medieval France, 987–1498*, London and New York, 1948, and *Cluniac Art of the Romanesque Period*, Cambridge, 1950; Alfred W. Clapham, *Romanesque Architecture in Western Europe*, Oxford, 1936; A. Gardner, *Medieval Sculpture in France*, Cambridge, 1931, and *English Medieval Sculpture*, Cambridge, 1951; R. de Lasteyrie, *L'Architecture religieuse en France à l'époque romane*, 2 ed., Paris, 1929, and *L'Architecture religieuse en France à l'époque gothique*, 2 vols., Paris, 1926–7; E. B. Smith, *Architectural Symbolism of Imperial Rome and the Middle Ages*, Princeton, 1956. Although not always accurate, George Ferguson, *Signs and Symbols in Christian Art*, New York, 1954, is interesting and very easy to read. All aspects of German art are considered in the handsome and beautifully illustrated volumes in the F. Bruckmann Verlag's *Deutsche Kunstgeschichte*, vols. I–V, Munich, 1953–5 (by E. Hempel, A. Feulner, T. Müller, O. Fischer, and H. Kohlhaussen)—not only are art and architecture dealt with, but also silverware, pottery, furniture, armor, tapestry, and jewelry (in vol. V by Kohlhaussen, on "Kunsthandwerk"). Raimond van Marle, *Iconographie de l'art profane au moyen-âge et à la Renaissance, et la décoration des demeures*, 2 vols., La Haye, 1931–2, also relates art to the manners and customs of daily life.

The serious reader will also wish some acquaintance of the following: Erwin Panofsky and Fritz Saxl, "Classical Mythology in Mediaeval Art," in *Metropolitan Museum Studies*, vol. IV, pt. 2 (1933); Kurt Weitzmann, *Greek Mythology in Byzantine Art*, Princeton, 1951; Oskar K. Wulff, *Altchristliche und byzantinische Kunst*, 2 vols., Berlin, 1914–24; Chas. Diehl, *Manuel d'art byzantin*, 2 ed., 2 vols., Paris, 1925–6; David Talbot Rice, *Byzantine Painting and Developments in the West before A. D. 1200*, London, 1948; Robt. Byron and D. T. Rice, *The Birth of Western Painting*, New York, 1931, on Byzantine and western form and iconography; W. R. Lethaby, *Medieval Art*, rev. ed., London, 1949, and New York, 1950; André Grabar, *Byzantine Painting*, Geneva, Skira, 1953; Otto Demus, *Byzantine Mosaic Decoration: Aspects of Monumental Art in Byzantium*, London, 1948; Ernst Diez and O. Demus, *Byzantine Mosaics in Greece*, Cambridge, Mass., 1931; O. Demus, *The Mosaics of Norman Sicily*, London, 1949 [1950], and *Die Mosaiken von San Marco in Venedig, 1100–1300*, Baden bei Wien, 1935. On music, see Fr. Anselm Hughes, ed., *Early Medieval Music up to 1300* (*New Oxford History of Music*, vol. II), London and New York, 1954; G. Reese,

Music in the Middle Ages, New York, 1940; J. Chailley, *Histoire musicale du moyen-âge*, Paris, 1950; and V. Sesini, *Poesia e musica nella latinità cristiana del III al X secolo*, Turin, 1949.

Finally, since Taylor devotes some attention to Byzantine civilization (and casts a few unmerited aspersions upon it), we may note: George Ostrogorsky, *History of the Byzantine State*, trans. Joan Hussey, Oxford, Blackwell, 1956, chiefly political and institutional, well organized and well disciplined throughout; A. A. Vasiliev, *History of the Byzantine Empire*, Madison, 1952, aims at a broad coverage; Louis Bréhier, *Le Monde byzantin*, 3 vols., Paris, 1947–50, excellent but rather dull to read; Norman H. Baynes, *Byzantine Studies and Other Essays*, London, 1955, very instructive; Karl Krumbacher, *Geschichte der byzantinischen Litteratur*, 2 ed., Munich, 1897, long out of date, but still the best available work; G. Montelatici, *Storia della letteratura bizantina*, Milan, 1916; also K. Lechner, *Hellenen und Barbaren im Weltbild der Byzantiner*, Munich, 1955; Basile Tatakis, *La Philosophie byzantine* (in Émile Brehiér's *Histoire de la philosophie*, fasc. suppl. XI), Paris, 1949; P. E. Stephanou, *Jean Italos: philosophe et humaniste* (Orientalia Christiana Analecta, no. 134), Rome, 1949; Jules Gay, *L'Italie méridionale et l'empire byzantin*, Paris, 1904; Gerhard Rohlfs, *Griechen und Romanen in Unteritalien*, Geneva, 1924, and *Scavi linguistici nella Magna Grecia*, Halle and Rome, 1933; Raffaele Cantarella, *Poeti bizantini*, 2 vols., Milan, 1948, an anthology; Silvano Borsari and Marcello Gigante, "Poeti bizantini di Terra d'Otranto nel secolo XIII," *La Parola del Passato*, VI (1951), 287–315, 367–90, and Gigante, *Poeti italobizantini del secolo XIII* (in the Collana di studi greci, no. 22), Naples, 1953; Alberto Vaccari, *La Grecia nell' Italia meridionale* (Orientalia Christiana, III, no. 13), Rome, 1925. For Byzantine connections with the West in general, see three recent articles by G. P. Bognetti, Franz Dölger, and R. S. Lopez, in the *Relazioni* of the tenth International Congress of Historical Studies, vol. III (Florence, 1955), 3–163, and Kenneth M. Setton, *The Byzantine Background to the Italian Renaissance*, in *Proceedings of the American Philosophical Society*, vol. 100 (1956), 1–76, with extensive bibliography. Many articles on Byzantine influences on southern Italy are published in the *Archivio storico per la Calabria e la Lucania*, I (1931) ff. For a brief, interesting study of the early Byzantine Church, see George Every, *The Byzantine Patriarchate, 451–1204*, London, 1947; almost equally brief is Ernest Barker, *Social and Political Thought in Byzantium from Justinian I to the Last Palaeologus*, Oxford, 1957, which contains selections translated from the Greek sources.

K. M. S.

INDEX